W9-CHK-473

THE
TWENTIETH
MAINE

THE
TWENTIETH
MAINE

John J. Pullen

STACKPOLE
BOOKS

To my parents

Copyright © 1957 by John J. Pullen, renewed 1985
New Materials Copyright 1991 by John J. Pullen
New Foreword Copyright © 2008 by Stackpole Books

Published by
STACKPOLE BOOKS
5067 Ritter Road
Mechanicsburg, PA 17055
www.stackpolebooks.com

All rights reserved, including the right to reproduce this book or portions
thereof in any form or by any means, electronic or mechanical, including
photocopying, recording, or by any information storage and retrieval system, without permission in writing from the publisher. All inquiries should
be addressed to Stackpole Books, 5067 Ritter Road, Mechanicsburg, PA
17055.

Printed in the United States of America

10 9 8 7 6 5 4 3 2 1

Stackpole edition

*Cover painting by Don Troiani,
www.historicalimagebank.com*

Cover design by Tessa J. Sweigert

Library of Congress Cataloging-in-Publication Data

Pullen, John J.
  The Twentieth Maine / John J. Pullen. — 1st ed.
    p. cm.
  Originally published: 1st ed. Philadelphia : Lippincott, 1957. With new
foreword.
  Includes bibliographical references and index.
  ISBN 978-0-8117-3524-7 (v. 1 : alk. paper)
  1. United States. Army. Maine Infantry Regiment, 20th (1862–1865) 2.
Maine—History—Civil War, 1861–1865—Regimental histories. 3. United
States—History—Civil War, 1861–1865—Regimental histories. I. Title.
  E511.520th .P8 2008
  973.7'441—dc22
                                    2008019889

CONTENTS

ILLUSTRATIONS

Photographs grouped in this order following page 148

MAPS

DRAWINGS

FOREWORD

When advertising executive and former reporter John J. Pullen published *The Twentieth Maine* in 1957 he revived a long dormant interest in that storied unit, its remarkable leaders, and its redoubtable volunteers. A gifted writer and diligent historian, Pullen inspired a new wave of regimental histories, leading Bruce Catton to declare *The Twentieth Maine* as "the best unit history of the Civil War." Over fifty years later, the work still stands as a classic in the literature. Pullen, a native of Maine who served in World War II, had great material to work with, but it was his novelistic rendering of the 20th's story that made for the gripping tale that captivated writers, filmmakers, and documentarians, as well as legions of visitors who regularly flock to Gettysburg National Military Park to relive the unit's defense of Little Round Top on July 2, 1863.

The 20th Maine was created when President Lincoln called for three hundred thousand volunteers to replenish the losses the Army of the Potomac suffered in the Peninsula Campaign. Recruiting proved far harder than in the early days of the war, and the 20th was hastily patched together with companies originally scheduled to join other Maine regiments. By late August 1862 the 20th was formally organized with West Pointer Colonel Adelbert Ames as commander and Lt. Col. Joshua Chamberlain, a thirty-three year old professor of rhetoric at Bowdoin College as second in command. Both would earn higher rank, and Chamberlain was awarded the Medal of Honor for his heroic actions at Gettysburg. As important as the leaders were to the immediate success and ultimate fame of the Twentieth, Pullen rightly concentrates on the lives and actions of ordinary enlisted men and lower ranked officers. The farmers, fishermen, and lumberjacks who comprised the companies that formed the 20th came from every part of the beautiful and rugged "Pine Tree State." Drawing from letters, diaries, and other sources, Pullen described the majority of them as "well informed, surprisingly well educated, and fully cognizant of the main issue." (p. 12) The main issue, as the men understood it, was the salvation of the Union. Assigned to the 3rd Brigade, 1st Division, V Corps in the Army of the Potomac, their patriotism would be sorely tested from 1861–1865 as they were exposed to the rigors of training, camp life, endless marching and combat action.

Still green when they were held in reserve at Antietam, the 20th saw hard fighting at Fredericksburg in December of 1862 as part of the bloody assaults made by Union troops on the Confederate position on Marye's Heights. The devastating loss at Fredericksburg, Pullen claimed, proved critical to building the unit's fighting morale: "They had lost four men killed and thirty-two wounded. They had not been disorganized. They had maneuvered and fought as a cohesive, thinking unit. They knew now that they were a regiment." (p. 59) The 20th Maine earned plaudits for its courageous actions on Day 2 of the battle of Gettysburg, which left 130 killed or wounded. By the time Lee launched the Pennsylvania Campaign in June of 1863, Joshua Chamberlain led the regiment, under Colonel Strong Vincent's brigade in the V Corps. Marching hard and fast from Maryland, the 20th arrived on the field late in the afternoon of July 1, hungry, thirsty and exhausted. Alerted to a dangerous weakness on the far left of the Union position, Vincent told Chamberlain on July 2, "This is the left of the Union line. You understand. You are to hold this ground at all costs!"(p. 111) Defending Little Round Top against an aggressive Confederate assault by the 15th Alabama, Colonel Chamberlain and his outnumbered men helped to stop the Federal line from being rolled up by the Rebels. "Seldom if ever before," writes Pullen, "had one small regiment been in such a fantastic spot." (p. 127) One soldier recorded the regiment's achievement: "Ours was an important position, and had we been driven from it, the tide of battle would have been turned against us and what the result would have been we cannot tell." (p. 127)

The unit did not rest on the laurels earned at Gettysburg and went on to fight in many other battles, among them The Wilderness, Laurel Hill, North Anna, Bethesda Church, Petersburg, Weldon Railroad, Hatcher's Run and Quaker Road. By the end of 1864, Pullen records the changes that overcame the 20th: through brutal attrition at least half of the 425 men were newly arrived recruits. One veteran lamented, ". . . how many forms had vanished! How many voices had been hushed!" (p. 236)

It was somehow fitting that the 20th Maine was active in the Appomattox Campaign that closed out the conflict. Their revered commander, promoted to brigadier-general, had been given the honor of accepting the Confederate surrender on April 12, 1865. Chamberlain made sure the 20th Maine was part of the ceremony. The unit also participated in the Grand Review held in Washington D.C. before being mustered out on June 4, 1865.

John J. Pullen's *The Twentieth Maine* offers a captivating account of the tragedies and triumphs of one remarkable volunteer regiment's experience in this most sanguinary of American wars. Skillfully interweaving social and military history, Pullen provides readable clear context to battles and campaigns while tracing the personal impact of war on the men. Pullen shows why and how the 20th Maine emerged as a true "fighting regiment" and became known for the quality of both its officers and enlisted men.

Upon his first viewing of the unruly, undisciplined group of recruits that would become the 20th Maine, Colonel Adelbert Ames famously remarked with disgust, "This is a *hell* of a regiment." After proving their mettle so often throughout the war, Pullen notes that Ames, now deeply appreciative of their record, could utter the same line, but with a different accent, "This is a hell of a *regiment!*"

Joan Waugh
Professor of History
UCLA

CHAPTER ONE

How D'Ye Do, Colonel

WHEN, in August of 1862, Colonel Adelbert Ames went to Portland, Maine, to take command of a new volunteer infantry regiment, he was a little more than fourteen months out of West Point and a year out of the first battle of Bull Run, where he had received a painful wound. Thus it had been impressed upon him in two ways—one theoretical and the other practical—that discipline is a mighty good thing to have among your soldiers when the shooting starts. And therefore Colonel Ames was disgusted and horrified when he arrived at Camp Mason, near Portland, and got his first look at the troops gathering there for the 20th Regiment Infantry, Maine Volunteers.

Instead of saluting, a man would say, "How d'ye do, Colonel!" often as not leaning against a wall or tree with legs crossed, for a Maine man will not ordinarily waste energy holding himself erect if there is an inanimate object handy to do that for him. The military posture of one man, standing in ranks, was so abdominally atrocious that Colonel Ames roared at him, "For God's sake, draw up your bowels!"

The men wanted to act like soldiers but obviously none of them had the slightest notion of military affairs. They had no uniforms or arms and little equipment. Yet they had organized a guard and were trying to hold formations. At one guard mount, the Officer of the Day was clad in a brown cutaway, striped trousers and silk hat. He carried a ramrod for a sword.

Both the officers and the men seemed to think that a regiment should be run something like a town meeting. Orders consisted of long explanations, then there would be conferences and dis-

1

cussions and, finally, agreements between the officers and enlisted men. True, the agreements seemed to be carried out; the men themselves took a great deal of responsibility for this, and in cases of disobedience the offender was likely to be knocked down and perhaps kicked if the offense was of a particularly flagrant nature.

Colonel Ames, not a mild-tempered man to begin with—and with so much to be done, the Union to be saved, a brigadier generalship to be won, and all that—found himself losing what patience he had. He barked, "This is a hell of a regiment!" Then he straightaway set about putting the 20th Maine into some semblance of a military organization.

After a little preliminary drilling, the Colonel attempted to hold a parade, so that he could get the 20th Maine lined up and see what he had for soldiers. This was interrupted, noisily. In their martial ardor the men had organized a fife and drum corps in which the fifers and drummers all seemed to fife and drum independently but with great power. Just as the Colonel took his place in front of the drawn-up troops, the fife and drum corps suddenly and prematurely moved from its position and came tweetling and thundering down the line, making an appalling racket. To the company commander nearest him Colonel Ames shouted, "Captain Bangs, stop that damned drumming!" Captain Isaac S. Bangs couldn't hear him for the noise, nor could anyone else. In a rage, Colonel Ames charged the drum corps with his sword and scattered it sufficiently to make himself audible.

If Ames had been asked to pick a regiment that was earmarked for great deeds, he certainly wouldn't have picked the 20th Maine in that August of 1862 as having any date with Destiny. Yet in numbers, at least, Ames could see that he had a regiment that conformed to the table of organization prescribed by law. The Civil War volunteer regiment consisted of ten companies, each having from sixty-four to eighty-two privates, thirteen non-commissioned officers, a wagoner, two musicians, a captain and two lieutenants. The regiment was commanded by a colonel, aided by a lieutenant colonel, a major, and a small regimental staff of commissioned and non-commissioned officers.

All these positions had been filled by individuals with varying degrees of competence. Starting at the top there was Ames himself—a West Pointer and a Maine man, thus both able and eligible to command the regiment. Ames had already made a distinguished record for bravery and what Maine people would call "stick-to-it-iveness." Serving with a battery at the first battle of Bull Run, he had taken a Minié ball through the thigh, but had refused to leave the field, being lifted on and off a caisson as the battery changed position, and continuing to give fire commands until his boot ran full of blood and he keeled over from exhaustion. Able, intelligent, intensely ambitious, Ames had been mentioned in official reports and marked as a young officer who was on the way up. For his performance at Bull Run he would later be awarded the Congressional Medal of Honor.

The lieutenant colonel of the regiment was a man worth looking at twice. This was Joshua L. Chamberlain, age thirty-three, a graceful, erect gentleman of medium but strong build, with a finely shaped head, a classic forehead and nose, a moustache that swept back with a distinguished flair, a resonant and pleasing voice. To Chamberlain the war would be a great adventure. He was destined to become one of the most remarkable officers in the history of the United States—a veritable knight with plumes and shining armor. He came of English and Norman stock; his people had been among the earliest settlers; and he combined a great deal of solid strength and common sense with dash and gallantry that may well have come to him from the French roots of the family tree. Chamberlain also had a talent for doing the impossible which seems to have been encouraged by his childhood training. One of the tenets of this training was that if something was said to be impossible, a man was supposed immediately to go at it, and do it. Clearing stones from the family farm in Brewer, when Joshua and his brothers reported to their father that they'd left a rock on the field because it was too heavy to move, the elder Chamberlain would say simply, "Move it," and the boys would go back and move it. (One of these brothers, Thomas, was also in the 20th Maine as a sergeant.) As another instance of this unwonted perseverance, when young Joshua wanted to learn to play the bass viol but couldn't afford to buy the instrument, he made a crude viol and bow, and sawed away

3

until he could play tunes. And when he desired to learn Greek, he shut himself up in the attic and studied from morning until night, until he had learned the complete grammar textbook by heart.

After graduating from Bowdoin, Joshua had taken a three-year course at the Bangor Theological Seminary, meanwhile teaching German language and literature to classes of young ladies, serving as supervisor of schools in Brewer, running a Sunday school, and leading a church choir. Later he had joined the faculty of Bowdoin College, where he had taught rhetoric, oratory and modern languages. The college had not wanted Professor Chamberlain to go to war, so he had taken a two years' leave of absence for the purpose of visiting Europe and had instead visited the state capital in Augusta, where he secured a commission as lieutenant colonel of volunteers. The Governor had wished to make him a colonel and give him a regiment, but he'd said no, he'd start a little lower and learn the business first.

Although trained to be a minister of the Gospel, Chamberlain seemed to show a most un-Christian aptitude for military affairs, and Ames thought he might do well.

The major, Charles D. Gilmore, had seen service as a captain in the 7th Maine, a regiment that went into the field in 1861. Gilmore was evidently a man of some managerial ability. He had contrived to get himself a transfer back to Maine, a leave of absence and a promotion to major in the 20th Maine all at one stroke. For some time he had been the only uniformed person in camp and had looked extremely lonesome.

Among the company commanders one of the most notable, as it would turn out, was Ellis Spear of Wiscasset. A frail-appearing, bearded young schoolmaster, Spear didn't look as though he could withstand the rigors of army life a month, but he was actually tough as leather and what he lacked in physical stamina he would make up in determination. In many ways, Spear was much more typical of the good volunteer officer than was Chamberlain. To him, war was far from being romantic; it was instead a dull, ugly job that had to be done in spite of all its horrors and official stupidities. Possessed of a dry sense of humor and a Yankee gift for understatement, Spear was the type of Maine man who, if you ask him how he is doing and he happens to be doing very well indeed, will reply, "All right." Ellis Spear always took the conservative view of both men and events.

As for the enlisted men, as Colonel Ames walked up and down the ranks of his first parade he could begin to see certain possibilities. There were many—obviously passed by patriotically blind examining physicians—who had no business in the army. But there were others who looked very rugged indeed. These were flat-bellied, hard-muscled fellows from the farms, forests and coast towns. There were among them many who eked out a living on the farms in summer and in the woods in winter, and it was a muscular life in both places. On the farm power was provided by the man, the ox and the horse, and the work—lifting rocks, pitching hay, manhandling the crude farm tools—was a personal struggle against the laws of inertia and gravity. In the woods it was all axe work. Even that doubtful laborsaver, the two-man crosscut saw, was not in general use. Men who worked in the lumber camps of that day got up before dawn, walked through deep snow four or five miles to their work, started chopping as soon as there was light enough to see, ate a frozen lunch, and worked until the light faded. To many of Ames' soldiers hardship was not strange; it was the ordinary and accustomed way of life.

So there were tough men in the ranks of the newly formed 20th Maine. Not many six-footers among them; a good guess would place the average at about five feet eight inches, but that was all to the good; experience had shown that tall men did not stand up as well on the march as the small- or medium-sized soldiers.

In addition, many of the Maine soldiers were already familiar with firearms. And they *were* volunteers, even if strong persuasion had been involved in their enlistment. The year before, in 1861, Maine had had no trouble in raising regiments; young men had rushed to the colors in the first flush of war excitement, when it seemed that the rebellion would be put down within a few weeks. But in the July of 1862, when Father Abraham called for "three hundred thousand more," it was a little harder to round up the requisite number.

5

Usually, ordinary citizens, with authorization from the Governor, did the recruiting and paid their own expenses. The recruiters were men of all classes: ambitious young lawyers, budding politicians, schoolteachers who thought they knew something about discipline, farmers, clerks, youngsters just out of college. There was a sort of understanding with the Governor that if they succeeded they would get commissions. In the Civil War volunteer regiment, all the officers were appointed by the Governor—often on the basis of political rather than military merit. Regular Army commanders contemplated the system with positive horror. Referring to the commissioning of untrained officers by governors, Major General Emory Upton wrote, "In no monarchy or despotism of the Old World do the laws give to the ruler such power to do evil." Once the regiment was in Federal service, higher commanders had ways of getting rid of incompetent state officers, but then the Governor might appoint another one just as incompetent as a replacement. Within the regiment itself there was much political activity—manipulation of influences and supposed influences in order to obtain commissions or promotions from the Governor. And not only was politics active in the regiment, but the regiment was active in politics. The 20th Maine, for example, in 1863 would hold a meeting and send a resolution back to Maine approving one candidate for governor, and roundly condemning another.

Ellis Spear, who helped raise Company G of the 20th Maine in Lincoln and Sagadahoc counties, could foresee some of the complications. He described the work as a process of "log-rolling" among the neighbors. There had to be persuasion, promises, and deals of various kinds which would not leave him an enviable position when it came to future discipline. Thus, the test of a line officer was whether or not he was an effective salesman and diplomat. In military matters, he was as green as the men he was trying to enlist. Thinking about it later, Spear could only credit the recruiting officers with great enterprise and audacity, "for such certainly were required in a young man given to serious reflection, who should propose to organize a military company, and to command it in the field, when he scarcely knew a line of battle from a line of rail fence."

6

There were other and more immediate perils, such as wrathy mothers. One woman charged with a pitchfork and drove the recruiting officer from the premises. And there were additional difficulties that could be overcome only through methods that would not bear strict investigation, in the absence of adequate methods for raising troops.

Like most of the states, Maine had entered the war in a woeful state of unpreparedness. Only twenty years before there had been a thriving militia—699 organized companies in the state. And this had been militia in the old "minute man" sense of the word, as originally envisioned by the framers of the Constitution and by Congress. The men had armed and equipped themselves at their own expense, had elected their own officers and held musters in the spring and fall for training and inspection. The older men in the 20th Maine remembered the muster, an occasion which was a sort of combined Fourth of July and country fair. Around the drill field there had been refreshment booths, dancing floors, shows, games, sleight-of-hand performances, auction sales and wrestling matches. And there had been martial splendor of a safe and satisfying kind—soldiers parading up and down to the music of fife and drum, officers resplendent in their fancy uniforms, a few old soldiers of the Revolution watching critically from the sidelines. It had all been a great event—one of the few holidays of the year, looked forward to for weeks, talked about for weeks afterward. But by the time of the Civil War, musters and other training had long since been discontinued and the militia was little more than a memory of plumes and epaulettes, sideshows, cider and gingerbread. As John Hodsdon, Maine's Adjutant General, put it, "Long years of uninterrupted peace had led us to believe that it was our privilege to enjoy all the advantages of a free government, the best since the world began, without adopting any measures for its protection and perpetuity, just as we enjoy the light and the heat of the sun."

Actually, the situation was even worse than it looked on the surface. Until the passage of the Enrollment Act, calling for national conscription in 1863, the basic legal authority for the raising of a large army was the Federal government's ability, under the Constitution and existing laws, to call out the militia, or state troops. (Expansion of the government's own force, the U. S. Regulars, was also possible but was never seriously considered; the specter of a large standing army still haunted the nation.) In order to provide for a uniform militia establishment throughout the states, Congress in 1792 had enacted legislation which ordered, among other things, that all qualified men in the nation between the ages of eighteen and forty-five, with certain exemptions, were to be enrolled by the captains or commanding officers of their local militia companies.

At the outbreak of the war there was a nominal enrolled militia in Maine of around sixty thousand. But most of these men were subject to no peacetime duty or training whatever. Aside from a few volunteer companies, the militia existed on paper only. And there was even some doubt about the legal validity of the paper. As the Federal law then stood, the men were supposed to be enrolled by military officers—the captains or commanding officers of the local companies. But most of Maine's militiamen had been enrolled simply by the assessors of the towns and cities, in conformity with a section of the state law which did not agree with its Federal counterpart.

Fortunately the insubstantial nature of the militia was not an immediate danger in the early days of the war. In 1861, men were trying to get into military service, not out of it, and the government was hard put to find places for all the patriots who came forward. This gave rise to the authorization of a third type of military organization for the Civil War—the volunteer force. But Congress was still unwilling or afraid to invade states' rights too far. Although in the service of the United States, the volunteers were still considered by many to be another form of militia. The volunteer regiments were raised and officered by the states. They took their names from the states, and while making up almost all of the armed force, still remained essentially state troops.

In the meantime, while the first volunteer regiments were being raised, a somewhat tighter legal net was being cast for the militia. By midsummer of 1862, when the 20th Maine was being assembled, there were provisions for properly enrolling men in the militia and for drafting them from the militia into Federal service. This served primarily as a threat. If enough troops could not be raised through volunteering, they could be drafted as militiamen. Thus, the Federal government could put pressure on the state, and the state could put pressure on its towns and cities in the form of quotas for required numbers of men. Every possible effort was made to avoid the draft. A quota, being a number, could be filled by a number; and getting the equivalent in live bodies became the chief consideration of everyone from the Governor down to the town officials. Examining physicians could be persuaded that patriotism was sufficient evidence of physical fitness. If a man was warm, moving under his own power, and patriotic enough to sign his name on the enlistment papers, certain defects could be overlooked. One man, for example, was too short; but he got into the 20th Maine by virtue of a pair of high-heeled shoes. As the heels wore out, he shortened down considerably, but it is recorded that he made a good soldier after all. Another passed muster in a beard dyed glistening black; shortly afterward a widening band of gray appeared and he grew old prematurely.

The first problem, however, was to ignite the necessary feeling of patriotism. It was soon discovered that there was nothing like money for doing this. Bounties were offered by the cities and towns in addition to those from the Federal and state governments. A dollar was hard to come by in Maine, and if a man could be patriotic and lay a little away at the same time, he might as well. In an attempt to fill their quotas, many of the towns were in effect bidding against each other, so it paid to shop around and there was much switching of names and numbers on papers.

This led to some real headaches for the man who was supposed to keep the records straight, Adjutant General John L. Hodsdon, and when he wrote his report at the end of 1862, he was burning up about it. Although he fought the war with pen and paper in Augusta, Maine, General Hodsdon appears to have been one of its unsung heroes. He complained that statistical records of all kinds were sadly deficient and incomplete in America. He could remember old soldiers of the Revolution and the War of 1812 who had died in want because their rights to pensions and other claims could not be established for lack of adequate records. He

9

had, in addition, a deep sense of historic justice in thinking of the men who were going to bleed and die and disappear in this big new war, and he wanted, as he put it, "to present a continuous and perfect record of the share of our State in the present glorious struggle for the honor and integrity of the union, and afford, so far as is practicable, the due meed of praise to every person participating in it, however humble his position."

As he struggled to compile and publish his "continuous and perfect record," Hodsdon was beset by many difficulties, such as illegible, lost and neglected returns from careless and forgetful correspondents. But some of his worst troubles were caused by the bounties. The papers turned in to his office were supposed to show the recruit's place of residence as well as other needed facts. Each volunteer for three years' service was enlisted upon a separate contract, and these papers were usually sent along with a group of recruits to their regimental rendezvous in charge of a recruiting officer or some other authorized person. It was usually upon delivery and mustering-in of the men in camp that the bounties were paid, although in some instances the recruits were paid in advance.

Hodsdon described what often happened: "Upon their arrival at the camp, the officer in charge finds the agent of some city or town 'where wealth accumulates but men decay,' prepared to pay a much larger bounty than that offered by the place from which his squad was sent; by supplying him with the men under his charge, he secures a larger bounty for them than that which they had contracted for, with a bonus to himself usually, of from twenty-five to one hundred dollars per man. To effect this arrangement, either the place of residence given on the enlistment papers was changed, or new enlistments were substituted from the assertion of the recruits, upon due instruction, that the quotas of their towns were full, or that they had no legal residence in the State. Not infrequently during the negotiations, the agent of some other town offered a larger bounty, occasioning the substitution in the enlistment papers of still another place of residence, so that some papers when they were deposited in this office exhibited three or four different towns as the residence of the recruit, all but one of which shows an attempt at obliteration."

Endless confusion resulted. Often, when the authorities of a town from which recruits had been sent came into camp to pay them the bounty agreed upon, they found them credited upon the quotas of other towns. Or worse yet, where quotas were filled and bounties paid in advance, towns were often surprised to get notices that they were short a number of men. Controversies arose between towns which, as Hodsdon said, "embodied all the zeal, bitterness and contradictory evidence usually attending pauper lawsuits."

In his report for that year, 1862, Hodsdon estimated that in addition to bounties paid by the Federal and state governments, Maine cities, towns and plantations had paid more than $1,500,-000. This money even corrupted some of the earlier volunteers, who presumably had enlisted for pure patriotism in 1861. Many procured discharges by any available means and came back to Maine. Here they re-enlisted to get some of the gravy.

A great deal of the bounty money went into the pockets of brokers and agents who negotiated between the towns and the available recruits. Often broker and volunteer divvied up the money half and half. The municipal authorities themselves were not above reproach. Many of them were interested in filling their quotas in any way they could, without regard to the interests of the nation. The system of voluntary enlistment was proving itself to be unrealistic, and the bounty payments were in Hodsdon's opinion a deep and lasting disgrace.

And yet most of the volunteers were far from being crooks or mercenaries, and not all the towns lagged in their responsibilities. The Adjutant General cited seventy-nine towns, cities and plantations that not only sent their quotas but sent from one to twenty-five more soldiers than they were asked for. The town of Enfield, with 329 inhabitants, had fifty-four in the service. One Enfield man sent six sons, then went himself. The town of Portage Lake had only one able-bodied man left in it. And again it must be remembered that people were persuading, but no one was forcing these men to go; they were volunteers.

It is difficult, at this distance in time, to analyze their deeper motives. Many undoubtedly enlisted from boredom—to get away from bleak farms, lonely forest clearings or ugly wives. Many volunteered simply because there was a war on and men were going to it. But many enlisted in a sort of patriotic frenzy. It can well be imagined what emotions would be aroused today if there were an attempt to break up the United States by force. That feeling, comparable to the instinct of the hive or the herd to save itself, was perhaps intensified by the fact that the nation was smaller, younger, and at that time not too far removed from foreign domination.

The regimental staff did not include an Information and Education officer to tell the men what they were fighting for. None was needed. Many of the men of the 20th Maine seem to have been well informed, surprisingly well educated, and fully cognizant of the main issue. If the South won, there would be no reason to expect a continuance of the United States of America. And they might soon have no country.

This was an intolerable thought. Just how intolerable it was we can probably never understand, unless some day we unhappily find ourselves in the same position. But judging by the letters these men wrote, the efforts they put forth, and the hardships that failed to deter them, we can understand that they were very much in earnest in their devotion to the Union.

As the war progressed and they saw that Southern men were fighting for ideas that seemed to *them* equally important, the Maine soldiers thought more deeply, and some of them realized that it was not a simple question they were fighting to settle. But through it all they clung to their determination that the Union must be preserved, and in this resolve—as they would prove in the election of 1864—they identified themselves very closely with the President.

In the character of its men, the regiment approached a fairly good cross section of the entire state, although its volunteers came mostly from the smaller villages and rural sections. The 20th Maine was the last of the three-year regiments raised in Maine in response to the President's call for three hundred thousand volunteers in July of 1862. Apparently it was formed from detachments originally enlisted for the 16th, 17th, 18th and 19th regiments, and afterward found to be unnecessary to complete those organizations. The "leftovers" came from scattered localities. Companies E, G, I and K came from many little towns lying in the arms of the ocean along the deeply indented coast. Companies A, C, D and F were harvested from the farmlands of south-central and western Maine. Company B came from a big-woods county, Piscataquis—as also did Company H, journeying down from Aroostook County, forest-sequestered region from which it was a one-hundred-mile trip by stagecoach before they came to the railroad at Bangor.

Geographically, this was the background of the 20th Maine, and when the regiment had left home far behind, it could dream of many things: of gulls crying and green waves crashing on a stony shore; of forest silences so deep they seemed to have an audible presence; of oxen and bow-necked horses pulling plows and turning the green sod of spring, with birds foraging behind in the furrows; of axes ringing in a winter dawn and tall trees falling with lingering smashes; of deer running in high bounds and partridge rocketing up over hardwood ridges; of endless crops of stones, and stone walls lined with hazel bushes; of one-room schools with a water pail in the corner, a stove in the center, and scholars studying with a drowsy hum; of white farmhouses with lilacs in the yard; of gristmills and blacksmith shops; and fishing boats bobbing on a wind-swept ocean.

. Racially, with few exceptions, the men were what the people of Aroostook, borrowing an expression from the terminology of the potato, would call "the old seed-ends." After the war the Adjutant General tabulated the nativity of all Maine troops, and it figured out that about eighty-five per cent had been born in New England. The rest were overwhelmingly English, Scotch and Irish in their origins. The same report classified occupations as around thirty-two per cent agricultural, twenty-nine per cent mechanical, twenty-four per cent laborers, eleven per cent miscellaneous (which included seamen), two per cent commercial and two per cent professional. With so few men from the cities and larger towns, the 20th Maine probably was composed of an even larger percentage of native stock, with farming, fishing and lumbering predominating among the occupations. The names in the muster rolls also reflect an old-time character of population, culture and way of life. Along with the Georges and Williams, there were the Aarons, Abials and Arads, the Ebenezers, Elijahs, Elishas, Ephraims and Ezekiels, the Isaacs, Isaiahs and Israels, the Jobs, Joshuas and Josiahs, and so on down to the Zachariahs.

In age, the men of the 20th Maine (just under one thousand in all) ranged all the way from eighteen, the lower legal limit, to forty-five, the upper. Sixty-seven of the them were forty and over. The oldest rifleman listed on the records was Glazier Estabrook of Amity, forty-five. Glazier was a small man but full of fight and terribly strong. The older people in Amity remember stories. One: Long after the war, when Glazier was getting on in years, he got into a fight with a man at a lumber camp on Jimmy Brook, got him down, and began beating him with his fists. When bystanders dragged him off he cried, "Oh! Let me give him just another touch of the live oak!" Glazier fought all through the war and, after Gettysburg, made corporal and the color guard.

All this was the raw material waiting for Colonel Ames. The men, he soon realized, would never be regulation, government-issue soldiers. They were too independent, for one thing, and although acknowledging the necessity for obeying orders, they could not help resenting invasions of their "rights." For example, a private, when admonished by his company commander for a lack of personal cleanliness at inspection, would retort that he thought it was "cussed mean business to go around and peek in other folks' ears." But they were enthusiastic and willing. Many of the officers showed promise, even though they had not been selected on the basis of military merit. (Ellis Spear believed the Governor commissioned them after thinking it out in this fashion: "These fellows who have recruited so many men and have actually landed them in camp must have military qualifications.")

In the few days Colonel Ames had before the regiment was to move to the theater of war, everything seemed to happen all at once. Commissions for the officers arrived from Augusta. A Regular Army officer appeared and mustered the regiment into the Federal service. The uniforms came and were issued. The usual uniform in the Civil War was dark blue coat and light blue trousers. But initially the 20th Maine wore *all* dark blue—coat and trousers alike. This effect must have given the regiment, as seen in the distance, something of the appearance of a group of railway conductors on an outing. Ellis Spear recalled that "the diverse effect of all these new clothes was remarkable. Of course there was no such blaze of glory as that which now appears upon the Avenue on occasions of official display; but compared with the sober drabs of civil life, the blue cloth with the gold buttons and the new shoulder-straps were comparatively gorgeous. Some whose youth was more easily affected by the unusual display assumed airs of importance; others wore their honors with meekness, and some went about with a settled determination expressed upon their faces to attend to business and to ignore as far as possible these honors and glories thus suddenly thrust upon them. The camp put on a military appearance, and the regiment, if not a lion, was at least clothed in the skin of that formidable beast."

The skin was too tight in places, and at others it hung loosely. One soldier wrote later that he was sixteen years old (his age appears on the rolls as eighteen) and stood over six feet and weighed 150 pounds. To get a uniform that was long enough to cover his beanpole frame he had to take one that billowed out around the waist, leaving room enough for another soldier inside.

The regiment would be equipped partly by the state, partly by the United States government. In addition to his uniform, each man would get from the state a woolen blanket and a rubber blanket . . . a haversack, knapsack and canteen . . . a tin plate, tin dipper, knife, fork and spoon . . . and if he were lucky he would get a towel. From the Portland peddlers the men were also buying patented drinking tubes, pencils, stencil plates and ink, stationery, combs and brushes, revolvers, murderous-looking knives, money-belts, patent medicines and everything else that could possibly be imagined as helpful in crushing the rebellion. Colonel Ames knew that most of this stuff and much of the government-issue material, too, would probably be scattered along some Virginia roadway on the first hard march.

As for arms, the 20th Maine was scheduled to draw muskets and ammunition in Washington. Colonel Ames went through the list of other regimental property, and it didn't take him long.

He noted such items as camp kettles . . . wall tents . . . spades
. . . axes . . . hatchets . . . mess pans. With no time for training,
with 965 officers and men who were completely raw militarily,
and with scanty equipment that included ten drums, five
bugles, ten pounds of nails and a handsaw, Colonel Ames was
supposed to represent himself as the commander of an infantry
regiment and report, forthwith, to the Commanding General,
Army of the Potomac.

The 20th departed quietly from the State of Maine. Probably
because of the scattered nature of its origin, it was not, as Joshua
Chamberlain noted, one of the state's favorites; no county
claimed it; no city gave it a flag; and there was no send-off at
the station.

As the troop train rattled southward and Colonel Ames brooded
upon the military shortcomings of its passengers, the young
West Pointer might have been reassured by the prophetic words
of Alexis de Tocqueville, a perceptive Frenchman who had visited America some years before. De Tocqueville had observed
that discipline for many European soldiers was only a continuation of social servitude, but the American fighting man would
be another breed of cat. He wrote, "A democratic people must
despair of ever obtaining from soldiers that blind, minute, sub-
missive, and invariable obedience which an aristocratic people
may impose on them without difficulty. The state of society does
not prepare them for it, and the nation might be in danger of
losing its natural advantages if it sought artificially to acquire
advantages of this particular kind. Among democratic commu-
nities, military discipline ought not to attempt to annihilate the
free spring of the faculties; all that can be done by discipline is
to direct it; the obedience thus inculcated is less exact, but it is
more eager and more intelligent. It has its root in the will of
him who obeys; it rests not only on his instinct, but on his reason; and consequently it will often spontaneously become more
strict as danger requires it. The discipline of an aristocratic army
is apt to be relaxed in war, because that discipline is founded
upon habits, and war disturbs those habits. The discipline of a
democratic army, on the contrary, is strengthened in sight of the

enemy, because every soldier then clearly perceives that he must be silent and obedient in order to conquer."

But all this could be clearer to a foreign observer than it was to natives facing the nation's first big war. There was still a picture of battle wherein brilliantly uniformed men moved to the music of bands and executed Napoleonic maneuvers—with a smaller picture of the soldier saying "Sir" to officers, clicking his heels, and turning to carry out orders without question or hesitation even into the jaws of death. If he had reflected upon it, the Maine man would have agreed with de Tocqueville. He had about as much chance of being the classic soldier as he had of becoming a ballet dancer in the Paris Opera. For he certainly wasn't going to say "Sir" to the officer who was just old Tom or Joe from down the road. Clicking the heels was just plain silly. As for carrying out orders without question, sometimes old Tom or Joe didn't show very good sense. So the glamorous picture would begin to disintegrate even as he first thought about it.

As many men have been, the volunteer was somewhat enamored of war. He had read of war. He had heard of war. But he knew absolutely nothing about it, except that there was a war on; that it was a serious thing for the country; and that it had better, some way or other, be won.

CHAPTER TWO

Dan, Dan, Dan, Butterfield, Butterfield

ASHINGTON in late summer of 1862 was hot and humid, with mutterings of thunder, currents of fear and hope running through the stifling atmosphere. Fear because Union troops under Pope had just come tumbling back into the defenses of Washington after their defeat at the second battle of Bull Run. Hope because "Little Mac" McClellan was again in command, and the strange inspiration of his personality had lifted men's hearts in the expectation that maybe now, after all, victory was just over the horizon—hope also because the tide of Northern manpower was running strong, and fresh new regiments were arriving. Private William T. Livermore of the 20th Maine noted in his diary, "Everything looks warlike here . . . flags flying from every hill and for miles the fields are white with tents and troops and army wagons and artillery and cavalry and horses and mules without number."

The 20th had come from Maine by rail and steamer, arriving in Washington on Sunday, September 7. The regiment spent the night in a vacant lot near the U.S. Arsenal, on what Ellis Spear described as "a downy bed of dead cats, bricks and broken bottles." Next day the men drew muskets and ammunition at the arsenal; then the regiment started for Fort Craig, on Arlington Heights. Acutely conscious of the fact that they were country boys in the big city, the Maine soldiers wanted to make a good impression. But the drum corps got out of time, the men got out of step, and the march turned into a frustrating draggle, with onlookers laughing and old soldiers jeering along the way. By the end of the march the regiment had straggled so badly that

18

Ames could no longer contain himself. He shouted, "If you can't do any better than you have tonight, you better all desert and go home!" This remark did not endear him to the volunteers.

Having reached Fort Craig, the next matter of interest was the organizational assignment of the regiment. The military structure into which the 20th Maine was to fit was one that had not changed very radically since the days of Napoleon. The Army of the Potomac was divided into corps. Each corps was, in effect, a little army.

The corps was composed of two or more divisions, usually three.

The division was normally made up of three brigades.

The brigade, as originally organized in the Army of the Potomac, had four regiments.

The regiment was the basic building block of the army and the fighting unit. With the exception of a few U. S. Regulars, numbering at the end of 1862 less than three per cent of the total force, the regiments were mostly volunteers, taking their names from their parent states, having their own flags and in a sense their own souls and personalities.

Normally a regiment would leave its home state with around a thousand officers and men. If all the regiments in a corps were at full strength, the corps might have around thirty-six thousand men—a force capable of decisive effect on any battlefield. However, the "if" was a big one. Hard marching, exposure, and disease might reduce the regiment to seven hundred men within a few weeks; continued sickness, desertions, straggling and the first battle might take another two hundred; a few months more of combat and the regiment was likely to be down to a third of its authorized strength.

Most of the states at this time had no system of automatic replacements for existing regiments. Instead, new regiments were made up and sent into the field—which, incidentally, gave the Governor a batch of new commissions to hand out. About the only way an old regiment could get more soldiers was to detach a recruiting party and send it home to enlist new men. Sometimes a Maine officer on leave would undertake this duty voluntarily; he would gather up a group of recruits and take them back with him to the regiment, not even bothering to report his acquisitions to the state. But these hit-or-miss methods did not work well, so the regiment never did get back to anywhere near its authorized strength.

Therefore, because it was built on regiments, the ideal army organization had to be modified. In order to have a brigade that amounted to anything in size, it was often necessary to increase the number of regiments. The brigade to which the 20th Maine was assigned had six regiments at this time. It was the 3rd Brigade, 1st Division, Fifth Corps, known as Butterfield's Light Brigade. It had been through the Peninsular campaign and the men had a reputation for being good fighters and a less enviable one for efficient foraging. "Butterfield's Thieves," a soldier in another brigade had called them. It seems there was a question about taking some chickens, and the soldier settled it by saying that Butterfield's Thieves were coming along behind and "if we don't take them, *they* will."

The brigade was unusual in other ways. Ordinarily, most of the soldier's loyalty went to his own regiment; the brigade was merely a tactical unit in which he fought and maneuvered. But Butterfield's Brigade had a family feeling all its own. General Daniel Butterfield no longer commanded it, but he was one who left an impression on the brigade—and on the army—that was all out of proportion to his actual ability as an officer.

Butterfield was a composer of bugle calls. Bedding down with the brigade at night the Maine men heard a sad, strangely haunting call that seemed to say, "Go to sleep . . . all is well . . . all is well . . ." and they felt as though the army had taken them in among its own. This call, according to Oliver Norton, the brigade bugler, was one that General Butterfield had composed while the army was at Harrison's Landing after the Peninsular campaign. The regulation Lights Out call had displeased Butterfield. It was too official-sounding. He wanted something that would convey the mood of putting out the lights and lying down to rest in the silence of the night. So he composed this new call for use in his brigade. Other buglers heard the call and eventually it spread through the entire army. Today it is the official Taps. It has a strong funereal significance to the general public because of its association with military burials. But to most army people the call is still—as Butterfield intended it to be—a benedictory good night, best heard, perhaps, on one of the old western posts, like Riley or Sill, when the stars hang low and yellow, when 'the noises of the day have ceased, and a cool breeze is starting to come in across the parade ground. Then, down through the years in its true sense, comes Butterfield's Lullabye, the one expression of tenderness the army ever allows itself.

This the 20th Maine heard and felt, and they also heard for the first time Butterfield's famous Brigade Call. In the Civil War the bugle was a primary instrument of communication and command, along with the drum. Casey's *Infantry Tactics* prescribed twenty-six general calls for all troops and twenty-three special calls for skirmishers, including such detailed bugle-orders as Lie Down and Rise Up. When regiments or brigades were drilling or maneuvering in close proximity there was a tendency towards confusion—a call for one unit was likely to be heard and responded to by another. To forestall this in his own brigade, General Butterfield composed a brigade call. This was a brief series of notes which was sounded twice before the call for any operation or movement to be executed by the 3rd Brigade. The men put words to it:

DAN, DAN, DAN, BUTTERFIELD, BUTTERFIELD.

Or sometimes, if the going promised to be rough:

DAMN, DAMN, DAMN, BUTTERFIELD, BUTTERFIELD.

Of course they heard it thousands of times before the war was over and it became deeply ingrained in their consciousness—a sort of automatic alert. A quarter of a century later, during a reunion at Gettysburg, a bugler went up on Little Round Top and sounded the old Dan Butterfield call. Veterans who had been scattered all over, examining half-remembered positions, came hurrying to the hill in answer to the call, many with tears in their eyes. Echoing sharp and clear among the rocks and trees where they had fought, it had awakened the memories they were seeking with a sudden and breath-taking sense of reality.

There was another call the 20th Maine was to hear often—The

General, the signal for soldiers in camp to strike tents and prepare to march. It sounded on September 12, and they started on
the forced march that was to lead to Antietam. The weather
continued unusually hot and oppressive. The Maine boys weren't
used to it. As they pushed forward at the route step, sweat ran
down their backs, down their legs, into their shoes, where the
ill-fashioned leather was rubbing up blisters the size of silver
dollars. Hardly a breeze stirred. Dust rose up and hung over the
road in thick, suffocating masses. Columns of dust traced the
roadways in the air, from horizon to horizon, as the Army of
the Potomac pressed northwestward. The 20th Maine suffered,
sweated, choked and after a while began to divest itself of some
of the excess equipment picked up from the peddlers. Then some
of the men began to throw away blankets; it was hard to comprehend, in this heat, how a man would *ever* need a blanket.
The march that day was about sixteen miles, and even stripped
down to light marching order, the 20th Maine didn't make it.
By nightfall, hardly a corporal's guard was left.

This experience was by no means limited to the 20th Maine.
There was another new regiment which had joined the corps at
the same time—the 118th Pennsylvania, otherwise known as the
Corn Exchange Regiment because it had been raised through
the efforts and considerable financial resources of the Corn Exchange in Philadelphia. The two regiments, from Maine and
Pennsylvania, would have much in common throughout the war,
and on this day they were sharing the same foot-blistering introduction to army life. One dusty, demoralized private of the 118th,
trudging wearily along in the sunset, saw the division commander, Major General George W. Morell, and made bold to
inquire, "General, can you tell me where the 118th Pennsylvania
is?"

"Certainly, my man," replied the General. "Everywhere between here and Washington."

In another regiment of the division, one of the new companies
had no officers and only one man left at the end of the day. The
remaining soldier made a pardonable demonstration of his accomplishment. When the regiment bivouacked in column of
companies, it is recorded that the one single man "executed un-

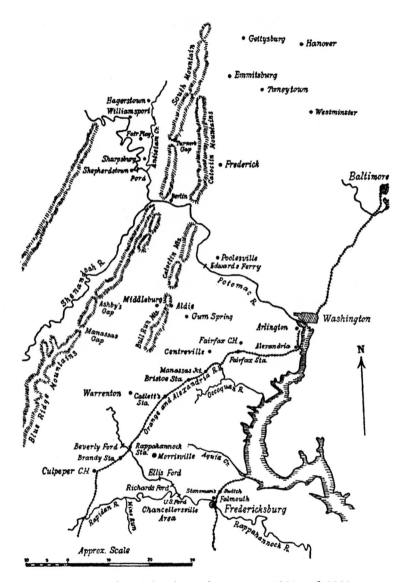

Theater of War for the 20th Maine in 1862 and 1863

der his own command the company right wheel, dressed his ranks, stacked his arms (by plunging the bayonet into the ground), called the roll, broke ranks, supped, and slept the sleep of the just."

Flesh failed, temporarily, but the spirit was more than willing. The coolness of evening revived many of the fallen, who got up and struggled on. The night was full of wanderers and wakers of sleeping men, asking the anxious question that will go on through nights forever where armies move, "Hey soldier, what outfit is this?"

The 20th Maine collected itself during the night. In the morning the regiment marched with nearly full ranks. That day it did twenty-four miles. The prospects improved. Out in the fertile countryside it seemed cooler. The landscape was rich and colorful under the mellow September sunlight. There were pretty villages and pretty girls along the way. Many of the people were friendly, offering the soldiers fresh-baked bread, fruit and cool water.

On September 14 there was audible evidence that something more ominous lay ahead, a disturbance of the atmosphere off to the northwest, which gradually increased to the soft, thudding thunder of distant artillery fire. They passed through Frederick, Barbara Frietchie's home town, now bright with waving banners. And beyond Frederick they came to their war through a series of magnificent vistas. Ascending the Catoctins they saw, across the green-and-gold patchwork of a fertile valley, another height of land rising—the long blue-shadowed South Mountain range, where there had been fighting ahead of them. They met their first Confederates, prisoners being escorted to the rear who impressed Private Theodore Gerrish of Company H as "lank, slouchy looking fellows, clad in dirty gray uniforms." They ascended the slopes over South Mountain, through Turner's Gap. Seemingly, a small hurricane had been through the gap. They noted torn-up earth, white-gashed trees and fallen branches, splintered barns. Burial parties were at work, leaving the Confederate dead until last, and of these Private Gerrish remembered that "they lay, as they had fallen, in groups of half-a-dozen each, and single bodies scattered here and there, all through the scattering oak growth that crowned the crest of the hill. They were of all ages, and looked grim and ghastly. Old men with silvered hair, strong men in the prime of manhood, beardless boys, whose smooth, youthful, upturned faces looked strangely innocent, although sealed in a bloody death."

Again, from the western slope of South Mountain, on the afternoon of the sixteenth, there were breath-taking views as they descended—glimpses, through Turner's Gap, of the Army of the Potomac stretched out ahead of them. From the heights it looked like a toy army—tiny horses, miniature cannon and white-topped wagons, dusty-blue columns of infantry, a vast array extending off into the distance toward a stream called the Antietam. Just beyond the Antietam was the little village of Sharpsburg—and the army of Robert E. Lee.

They descended South Mountain and joined the forces below. Next morning found the 20th Maine men resting behind what came to be known to them as the Middle Bridge, the Fifth Corps being held there in reserve while the right wing of the army began the assault across the stream. On a ridge in front of them Union batteries began to hammer. From across the Antietam arose a mighty clamor. The Maine men waited, and the tension mounted intolerably. Some of them went up on the ridge to get their first look at a battle.

They were surprised to find that it looked a great deal like pictures they had seen, with little fire-winking puffballs appearing in the air, tremendous quantities of smoke, and a soiled, gray look all over the landscape. The country appeared to be fairly open; across the Antietam in the distance they saw cornfields, pastures, patches of woods. Running along an irregular line from the right was what looked to be a bad grass fire, rapidly getting out of control. Dark masses of men moved here and there, giving out blinkings and rattlings that occasionally deepened to a roar where the smoke was thickest. Everything seemed to be in slow motion on the ground, but the air was alive with quick flashings and thunderous shakings. Smoke from a distant battery appeared: *puff——puff, puff, puff——puff, puff,* and after an interval the sound reached them in the same rhythm: *pum——pum, pum, pum——pum, pum.* A caisson blew up with a silent orange flash, throwing fire and splinters high into the air . . . also an old suit of clothes that flopped in the sky . . . and tiny blacknesses, specks and strings falling; then the sound of the explosion came with an identity of its own, a soft, brushing shock-wave felt on the forehead and cheeks, a slight jarring under the feet.

Dirt spattered on the ridge near them, and a large object swished past, striking again behind them and bounding off into the rearward distance. Cannoneers of the Union batteries near by began giving the spectators hard looks. The Confederate batteries across the stream were mostly concentrating their fire on the attacking infantry in their immediate front; however, if a profitable long-range target showed up over here on the ridge, it was always worth a shot, so the artillerymen told the sightseers from the infantry to get the hell back down the hill; they were drawing fire.

The walking wounded started coming back—men with shocked, staring faces, croaking in the doleful manner of walking wounded about impending disasters up ahead. On top of the ridge, just at the edge of safety, one of the hobblers sat down to pull a shoe off his wounded foot. Behind him a round, black object came bouncing like a rubber ball; there was a soft, smashing sound; the man collapsed with odd violence into the semblance of a large, bloody rag doll; and the solid shot bounded again, sailing lazily over the heads of the Maine soldiers. In the backwash of the battle, there were other horrid and dismal sights, but when night came the Fifth Corps, with the 20th Maine, was still in reserve.

Among the many criticisms directed at McClellan for his conduct of the battle of Antietam has been the accusation that he let the Fifth Corps stand idle when it, along with other available troops, might have turned the tide. Whoever would attempt to unravel and reweave the strands of history must be led inevitably to patterns that are endless in the conjecture they allow. But considering only the thread represented by the 20th Maine, this regiment could thank its lucky stars for McClellan's excess of caution. For there had been no time to give the 20th even rudimentary training; it was still a shambling mob, and efficiency in drill was something more than a parade ground requirement in the Civil War. To deliver effective fire and defend itself, a regiment had to be able to maneuver in formation, and Antietam, one of the bloodiest and most violent battles of the war, was no place for an outfit that was likely to get its feet tangled up.

Fortunately, also, the actual baptism of fire for the 20th Maine came under circumstances that were not excessively trying. This took place on September 20, when a portion of the Fifth Corps crossed the Potomac in an attempted pursuit or heavy reconnaissance action near Shepherdstown, where the main body of the Confederate army had recrossed into Virginia. Marching down in their turn to the river, the Maine men saw that it was fordable, flowing between high bluffs on either side. On the Maryland side (the side held by the Union army), the Chesapeake & Ohio Canal ran parallel with and close to the river. The canal was dry; the Confederates had tapped and drained it.

The water in the Potomac was low. There was a neglected dam across the river, the outer face greasy with green slime where it sloped down into the water. Beyond the other shore the wooded bluffs rose, ending in a ragged rim against the sky. Beyond that, somewhere, were the rear elements of Lee's army.

Those with an eye for topography and the similarity here to the much-written-about-and-discussed Ball's Bluff hoped that they weren't getting into another disaster like *that*. At Ball's Bluff, eleven months before, a Union force had been hurled over a precipice and into the river in a massacre that set the whole North buzzing with horror and indignation.

By the time the 20th Maine arrived at the river, part of the Union force had already crossed and climbed the bluffs. The regiment stood awaiting its turn to cross, with the officers talking too much and too fast and saying, "Steady, men," a little too often. Ahead of them, just over the rim of the bluffs on the Confederate shore, the racket of gunfire was banging against the sky, and soon they were aware of faint howlings and whistlings in the air above them. The imminence of personal death began to develop its involuntary, uncontrollable physiological reactions—the too-fast, too-hard pounding of the heart, the dry knotting of the stomach, and a general shakiness that made them aware of why the old biblical fellows had spoken so often of girding up the loins—a man's loins, they found, could get mighty loose.

Even to the inexperienced eyes of the Maine soldiers it was soon apparent that operations were not proceeding according to plan. Union cavalrymen were pounding back across the river, whipping their horses through the shallows and gazing over their shoulders apprehensively. Union infantry also seemed to be retreating. And artillery which had been getting ready to cross was now going into position and opening fire from the Union shore. But the 20th Maine had received no orders to halt, so the regiment started for the river to begin its crossing.

In his diary that night, Private William T. Livermore wrote a description of what happened. The ordinary Civil War diarist in the ranks was no Richard Harding Davis, and his accounts are often unsatisfactory. ("June 24. Cloudy. We advanced ½ mile and a terrible battle was fought. June 25. Fair. Another terrible battle was fought today.") But Corporal Livermore had some talent for writing as well as a great deal for fighting and he left us a good account of his experiences in the river crossing. ". . . We saw the cavalry coming in on the run from the other side and we soon found that they were retreating and our artillery that was waiting to cross took their position and opened. But we went on and met the river full of cavalry and infantry. But we went on under the greatest roar of artillery. The shells from our batteries would go so near our heads it seemed as though it would take the hair off from my head, and the air was full of shells and some of our own burst overhead and wounded some of our own men. And the rebels shot and shells made it a fearful scene as we went down the bank and walked up a few rods to get a chance to cross. And a piece of shell went through the co. just ahead of me and just grazed the head of Lieut. Lyford, and the next instant a bullet came and struck the toe of Corp. Waterhouse and knocked his toes back under his foot. His toe was not more than 8 inches from my heel. It threw the mud onto my legs and I rubbed my legs to see if it did not hit me, but I turned round and saw Waterhouse fall out. . . ." Despite this shock to his morale, Livermore continued, but when the 20th Maine reached the far shore most of the other troops had turned back. By now the counterattacking Confederates, having precipitated the Union retreat, were making their way to the edge of the bluff and firing down at the fleeing Federals. An order finally came for the 20th to get back to the Maryland bank. There was a great harrying of bugles, shouting, and the beginning of confusion.

As the Maine regiment recrossed, bullets were falling into the river. Fearful of panic, one of the officers stopped his horse in the water, turned about, and sat there calmly, urging the men on. He wanted to set them a good example, but a private soldier of the 20th unwittingly outdid him. The private was a fussy little man, and before entering the river he had taken off his shoes and stockings and packed them away in his blanket roll. Now, before going back, the little man sat down on the bank to roll up his trouser legs a few inches higher, the officer watching with incredulous anxiety. The little private started gingerly into the river, bullets going *spat, chug* into the water around him. One of the trouser legs fell down. The man turned and went back to the enemy shore to roll it up again. The officer, able to stand it no longer, hustled the fussy little man across the river.

While engaged in similar duty, supervising the retreat across the river, Lieutenant Colonel Chamberlain's horse was shot under him. This was the first of a long series of unfortunate animals associated with the Maine officer. Confederate marksmen aiming at Chamberlain almost invariably hit his horse instead, until later in the war, when they succeeded in bringing down both horse and rider on a couple of occasions.

In its retreat across the river, the 20th Maine behaved remarkably well. There was no disorder even when the regiment, still under fire and with three men bleeding from bullet wounds, had gained the Union shore and taken cover in the dry canal—which made an excellent entrenchment.

The other new regiment in the division, the Corn Exchange Regiment from Philadelphia, had been less fortunate. The Corn Exchange men had got up over the bluff, into an advanced position in the fields beyond, and were trying to stand off the Confederate assault when it was discovered that about a quarter of their muskets—defective Enfields—would not fire. The Corn Exchange Regiment had had no appreciable drill or instruction, yet it battled gamely for a while and then, with the enemy in close pursuit, came tumbling back down the bluff, a mass of blue figures that seemed to fall apart and slide down the slope. Confederates appeared on the rim of the bluff, shooting down into the Pennsylvanians. Many were hit as they tried to cross on the old dam; their bodies caught in the ruins or bobbed away downstream in the shallow, swift-running river.

But it wasn't going to be another Ball's Bluff. Union artillery blasted the Confederates, and an excited yammer of musketry ran up and down the canal as troops behind this ready-made line of breastworks opened an effective covering fire. Under this protective fire, most of the Corn Exchange Regiment got back safely. Previously the Philadelphia regiment hadn't been too warmly received in the division; the rumor was that its presence at the front was largely explained by the big bounties offered by the Corn Exchange. But here at Shepherdstown Ford, it had done most of the fighting and suffered most of the casualties, and from here on, as one of the Pennsylvanians noted, "opprobrious allusions were changed to plaudits."

With the shot-up Corn Exchange Regiment back on the Union shore, there was a lot of firing back and forth across the river for the rest of the day. Few people were getting hurt, and the affair from then on turned out to be rather enjoyable—excepting some trouble with one of their own supporting batteries. This battery, which must rank as one of the most inexpert of the war, was just about as far behind them as the enemy was in front. Yet the gunners were getting bursts at points less than fifty per cent along the trajectory, and so the 20th Maine and the rest of the brigade were receiving a shower of metal from their own artillery, a matter most annoying to infantry. A delegation went back to confer with the defenders of the Union who were manning this battery; shortly afterward it fell silent with dramatic suddenness.

That night the Confederates withdrew from their front, and that was Antietam for the 20th Maine. Except for one all-important event. They saw Lincoln at Antietam. On October 1, the President arrived to see McClellan and to spend several days with the army. A review was held in his honor. Joshua Cham-

berlain believed that Lincoln always had a great desire to see
the Army of the Potomac together—that to him the Army in mass
had a power and a presence far beyond the aggregate of its
individual units, and that between it and the President there
developed an almost mystic bond. At Antietam, according to
Chamberlain, the men conceived an affection for Lincoln that
was "wonderful in its intensity."

As the reviewing cavalcade passed down the lines, Lincoln
and McClellan made a picture which the men of the 20th Maine
must have remembered long afterward—especially when the two
leaders confronted each other in the election of 1864. Physically,
the contrast was striking: McClellan—trim, dashing, romantic,
with his cap cocked at a jaunty angle; Lincoln—angular, un-
gainly on his borrowed mount, with his deep-lined, bearded face,
his shadowed eyes. Spiritually there was a contrast too. McClellan personified the glory of war, with all the trappings inherited
from European tradition, a glamour that was soon to fade for
these men of the 20th Maine. Lincoln—with his rural, woodland
and small-town background—was nearer home; he had something to remind them all of what they were or what they had
been; he was America itself, a giant emerging from the wilderness with all his imperfections pathetically laid bare, and it may
be imagined that they took him to their hearts with a fierce, protective pride. The glory would fade. But the pride would last,
even to the mud of Petersburg, when war became as unglamor-
ous as murder in a back alley.

In front of the 20th Maine, Lincoln took notice of Chamberlain's horse, a beautiful dappled-white animal, and he paused a
moment to call it to McClellan's attention. In his high silk hat,
Lincoln made a figure nearly seven feet tall. Here on his horse
he seemed to tower against the sky. There was only a moment
before he passed, and it is so long ago that it is hard to say what
the men felt. We have only a brief description from Chamberlain, written much later. On their yellowed pages the words today look over-sentimental and perhaps inspired by hindsight.
But they must be respected and granted some validity as a reflection of emotions we are no longer in a position to understand.
Chamberlain remembered that "we could see the deep sadness in

his face, and feel the burden on his heart, thinking of his great commission to save this people, and knowing that he could do this no otherwise than as he had been doing—by and through the manliness of these men—the valor, the steadfastness, the loyalty, the devotion, the sufferings and thousand deaths, of those into whose eyes his were looking. How he shrunk from the costly sacrifice we could see; and we took him into our hearts with answering sympathy, and gave him our pity in return."

And so this was an important day for the 20th Maine at Antietam. And there were others. After a spell of picketing near Shepherdstown Ford—very pleasant duty in the shady glens, with the autumn-colored hills towering up before them—they moved to an encampment near the old Iron Works near the mouth of the Antietam. Here Colonel Ames finally got the chance to give the regiment its much-needed military education.

There was a lot of civilian independence in the enlisted men of the 20th Maine that neither Ames nor anyone else would ever be able to eradicate. One of their habits, at the outset, had been to hang around the commissioned officers' tents, as though these were country post offices where citizens had the privilege of gathering to chew tobacco and discuss the latest news. Ames had put a stop to this and many other civilian habits. But weeks later, even after the regiment was a fairly well-trained unit, incidents would keep popping up. Once a man was cooking apples at his tent when an order was given to fall in for inspection, and in his haste to obey, the soldier accidentally tipped the pan over and messed up his rifle. Wiping it off as best he could, he ran to the formation. An inspecting officer from division headquarters came down the line, grabbed the rifle with military smartness, and found his white gloves all covered with a sticky substance. The inspector lost his temper and profanely demanded to know what that stuff was on the gun. The enlisted man apparently thought it wasn't sensible to take on so, over a thing like that, and told the officer reprovingly, "It is *nothin'* but green apple sass, sir!"

And another time a man in ranks was called on by an officer to explain why he was always loudly crunching a piece of flinty hardtack in his mouth. "The juice, sir!" he called back cheerfully. "I am very fond of the juice!"

But in spite of all this, Colonel Ames was determined to hammer the 20th Maine into a fighting unit. The 20th had come into the war with traditional American unpreparedness for such matters, and it had nearly everything to learn. Even in the procedure of loading its weapons, the 20th needed training. Between firings of the muzzle-loading rifle a man had to go through all these manual operations: he had to reach into his cartridge box and get a cartridge, which consisted of a charge of powder and ball wrapped in paper; place one end of the cartridge between his teeth and tear it open; empty the powder into the barrel and insert the ball with pointed end uppermost; draw the rammer out of its pipes beneath the barrel; ram the ball home; return the rammer; half-cock the hammer and remove the old cap; reach into the cap pouch, get a new cap, and press it down on the nipple.

At a turkey shoot, or in the leisure of hunting in the Maine woods, shooting a muzzle-loading rifle was a simple enough procedure. But strange things could be done in the brain-fogging frenzy and fear of battle. In his terrible excitement, a man could neglect to withdraw the ramrod from the barrel, so that it sailed off through the air with a dismal twang when he fired, leaving him without the means of properly loading his rifle again. Or he might forget to remove the old cap and put on a new one; then with the noise all around him he might pull the trigger, think he had fired, and ram in another charge on top of the first one, and perhaps do the same thing again. (Often muskets were found on the battlefield crammed to the muzzle with unfired charges.)

The answer was training . . . so that a man would form the habit of loading his rifle with the complete and proper sequence and this habit would persist even though the rifleman's mind went temporarily blank under the emotional stresses of combat. This training was provided for in the School of the Soldier, in a "by the numbers drill," LOAD IN NINE TIMES, which organized the movements into nine consecutive operations, performed over and over until they became, as it were, automatic.

Besides instruction in the handling of weapons, the School of the Soldier also included the different steps and movements of facing, alignment and marching. When the individual soldier was trained to the point of maneuverability, then came the School of the Company, and this was the basis of maneuvers by larger units.

The idea, of course, was to get all these soldiers into the best arrangement from which to start shooting at or advancing on the enemy. The ultimate objective was to mass firepower. Today, with longer ranges and modern communication, fire can be massed from weapons located at widely dispersed positions. But in the Civil War, massing fire meant massing the men who delivered it. The drill-book line of battle consisted of riflemen in two ranks, one behind the other. Two paces behind the rear rank stood a line of lieutenants and sergeants who were known as file closers.

The file closers were placed as they were to direct the men and also, it must be said, to restrain them in case conservation of Federal manpower should prove to be an idea of sudden and irresistible appeal in the ranks. The position of file closer had its advantages. Sergeant Tom Chamberlain, writing home with the obvious intent of reassuring his sister, pointed out that "if you shoot a Sergeant you have to fire through two men first. A Sergeant never fires his gun until the men in front are killed & then not unless you want to show off."

Drawn up in two ranks, a unit could execute certain limited maneuvers, but the formation was too unwieldy for movements of any length or complexity. For such movements the formation was usually a column of narrower ranks, for example a "column of fours."

The ability to go from line of battle into column and from column back into line of battle, with a high degree of teamwork in all formations, was a tactical necessity. The various orders and prescribed movements for accomplishing this, as set forth in Casey's *Infantry Tactics*—the manual used by the 20th Maine—make the modern infantry drill regulations look as uncomplicated as a diagram in a dancing school advertisement.

Colonel Ames didn't know how long he would have before his

embattled farmers would be thrown into another full-scale scuffle like Antietam, so he trained the 20th Maine in some of the more elementary movements first, and left the fancy ones until later.

One of the first requirements in the School of the Company was to be able to "march by the flank"—that is, to go from line of battle into a "column of fours," heading off in a sideways direction, parallel to the original line. Here's how, for example, a movement to the right flank was accomplished. At the command, *Company, right FACE,* all faced to the right and the rear-rank men (now standing in a long file) side-stepped a pace to their right to make room for "doubling." In the procedure of "doubling," every even-numbered man stepped up to the right side of the man in front of him, so that four men stood abreast. This converted the formation into a column of fours. At the command, *Forward, MARCH,* the column moved forward and was then "marching by the right flank."

Meanwhile, it was important for a soldier to remember his number. There were only two numbers, 1 and 2, but even so, a few minutes after "counting off," a man could forget, and this would result in indescribable confusion. For example, with the column of fours moving by the right flank as we just left it, it might be desired to put the men back into the original line of battle. At the command, *Company, HALT—FRONT,* the men halted and faced to the left; then the even-numbered men had to remember to "undouble" and jump back into their places in line-of-battle ranks.

Or—to return to the column of fours moving by the right flank —the commander might want to put the men into line of battle facing with their backs to the original line. This could be done by means of a complicated maneuver known as "on the right by file into line." It was something like pouring a strip of molasses on the ground—or *two* strips, rather—out of a moving jug. In the process (don't even try to comprehend this) some men marked time, others continued to march; odd- and even-numbered men crisscrossed; ranks undoubled, and if there was any forgetting of numbers, total disintegration set in and the company turned into a mob of colliding men and clashing muskets.

These maneuvers, confusing as they may sound, were as nothing compared to the drills and evolutions for the next higher unit of instruction, the School of the Battalion. (This really meant School of the Regiment; the regiment while drilling was called a battalion.) With heads whirling, the men of the 20th Maine milled and marched up and down the dusty field with Colonel Ames shouting such nightmarish commands as:

"By the right of companies to the rear into column. Battalion, by the right flank—MARCH!"

or

"Close column by division. On the fourth division left in front. Battalion left-FACE! MARCH!"

It was dull, exhausting, enraging work—needful preparation for which the Maine men would thank the West Pointer later on —but while it was in progress there is evidence that they hated the Colonel's giblets. Still, there began to emerge a grudging pride of accomplishment and a certain *esprit de corps,* particularly traceable in some of the letters Sergeant Tom Chamberlain was writing home. On October 14, describing the men's feeling toward Ames, Tom wrote to his sister, "I swear they will shoot him the first battle we are in." Writing again on the twenty-sixth, Tom noted that Ames was hated "beyond all description" . . . and that "Col. A. will take the men out to drill & he will d'm them up hill and down," also expressing his own wish that Ames would either be put in state's prison or promoted to brigadier general—anything to get him off the back of the regiment. But on October 30, in a letter to one of his brothers, Tom wrote a bit boastfully, "Col. A. drills us sergeants every day to see who is fit to promote. I tell you he is about as savage a man as you ever saw. If I can't knock Frank Sabine drilling I will give it up. I drill the co. every day and do it up like an old soldier. I tell you we have to do it well or get a damning. . . ." A few weeks later, when Ames had made a good non-com out of him and was recommending him for a lieutenancy, Tom Chamberlain's feelings toward the Colonel would mellow somewhat.

The enlisted men were not the only ones who were getting strong doses of the Ames discipline. Some of the younger officers had not quite got themselves into perspective, militarily. As described by one of the men, "These had a peculiar way of looking sidewise at their shoulder straps, and the red sash around their waists, worn full width. They had a strut in their walk, and the swords . . . would trail along at quite a respectable distance in their rear. One glance would be sufficient to convince the most careless observer that each felt as if the destiny of the country depended largely upon their individual efforts."

On one occasion a couple of young lieutenants decided to leave a marching column and take a short-cut across a field. They hadn't gone far before a messenger caught up with them. He had an order from Colonel Ames placing them under arrest and sending them to the rear of the column. Next day one of the lieutenants wished to be relieved from arrest in order to make a trip into a near-by town. All he had to do, he figured, was to write the Colonel a note and get permission. He tore a piece of paper from a pocket notebook, scribbled his request, and sent it off to regimental headquarters by one of the men. Within a surprisingly short time he received in reply a Proper Military Communication. Lieutenant would please understand that officers in arrest got no special favors, and when communicating with these headquarters hereafter, the Lieutenant will use the correct military form and stationery of proper size. Signed, Adelbert Ames, Commanding, 20th Me. Vols. The youngster had made a discovery which has been rediscovered untold thousands of times by defenders of democracy. Namely, that one of the quickest ways to get yourself into serious trouble is to write a letter to your commanding officer in the good old democratic style beginning "Dear Colonel. . . ."

There was one bright exception to these awkward performances, however, and that was the conduct of Ames' second-in-command, Lieutenant Colonel Joshua Lawrence Chamberlain, who was finding himself right in his element. His brother Tom wrote home to say, "I wish you could hear Lawrence give off a command & see him ride along the battalion on his white horse. He looks splendidly. . . . Lawrence told me last night that he never felt so well in his life." Ames apparently took a keen interest in Joshua Chamberlain. On many nights, after Taps had sounded and the men were all asleep, a solitary candle burned in the headquarters tent where Ames was giving his lieutenant colonel a special course in tactics.

Meanwhile, the 20th Maine was having troubles of a less constructive kind. The regiment was in poor health. The weather had turned bitterly cold, and the men were not fully supplied with shelter tents. Sleeping on the frosty ground without adequate protection against chilling winds and rain, men felt the cold penetrate to their bones. Soldiers would be up before dawn, running up and down to restore circulation. The food, for the most part consisting of only salt pork, hardtack and coffee, was bad, and the cooking, done individually or in squads, was abominable. Worst of all, camp conditions were unsanitary; the army was not practicing the almost fanatical cleanliness that is necessary when large numbers of men live in close proximity.

The result was that here at the mouth of the Antietam the 20th Maine met its most powerful enemy: Disease. From the simple standpoint of life or death for the soldier, the medical history of the Civil War was its most important history. Disease killed twice as many soldiers as battles. And a regiment such as the 20th Maine, coming predominantly from rural sections, was the most vulnerable, at least in camp. Army doctors were in general agreement that soldiers from the cities, particularly those from the lower classes (who were accustomed to crowded and unsanitary quarters) far surpassed those with rural backgrounds in their ability to withstand the vicissitudes of camp life. Also—the country boy might be well developed physically, but even his strength held its handicaps. As one surgeon put it, "His muscles have more development than training. All his life a lounger . . . never assuming the absolutely erect position except momentarily, always resting himself by frequent changes of attitude, it is really a severe trial for his nervous system to 'stand at attention.' This shows itself in frequent syncope at dress parade. Standing erect, facing the declining sun, it is a very common thing for the rural recruit to find his head reeling until he astonishes the adjutant by falling prostrate and insensible." Once you got him on the march or in battle, the doctor pointed out, the countryman made a splendid soldier. But he had to be handled carefully in the early training, and the worst danger at this stage came from the several camp diseases for which the rural recruits had little natural immunity.

There were, of course, notable exceptions. Judging only from physical appearances it was hard to tell just who would survive. For example, Thomas Chamberlain went into the army weighing only 120 pounds. But in spite of the freezing cold and a diet of mouldy, maggot-infested hardtack, Tom gained weight. By the end of October he was up to 132 pounds. "What makes it strange," he wrote home, "is that I should have gained 12 pounds living on worms." Much to his astonishment and delight, he kept on gaining. But the regiment as a whole met disaster in its battle with disease.

One of the worst of these afflictions was measles. An epidemic was likely to sweep through a regiment during its first encampment. Frequently fatal in itself, the disease also had damaging effects in some of its aftermaths: bronchitis, pneumonia and exhaustion which opened the way for still other diseases. Diarrhea and dysentery were also scourges in camp as well as in the field. Records of deceased soldiers of the 20th Maine during this period show them dying of measles . . . "fever," a designation that might mean several things . . . diphtheria . . . diarrhea . . . dysentery . . . typhoid . . . "putrid sore throat" . . . "consumption" . . . and various other ills. The tremendous advances that have taken place in medical science since 1862 are starkly underlined by the fact that around three hundred of the Maine soldiers were struck down by illness. The survivors wrote of these days with a kind of terror and despair that is not found in any of their accounts of battles. There was, for example, the heartbreaking experience of trying to nourish a dying man back to health with hardtack. And there were burial ceremonies that were brutally brief. Back home there would have been, for a man's survivors, the comfort and familiarity of the family plot in the cemetery, hymns, words of consolation, the Maine hills standing by, and the neighbors lingering a while before harnessing up the horses to drive home.

But here it was all too quick: an escort marching with reversed arms to the beat of muffled drums, a few words from the chaplain, a volley and a speedy shoveling underground. It was hard to write home and explain how a man so healthy in August could now, two months later—untouched by the enemy—be gone. Cold rains fell and washed mud over the new graves; gray clouds blew across the windy sky; and everything seemed to be moving and changing . . . so fast, so fast.

Already the glitter of the soldier's life was fading, and the old, deep melancholy was setting in. One Sunday night Corporal Will Owen wrote home to his sister: "How I wish you could hear the music (I will call it) of this encampment tonight. Just stand out in the open air a little while and listen. Some of the companies are singing *I'm going home to die no more*, others *Come sing to me of Heaven*, etc., etc. All seems happy and all seems gay, but still could you look into their hearts you would see thoughts of the loved ones that they have left at home rise above their mirth and gaiety. Yet they are contented though not happy. Contented to do their duty let come what may, contented to bear their part in this war and sing sad thoughts away."

In the first days of November, the 20th Maine took up the march, along with the army, into Virginia.

BUTTERFIELD'S BRIGADE CALL.

Dan, Dan, Dan, Butterfield, Butterfield.

CHAPTER THREE

Never and Forever

A NY general who wishes to convey a meaningful picture of his own personality to the men of a whole army has a considerable problem in communications. In the case of Major General George Brinton McClellan, however, there can be very little doubt that what came through to the soldier in ranks was something artistically complete and wonderful. In a sense, McClellan had created the Army of the Potomac after the wreckage of the first battle of Bull Run. And he had created it in the grand manner, in keeping with romantic ideals. When McClellan rode past, staff galloping behind, with a jingle and clatter and flash of banners, the troops cheered and for the moment war seemed like a great adventure. Because McClellan called forth this comforting illusion, and because the men believed he looked out for them (he looked out for them a little too well, Lincoln thought) and for many other reasons there was great affection for McClellan in the Army of the Potomac.

But Little Mac's days were numbered. Slowly and leisurely the army moved south from the Potomac, along the east side of the Blue Ridge, skirmishing through the passes with the Confederates, who were moving along the west side in the same direction. The men of the 20th Maine who made this march remembered it as one of the most beautiful of the war. One night while they were in bivouac the moon came up and illuminated a scene that might have been created by one of the more romantic painters of the Hudson River school. Under the magical light thousands of small tents shone whitely. At intervals campfires colored the tents around them with patches of orange glow.

41

Whippoorwills are reported to have sung all night, and some of the men had trouble getting to sleep, it was all so Indian-summerishly beautiful and curiously moving.

It might, in fact, have been taken to symbolize the end of a brighter, warmer era, for on November 7 there was a heavy fall of snow and McClellan was removed from command—also Major General Fitz-John Porter, commander of the Fifth Corps and McClellan's right-hand man. Immediately there was an uproar in the ranks. The 20th Maine had not been with the army long enough to share wholeheartedly in the general affection for McClellan, but the men could sympathize with the emotional disturbances in older regiments of the brigade. Among the men of these regiments there was much profanity, loud talk and writing of indignant letters to persons of supposed influence at home. There were offers to march on Washington if McClellan would only take the lead, threats of vengeance, cries of treason and injustice.

Some of the officers, at noon on the tenth, went to a farewell reception for McClellan at the Fifth Corps headquarters. The deposed general shook hands all around and made the proper sort of speech: . . . surprised by the action . . . supposed it was meant for the best . . . soldiers should obey . . . everyone urged to do his duty to the new commander as loyally as to the old . . . prayers and good wishes to follow the greatest army this continent ever saw. The assembled officers blinked and blew their noses—tears in the eyes of nearly everyone.

The troops lined up along the road to see him go. As McClellan rode past there was a tumult of yelling, cheering and entreaty. At least one brigade broke ranks in a vain effort to impede his departure. Then he was gone and it was all over. The emotions, which seem to have had a surface quality, subsided quickly. One soldier in an old regiment reflected that losing a general was, after all, very much like losing a girl. There would always be another one along. They would be deprived of many other generals after that, but as one of the veterans wrote, they would never again be "fluttered" by the experience.

To the 20th Maine soldiers the whole thing had been an annoyance and a needless delay of the war. From Warrenton, Corporal Will Owen wrote home, "One day we had to bid farewell to Gen. McClellan which took all day, then we had to bid Gen. Porter goodbye which took another day, then Gen. Butterfield reviewed us and inspected us all. Gov. Washburn has been here and paid the Maine Regts a visit etc. etc. Thus has the week been spent—and thus has the *war* been carried on from the *beginning*—Grand Review, Inspections etc. Now they have superseded Gen McC just on the eve of a move or when the army *was* moving on with speed toward Richmond. Now there is a *halt* of the whole army around here. Soon the rainy season will come and then a long and very disagreeable winter must be spent—before anything can be done. I blame McC for not moving before he did and I blame the President for removing him after he did start."

They lay in camp at Warrenton for a week and then set off through mud and drizzling rain toward the southeast, arriving after various delays at a place known as Stoneman's Switch, it being on the railroad between Fredericksburg and Aquia Creek. Here the men of the 20th Maine discovered that their expedition to southern climes had not removed them from frigid weather—also that a Maine constitution is no particular protection against low temperatures. On the night of December 6, four inches of snow fell, and it was so bitterly cold that two of the 20th Maine soldiers froze to death in their shelter tents.

At Stoneman's Switch the regiment settled down for a spell of camp and picket duty, meanwhile waiting to see what their new army commander, Major General Ambrose E. Burnside, would be like. Typically, what came through to them was a mixture of impressions. Those who saw him riding through the area reported that he was a handsome man, a six-footer of burly build. Officers who met him thought that he was a frank, manly, well-educated sort of person. He had an open face, pleasant eyes. He wore a high-crowned, round-topped hat. His characteristic feature was a garland of whiskers that ran from ear to ear, passing luxuriantly beneath the nose, but leaving the chin bare. One observer noted that Burnside was a tremendously imposing man —*without intending to be*—and it was only after talking with him for some time that one discovered that his intelligence fell far short of matching his physical size and presence. With characteristic modesty, Burnside quite freely admitted this lack of competence—an admission that did nothing whatever to encourage confidence in his subordinates. And worst of all, in the light of these dubious qualifications, the new commanding general was energetic.

General Burnside was to get men killed in large numbers. In the course of his military career, he assaulted Lee's army in various ways: head on, around-the-end, and by tunneling under. In nearly all of these attempts he reaped more than any man's share of frustration, confusion and disaster. At times his trouble seemed to come from above—a lack of co-operation by higher headquarters. At other times it seemed to be a weakness in the chain of command below him, a situation often aggravated by the fact that Burnside's orders were sometimes not clearly stated and their execution was not closely supervised. And at still other times, events beyond the control of mankind seemed to conspire against him. But Burnside belonged to that most sorrowful classification of the unlucky—the man who is both unlucky and stubborn. Driven by his sense of duty, he would push through all obstacles and plunge into the soup.

Thus it is possible to go on and on about Burnside, somewhat unfairly, for it is easy to make decisions at a safe distance of nearly a century, but hard to make them on the knife-edge of the moment, as Burnside had to do. Included in any appraisal of Burnside should be a look into the ranks, and here an unexpected amount of sympathy reveals itself. An enlisted man of the 20th Maine, thinking about Burnside many years later, remembered him as a kind and honorable person who had a sort of nobility as a man, but who was a victim of the war and all these conditions of fate and his own character that were against him.

As they lay in camp near the Rappahannock it came down to the 20th Maine through the enlisted men's own channels of communication that Burnside was planning to cross the river at or near Fredericksburg and head straight for Richmond. A few obstacles had interposed themselves. First, the pontoons for bridges had not arrived in time; Washington had somehow neglected to

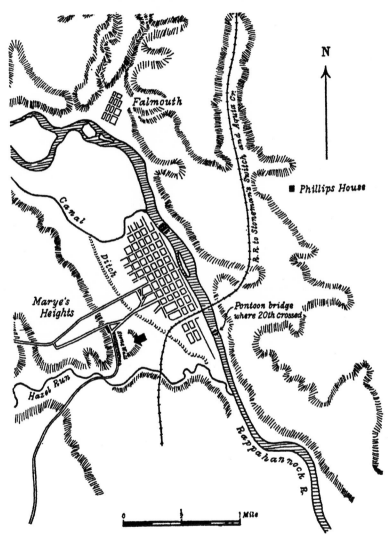

N

Falmouth

Canal

Ditch

Marye's
Heights

Hazel Run

R.R. to Stoneman's Switch and Aquia Cr.

Phillips House

Pontoon bridge
where 20th crossed

Rappahannock R.

0   ½   1 Mile

Fredericksburg, December 13, 1862
Arrow shows where the 20th Maine attacked

follow through on the arrangements, or there had been a misunderstanding somewhere. Then, by the time the pontoons arrived, Lee had had time to entrench much of his army on the heights across the Rappahannock and had also occupied Fredericksburg, which lay on the Confederate side of the river. These fortifications could be seen plainly from the high ground on the Union side. Also, Professor Lowe went up in his balloon and made further observations, all confirming the strength of Lee's position. It seemed as though a prudent general would call the attack off or make it somewhere else.

But the rumors grew more and more ominous. It was reported that there was a huge pile of coffins near one of the freight stations. Ambulance trains were parked in large numbers. And wagoners were bringing up straw, made up in neat bundles to lay the wounded on. On December 10, the rumors turned into an order; *Get ready to move with three days' rations and 20 extra rounds of ammunition per man.* Then came the familiar process of hurry-up-and-wait, with army telling corps to be ready to move at a certain hour; corps, just to be on the safe side, telling division to be ready an hour earlier than *that;* division telling brigade to be ready still another hour earlier; and regiment getting up in the middle of the night. On the eleventh, reveille sounded for the 20th Maine at three o'clock, but the regiment did not move until daylight. Meanwhile, at five, while it was still dark, the sky off toward Fredericksburg had begun to glow with intermittent flashes coming from an indistinct source, like heat lightning, and there was a dull rumble of artillery, a fainter sputtering of rifle fire. Word came that the army was beginning its attempt to force a crossing of the river.

The morning was cool and frosty, the air perfectly still, smoke of campfires hanging low over the ground in a ghostly haze. The men formed, wearing overcoats, with knapsacks, cartridge boxes, blanket rolls and other gear slung and strapped on over the coats. As the regiment moved out in the Fifth Corps column, it gradually ascended to higher ground. The sun came up as a dusky, blood-red disk seen through the smoky atmosphere, and with the sunrise, the air began to stir, so that soon the land was clear and bright on its upper levels. At Fredericksburg the Rappahannock runs through a sort of trough, from which the ground rises on both sides in a series of terraces. While still a couple of miles distant from the river, the 20th Maine was marching over a high plateau. The trough of the river was submerged in fog, but up here the landscape was bathed in morning sunlight, and from every direction, it appeared, bright columns of blue were converging on Fredericksburg.

About a mile from the river the Maine regiment found the Fifth Corps halted and massing in a large field by a set of buildings (the Phillips House). The corps was evidently going to be held in reserve. As thousands of men tramped over the field, it gradually turned into a vast mud pie, and here the troops stood restlessly, with no dry spot to sit on, no way to rest. The only diversion was in watching the Phillips House near by, which Burnside was using as his headquarters, and which was the focal point of a continuing stream of excited couriers. From this point also news came to the waiting troops in various ways, and the news was all bad.

The word was that Burnside's engineers were trying to lay pontoon bridges across the river, but buildings on the opposite shore were swarming with sharpshooters and these were shooting the bridge-builders as fast as their boats appeared through the fog. The sharpshooters were completely hidden from the view of riflemen on the Union shore, and with all the smoke from the artillery, vision was getting worse instead of better. In midmorning there was a report that Burnside had ordered the fire of all cannon concentrated on Fredericksburg, to batter it down and drive the snipers out. Later the guns opened in the most deafening cannonade old veterans had ever heard. More than one hundred guns, emplaced in an arc facing the town, began hurling shells into the fog, the guns roaring in what one listener described as a continuous, shattering peal of thunder, tons of shells swishing off into the gray obscurity, the growl and crash of their bursting in Fredericksburg making an echoing undertone. Soon the gray in that direction was not all gray; there were columns of black smoke crawling up through it. The fog had mostly lifted by noon, and it could be seen that Fredericksburg was burning in a number of places. But the crackle of rifle fire was still coming from the buildings. Burnside's terrific bombardment had accomplished little except to settle the snipers deeper into their rifle pits and cellars, where they were still thick as fleas. And the bridge-builders were still stymied.

But late in the afternoon, the news arriving on the muddy field by the Phillips House was suddenly better. Union infantrymen had made an assault-crossing in boats and driven the sharpshooters out, thus clearing the way for the laying of the pontoon bridges.

But it was getting dark by the time all this had been accomplished, and the Maine soldiers had been standing on first one foot and then the other all day. Wearily, the regiment moved with its division back about a mile to the rear, where it went into bivouac for the night. They could see a far-spreading glow illuminating the sky over Fredericksburg. The city was still burning in many places from the shelling. Behind it, on the ridges across the river, Lee's men were cooking their suppers, thousands of camp fires adding to the glow in the sky. Downriver, other Union forces had placed additional pontoon bridges, and their fires, too, were flickering in the night. It was all very much like that new song some of the soldiers were singing—the one that talked about "the watchfires of a hundred circling camps."

In his successful crossing of the river, Burnside had evidently won the first round. But the Maine men had noted several things during the day that had disturbed them. For one thing, the Confederate batteries on the heights beyond the city had remained remarkably silent all day. Why was that? Had General Lee become frightened as he saw this vast army assembling to assault him? Had he ordered a retreat to Richmond? Not likely. Could it be, instead, that he was simply waiting to draw the Union Army into a fatal trap?

There was very little sleep in the 20th Maine that night. Around the campfires in that December of 1862 the names of Lee, Longstreet and Jackson had a heavy, solid sound—and the Big Three were known to be across the river, waiting. Had the Maine men known the plans and dispositions of these fine officers there would have been even less sleep.

The assault-crossing of the river had been accomplished in

the face of infantry fire from the buildings of Fredericksburg, but actually Lee had no intention of making a stand on the river line, for several reasons. For one, the narrow, deep bed of the river was at least a mile away from points where the Confederate batteries could be placed, but was within easy and unobstructed range of the Federal guns on the heights of the Union side. And for another reason, Lee had a much better position right where he was.

The Confederate forces were on and in front of low hills behind the built-up portion of the town, separated from it by a plain. The Yankees would have to emerge from the town and cross the plain. Advancing over open ground they would meet obstacles, including fences and a deep, wide ditch with bridges partially destroyed. There were swells in the ground that offered some protection, a railroad cut and a few houses, but for the most part it was terrain that offered excellent fields of fire for the defenders.

Weapons were sited with consummate skill. Infantry positions were high, but not so high that they made for plunging fire; the bullets would sweep out more or less horizontally and, failing to hit the men aimed at, would be more than likely to hit others. Both infantry and artillery were placed to deliver interlocking bands of fire, so that there was hardly any place where an attacking regiment could not be hit from the side when it got up close, or even from both sides at once. The gunners had performed something very similar to a modern field artillery survey in defense of a prepared position. They had measured the exact ranges to points where the streets gave entrance to the plain, to the bridges over the ditch, and to other places certain to provide concentrations of troops and profitable targets. They had ranged their weapons on obvious places of refuge; for example, it could be anticipated that large numbers of Yankees would take cover in the railroad cut. Very well, guns were sited to take care of *that*, and when enough bluecoats gathered in the cut, they could be disposed of in a wholesale quantity.

All positions were well dug in. And in front of Marye's Heights there was a stone wall just the right height for shooting over, with men standing in a sunken road behind it. There would be four or five ranks behind the wall, with the rear men loading and passing muskets to those in front so that a continuous sheet of aimed fire would be flashing out over the wall. All in all, the position was almost *too* good, for it seemed that the Yankee general, if he had any sense, would take just one look at it and then figure out a more advantageous, roundabout way of getting at them.

But Burnside was going right ahead with the attack. At this time the army was arranged—somewhat confusingly, divisions normally being parts of corps—into three Grand Divisions, each of which was composed of two corps. General Franklin had the Left Grand Division; he would attack downriver and try to turn Lee's right flank. General Sumner had the Right Grand Division, and he would attack frontally, from Fredericksburg. General "Fighting Joe" Hooker had the Center Grand Division—this including the Fifth Corps and the 20th Maine—and he would hold himself ready as a reserve, without crossing the river initially.

This was the line-up, and of course it all came in via the foot soldier's grapevine and was thoughtfully considered around the campfires of the 20th Maine that night. In the morning they moved to another position, this one farther downriver and across from the lower part of Fredericksburg, where one of the pontoon bridges had been placed. Here they waited for still another day while troops of Sumner's Grand Division clumped across the pontoon bridges and into the town. By night, Sumner's two corps were all in the town and, it was rumored, ready to jump off for the attack next morning. The 20th Maine put in another nervous night, getting what sleep it could, the men wrapped in blankets on the frosty ground.

Morning came in weirdly, with a river of dense fog lying in the lower part of the valley, covering Fredericksburg and the Rappahannock, giving sounds an unnatural loudness. In mid-morning the roar of Franklin's guns, downriver to the left, came smashing through the mist. The Maine men got up and began staring tensely toward Fredericksburg, waiting for Sumner to launch his attack from the town.

The mist was growing luminous; soon the buildings across the river emerged like dark cliffs, then more distinctly; and the hills beyond revealed themselves. Around noon, Sumner's leading division moved out of the town, making the attack in three brigade lines. To the watchers in the 20th Maine, the lines seemed to be somewhat disorganized by fences at first but re-formed and moved on, blue uniforms and regimental flags now bright in the clear sunshine, spots and streaks of color in the distance. Smoke and the growl of artillery came from the enemy heights. Parts of the formations appeared to fly into bits; gaps opened and closed; the lines became mixed. But they pushed on, closer to the hills, until a sudden fiery gleaming ran along the base of the heights, a continuous flickering that began and never stopped. The blue lines sank as though into the ground. Driblets of blue came streaming back, gathering in small clusters behind the houses and in depressions on the field.

Other lines moved out of the town and across the fields. A lot of smoke on the hills now, and a steady pounding like that of kettle-drums. The Union lines seemed to melt, as one officer described it, like snow coming down on warm ground. Within range of the stone wall, one group halted as though trying to fire a return volley. Instantly it seemed to disintegrate.

Another line and another crossed the field against the gleaming and flickering and smoke. From the distance the ground appeared to be slowly turning blue, as though someone with a giant paintbrush were spattering it steadily with blue specks. And more and more—brigade after brigade—advanced against the heights without wavering until all went down, bright flags toppling and falling, the blue on the field deepening. The Maine men began to curse reverently and some of them wept. Even when seen at a great distance, there is something tremendously moving about courage, and what they were looking at was courage in a pure, undiluted form.

Many years later Longstreet wrote of it with awe, but seemingly with little satisfaction, as though he had assisted in a suicide. "A series of braver, more desperate charges than those hurled against the troops in the sunken road was never known, and the piles and cross-piles of dead marked a field such as I never saw before or since."

In late afternoon the Fifth Corps went in to get and hold what ground it could, with brigades going here and there to support various units of the preceding attacks. As the 20th Maine crossed on a pontoon bridge, Chamberlain recalled that "the air was thick with the flying, bursting shells; whooping solid shot swept lengthwise our narrow bridge, fortunately not yet ploughing a furrow through the midst of us, but driving the compressed air so close above our heads that there was an unconquerable instinct to shrink beneath it, although knowing it was then too late. The crowding, swerving column set the pontoons swaying, so that the horses reeled and men could scarcely keep their balance."

Once into the town, the men were ordered to unsling knapsacks and leave them to be cared for by the quartermaster. Fredericksburg, which had been thoroughly looted by Union troops on the day before, was a shambles with windows broken, clothing, furniture and household goods scattered through the streets and the unpleasant burning-dump smells that a city has when it has been ransacked and set afire. The 3rd Brigade formed line of battle near the outskirts of the town, with its left on a railroad. A report of the brigade commander, Colonel T. B. W. Stockton, describes the terrain that lay in front of them: ". . . received orders just before sundown to advance, my left [flank] to rest on a small white house, just this side of a ridge or crest, some 500 yards this side of the enemy's position. . . . The distance over which we had to advance is probably over 1000 yards, the ground undulating, rising first to a ridge, and descending and rising again to the ridge we were ordered to."

Above this field, now littered with awkwardly sprawled blue forms, hazy with smoke and gray in the shadows of sunset, the sky was ringing and roaring as though ripped by an unseasonable electrical storm, and there were yowling and shrieking sounds everywhere.

As the regiment moved out, Lieutenant Colonel Chamberlain saw a Confederate battery swing its guns to sweep their front. The guns flashed, and the air around the 20th Maine was suddenly full of brief illuminations, shocking noise and masses of smoke that seemed to materialize from nowhere. Colonel Ames called to Chamberlain, "God help us now! Colonel, take the right wing; I must lead here!" And Ames calmly walked to the front. They were into the afternoon's mowing now, and it was a mess, with smashed bodies, ownerless arms and legs, and scattered equipment everywhere. Maine men were beginning to go down. Medical attendants who, as Chamberlain remarked, "also bring courage to their work," got busy with stretchers.

A man in one of the regiments which had preceded them, and which was now pinned down on the slope ahead, twisted in his prone position and looked back. He left a record of what he saw: ". . . the 20th Maine . . . coming across the field in line of battle, as upon parade, easily recognized by their new state colors, the great gaps plainly visible as the shot and shell tore through the now tremulous line. It was a grand sight, and a striking example of what discipline will do for *such* material in *such* a battle.

"Shortly after, a tall, slim colonel coolly walked over our bodies. 'Who commands this regiment?' he asked. Our colonel responded. 'I will move over your line and relieve your men,' he quietly rejoined. It was Colonel Adelbert Ames. . . . We fell back through their lines a few yards. The 20th Maine swept forward. . . ."

Fortunately for the regiment, it did not have to sweep forward much farther, and darkness was settling when the 20th Maine reached the ridge which was its objective. The men fired a few futile volleys, muzzle flames flaring in the dusk, then lay down to take cover behind the slight protection of the crest.

It turned out to be a rough night. The weather became intensely cold during the evening. A bitter north wind began to sweep the slopes. Many of the men had left overcoats and blankets behind in Fredericksburg with their knapsacks. Initially overheated by their exertions, they now became violently chilled.

For the wounded, who covered the field thickly all around them, the bad part was beginning. The anesthesia of shock had worn off. The terrible pain, thirst and cold were setting in. They began to moan. The moans of one man would be separated by intervals, but others filled in, so that the sound had a uniform level of deep-toned anguish and despair. In the brave light of the sun they had been men, but now in the dark they were little boys again. They cried for mothers, for water, for help, for death, for God—a vast and terrible monotone that seemed to Chamberlain like some sort of strange ventriloquism, coming from a source that could not be located, or from distances beyond the reach of the human senses, as though the darkened earth itself were groaning in agony. Out of this vast chorus of misery sometimes would filter the voice of a delirious man, cooing in gentle, happy tones, so that the whole effect for those listening was one of a feverish dream, and nightmares within nightmares, and all this suffered in a bone-biting hell of freezing cold. The cold soon silenced many of the voices; wounded men died and stiffened quickly. Others, more fortunate, were gradually being removed by hospital stewards and stretcher-bearers, who were carrying them back to the ambulances that had come up as close as possible under the cover of darkness.

And there were other searchers in the night. Freezing live men were looking for dead men, with the practical idea of removing garments no longer needed. The report that the Confederates despoiled Union dead is true. But much of the clothing was taken by Union soldiers who spent that bitter night on the field.

Lieutenant Colonel Chamberlain made a ghastly bed. "For myself it seemed best to bestow my body between two dead men among the many left there by earlier assaults, and to draw another crosswise for a pillow out of the trampled, blood-soaked sod, pulling the flap of his coat over my face to fend off the chilling winds, and still more chilling, the deep, many voiced moan that overspread the field. . . ." Now and then one of the searchers would come along and lift the flap of the coat off Chamberlain's face, and would sometimes express his disappointment at finding a live instead of a dead man, which did not make for the best of feelings between the two men thus confronting one another.

The wind roared and kept swinging a loosened window-blind in an abandoned house near by. As the blind flapped back and forth in hypnotic rhythm, Chamberlain thought it was saying, "Never—forever; forever—never!" He remembered the sound all the rest of his life.

For Private Gerrish, the night held a fiendish dilemma. "There was a singular conflict in our breasts. We were wishing the hours away, and yet dreaded to have the darkness disappear."

But dawn came, with a spatter of bullets. At daylight the Confederates made an attempt to drive them out from behind the slight rise of ground serving as their protection. Artillery fire came down, but the Maine men hugged the earth and lived through it, twisting carefully to load their muskets from this prone position. Late in the afternoon they had a real scare. Two or three hundred Confederates crept out from behind the right of the stone wall, took cover behind a descending bank on their left, and began to pour in a flanking fire.

Once again the dead served. On this flank they laid up a breastwork of corpses. It worked, but a man could get sick to his stomach, listening to the bullets thud into the dead flesh. Chamberlain saw a man lift himself only slightly by the prop of his hands and forearms; a hole appeared in the middle of his forehead and his head sank down bloodily. The order went along the line to keep absolutely flat. But a man in Company B, from madness or bravado, jumped to his feet, took aim and fired at a Confederate on the hillside above. Almost simultaneously there was a dull thud as a bullet struck the Maine soldier; he was dead a second after he pulled the trigger.

Cold and covered with mud, they lay on the ground all day. It would have been fatal to get up and retreat. Reinforcements could not reach them. Now and then they saw a staff officer trying to bring up orders, but his horse would be shot from under him by the time he reached the first crest behind them.

Finally night came again and with it instructions to withdraw into the town. But there was something they had to do before they left. The men dug shallow graves, using bayonets, pieces of shell and fragments of muskets to scoop out the earth. Then the 20th Maine buried its own dead. They also erected low headboards made of musket butts or pieces of board, carving names and home towns into the wood laboriously—and dangerously by the light of guarded matches. They were to follow this practice on nearly every battlefield of the war where the regiment lost men, and perhaps it was here where the dead had sheltered them that the sense of obligation was formed. Down into the deeps of nothingness these men had gone; but they too would serve beyond their time, and the 20th Maine reached out to them to form a curious bond. As the war went on, an increasing part of the regiment was dead and a decreasing part was alive, but both the living and the dead seem to have been parts of whatever it was that made up the consciousness of the regiment.

As they were completing the burial, there was a completely unnecessary touch of melodrama. The northern sky lighted up with shifting and flaring streaks of Aurora Borealis. This was taken by some of the more sentimental as being a final salute to the fallen, displayed in the sky over the State of Maine.

Chamberlain described the return march to the town. "We had to pick our way over a field strewn with incongruous ruin; men torn and broken and cut to pieces in every indescribable way, cannon dismounted, gun-carriages smashed or overturned, ammunition-chests flung wildly about, horses dead and half-dead still held in harness, accouterments of every sort scattered as by whirlwinds." And he noted that all this was not good for the nerves.

Back in Fredericksburg, they spread their blankets on the paving of the streets and tried to get some sleep. They hadn't accomplished much except to fire a few volleys and then lie in the mud for nearly thirty hours, but for some unaccountable reason Colonel Ames seemed pleased with the regiment. He walked around among the men where they lay and told them that they had done well. All day Monday they lay in the town, now packed with troops of all commands—mixed and demoralized. The household debris in the streets had been churned into trash. Confederate shells kept slamming into the town, and pieces of buildings flew off to add to the chaos. Someone said that General Burnside had ridden through the town with his hat pulled low over his eyes, the troops silent as he passed.

Shortly after midnight the 20th Maine received orders to move up to the extreme front again with the utmost silence. All conversation strictly forbidden. Tin cups to be taken off belts and other gear secured so there would be no rattling. It was a cloudy, dark night with another roaring wind, fortunately blowing from the direction of the enemy, which would tend to blanket the sound of their approach. Details had gone ahead to distribute entrenching spades and picks on the ground they were expected to occupy. It developed that the mission of the 20th Maine was to dig in and form one section of an advanced picket line covering some important movement of the army. They began to understand that this was an extremely delicate business. And it was even more delicate than they thought, for the Union army was retreating across the river, leaving them as a rear guard. If the Confederates got wind of it, they could be down on this thin line like a tidal wave, afterward sweeping on to turn Burnside's retreat into a final disaster.

But the wind was literally blowing the wrong way for the enemy. It brought fragments of their conversation to the 20th Maine as the regiment got up close, and it appeared that the Confederates, too, were anxious and nervous. The 20th Maine began to dig in on an extended line, each man scooping out a hole and throwing up a little earthwork in front. Lieutenant Colonel Chamberlain, crawling along in the darkness to make sure the line was taking proper direction, heard someone throwing gravel in a place that seemed a little out of alignment. He approached and called softly, "Throw to the other side, my man; that's where the danger is!"

A voice came back. "Golly! Don't ye s'pose I know which side them Yanks be? They're right onto us now."

It appeared that the Confederates had pickets out, too. However, Chamberlain hadn't been a professor of languages for nothing. In rich Southern accents he told the man to dig away but to keep a sharp lookout.

A little later in the night Chamberlain had further occasion to call upon his oratorical talents. A staff officer came floundering up from the left rear and called, "Where is the commander of these troops?" Chamberlain, who was in charge of this section of the line, answered him.

The staff officer then stupidly yelled, "Get yourselves out of this as quick as God will let you! The whole army is across the river!"

Chamberlain was aghast. The enemy picket line had undoubtedly heard this, and as a result he could feel panic stirring in his own troops. Instantly Chamberlain shouted, in a voice loud enough for the Confederates to hear, an order to hold steady and arrest "this stampeder"; that it was a trick of the enemy; and that they'd "give it to them in the morning." The 20th Maine had its share of intelligence as well as bravery; the regiment did not stir. In a low-voiced rage, Chamberlain went back and told the staff officer exactly what he thought of him. The staff officer whispered apologetically that he had had such a time getting up across the field he had almost lost his mind. This Chamberlain could understand. He told the officer to clear out and keep his mouth shut and his stupidity would not be reported.

Chamberlain now crawled over to Ames and the two of them made up a plan of retreat. For a while, they would hold the position to keep up appearances. Then every even-numbered man would dig briskly, while every odd-numbered man moved silently to the rear. This half of the regiment would move back a hundred yards or so and form a new line of battle ready to cover the withdrawal of the even-numbered men. These would then come back through the new line and form another line a hundred yards farther back. The leapfrogging process would then be repeated until the command was out of danger.

It worked, and Chamberlain's comment on the reaction will be of interest to all infantry commanders: ". . . the enemy, after a short, puzzled hesitation, came out from their entrenchments and followed us up as closely as they deemed safe, the same traits of human nature in them as in us causing a little 'nervousness' when moving in darkness and in the presence of an alert enemy, also moving."

Part way back the moon almost betrayed them. Clouds were riding fast on the driving wind, and small shafts of moonlight swept over the field without warning. An illumination like this caught them in the middle of one of their leapfrogging moves, reflecting brightly on the musket barrels, but a quick order to hit the ground saved them as a scattered volley whistled over their heads. For the remainder of the retreat they had to watch the sky as well as the ground, for the malignant moonlight would bring death racing in with it.

As they reached the edge of town, their feeling of being hunted and pursued was accentuated when a bloodhound began baying somewhere off in the darkness. They entered the shadows of the buildings with relief. Fredericksburg was deserted except for some of the badly wounded who had been left behind.

The pontoon bridge was covered with sods and brush which had muffled the sound of the night's crossing. Day was breaking when the 20th Maine moved across the river and up to the heights beyond. A dismal rain was falling. The regiment halted for a rest beside the road. Looking back across the river as the light strengthened, they saw again from a distance the terrible blue color of the slopes they had left. For the 20th Maine it had been bad, but not so bad as it might have been with less capable leadership. They had lost four men killed and thirty-two wounded. They had not been disorganized. They had maneuvered and fought as a cohesive, thinking unit. They knew now that they were a regiment.

Leaning wearily against a tree, Joshua Chamberlain was thinking about the battle, particularly about the handling of the Center Grand Division of which the 20th Maine had been a part. He reflected that the division had not been put in as a body. "They were sent by superior orders, in detachments, to support other commands, or as a 'forlorn hope,' at various times and places. . . ."

The Center Grand commander, General Hooker, came riding by. Seeing the muddy, beaten-up infantrymen beside the road, he called to Chamberlain, "You've had a hard chance, Colonel; I am glad to see you out of it!"

Chamberlain was tired, hungry, disgusted. Also, he was nursing a slight wound in the right cheek, so he was somewhat more than figuratively soreheaded. He called back, "It *was* chance, General; not much intelligent design there!"

Hooker responded with an edge in his voice. "God knows I did not put you in!"

Chamberlain then practically put his neck on the block. "That was the trouble, General," he shouted. "You should have put us in. We were handled in piecemeal, on toasting forks."

There was a shocked silence for a moment, the rain casting a gray haze over the ruin across the river. Then Hooker rode on without a reprimand. Somehow this didn't seem to be the time or the place for the chopping off of heads.

CHAPTER FOUR

Stuck in the Mud

ONNOISSEURS of military mud could doubtless hold a long and inconclusive argument as to which section of the world provides mud of the greatest efficacy in distressing and impeding an army. Many votes from two generations would go to the mud of France. But if the men of the 20th Maine could rise up and speak, they would surely say that there never has been any mud to compare with that in which the Army of the Potomac lived and moved, or tried to move, in the winter of 1862-1863. This mud could be thick enough to pull a man's shoes off, or soupy enough to allow a mule to sink out of sight. It could be slippery, or gluey. It was highly versatile.

An officer wrote, "Virginia mud is a clay of reddish color and sticky consistence, which does not appear to soak water, or mingle with it, but simply to hold it, becoming softer and softer, and parting with the water wholly by evaporation."

A reporter from *The New York Times* who was with the army gave his analysis. "The sand makes the soil pliable, the clay makes it sticky, and the two together form a road out of which, when it rains, the bottom drops, but which is at the same time so tenacious that extrication from its clutch is all but impossible."

Mud like this was one of the reasons why Civil War commanders were hesitant about moving around very much in winter. With the lack of paved roads, a few hours of rain could turn the best laid plans awry and make an even well-regarded general suddenly look like an idiot. Mud helped grease the skids for Burnside as commander of the Army of the Potomac—and this something more than figuratively.

And yet this mud could also be useful—for building purposes. Marching back to Stoneman's Switch after the defeat at Fredericksburg, the Maine men received welcome instructions to build permanent winter quarters. Putting a man into winter quarters was a simple and inexpensive matter at that time. The government simply gave him an axe and located his camp in or near a stand of timber. The soldier had everything else he needed, including mud for chinking log walls and mortaring a chimney. In the 20th Maine, four men teamed up to make a hut, in most cases. There were plenty of good axemen in the regiment, so getting the logs was easy. Some of the other regiments were not so fortunate in this particular skill. John D. Billings, that admirable chronicler of life in the Army of the Potomac, told about seeing one of the less skillful choppers at work. The man, wrote Billings, suddenly sat down, took off his boot, and shook out "a shower of toes."

In constructing the hut, the Maine men usually made an enclosure of log walls about eight feet square. The height of the walls was about three feet, added head room being obtained by excavation. A ridgepole was then put up, and the men buttoned together the four halves of their pup tents, or "dog tents" as they were then called, to make a cloth roof. The fireplace was made of stones, bricks, sods, or even of wood. If made of wood, it had to be lined with a thick layer of the clayey mud. The chimney was often made of short lengths of logs and was chinked and lined with mud. A barrel might be placed on top of the structure to extend the height of the chimney and provide a better draft.

The construction of bunks offered slightly more opportunity for ingenuity. A man could make his bunk of barrel staves laid crosswise on poles; or of springy saplings; or of grain sacks, if they could be begged or stolen from an artillery or cavalry camp. Hay, leaves or pine boughs made the mattress. For the making of furniture, empty hardtack boxes were highly useful. A box turned upside down with legs attached was a good-enough table. A box fastened to the wall was a cupboard. When the little house was finished, there was something hugely satisfying about it—a sort of elemental pleasure for the men in building a shelter with their own hands and taking refuge from the weather, sitting around the little fireplace while the snow fell and the wind howled outside.

When all the huts were erected, the 20th Maine had what amounted to a little district in a vast city of similar shelters. The regimental area, laid out according to regulations, was based on the "color line" where the regiment assembled for formations. Off this line at right angles went the company streets, each consisting of two facing rows of huts. Behind these were the huts of company officers and the regimental field and staff, all in orderly formation according to grade. The enlisted men's latrine, or "sink" as they called it, was at one extreme end of the area and the officers' at the other—distance being about the only way of giving facilities of this nature the proper designation of rank.

Night saw the fabric roofs of this little village glowing with the light of the fires within; morning found it covered with low-hanging smoke from the burning of the green pine logs used as fuel. The memory of a morning in camp would be that of the sun coming up red through the smoke, bugles and drums sounding, sergeants barking, men shivering and throwing long, cold-looking shadows as they stood reveille. And men coughing. A soldier recalled that "one of the wonders of these times was the army cough; what with the smoke of the campfires, the dust of the country, and the effect of the variable weather upon people living out of doors, there was a general tendency to bronchial irritations, which would break out into coughing when the men first awoke, and it is almost a literal fact that when one hundred thousand men began to stir at reveille, the sound of their coughing would drown that of the beating drums."

And always they were conscious of the mud in one form or another—either solid, semi-liquid, or very nearly gaseous. The ground would often be frozen hard as stone; then as the weather warmed up, it turned into mud; and finally the top surface dried and there were clouds of fine, reddish dust flying in the winter sunlight. During these days there was plenty to do. Colonel Ames had the men of the 20th Maine out drilling at every opportunity. And there was guard, picket and fatigue duty. Cutting wood for fuel was a daily task, and this grew to be a real problem within a few weeks. When the army went into winter quarters there

63

were fairly extensive stands of timber around Stoneman's Switch. Pine was so plentiful that the men cut the trees off at a height of three feet. Then as wood grew scarcer, they cut the stumps off close to the ground. And finally they were digging into the ground for roots, the country around the camp was bare and brown, and the forest had receded to a considerable distance. This meant that wood often had to be carried three miles or more. One soldier thought he had found the solution. He went down the railroad toward Aquia Creek, found a stump two miles from camp, and dragged it to a grade, up which the locomotives always moved slowly. When a flat car came along, he threw the stump aboard and climbed on himself. But when the car neared the camp, the train was going so fast that the soldier did not dare to jump. Instead, he threw the stump off, intending to return and get it later, but of course the stump was missing when he got back. Wood stealing was a popular practice. (Years later one of the 20th Maine veterans would take his little grandson along to an outdoor encampment of the G.A.R. in Maine, and the little fellow would wonder why the oldsters made such a point of stealing from each other's woodpiles. To the boy, the pursuits, mock rages and sham disputes would seem rather childish.)

There was one incident connected with wood cutting that left an unpleasant memory with the 20th Maine. Not all of the officers of the regimental field and staff, apparently, were of the same caliber as Ames and Chamberlain. The Quartermaster was a big overbearing officer who was heartily disliked by the men. One day while the rest of the regiment was absent from camp, the Quartermaster came across Sergeant George W. Buck, who had been excused because of illness and left behind in quarters. "Go get an axe and cut me some wood," ordered the Quartermaster.

There were two reasons why Buck should not have been required to cut wood: He was a non-com, and therefore not liable to fatigue duty. And he was sick. Buck refused for both reasons, whereupon the Quartermaster knocked him down and kicked him. Further, when the regiment returned to camp, he reported that Buck had been insubordinate. No witnesses had been present. The cards were stacked against the sergeant, and he was reduced to private, to the great displeasure of the regiment. He would be restored to his original rank in dramatic circumstances to be revealed later.

The principal duty of the regiment in the last days of December was picketing two or three miles in rear of the camp. The enemy being in the opposite direction and mostly on the other side of the Rappahannock, this was peaceful work, and pleasant —away from the dust and smoke. The weather after Christmas was sunny and cold, the air invigorating, the ground firm underfoot. The one exception to routine duty was a reconnaissance as the old year was ending—an affair which was conducted with great secrecy and which mystified the private soldiers no end.

On the afternoon of December 30 the 20th Maine fell in with three days' rations and a full supply of ammunition. Moving out of camp with the 3rd Brigade, they found that the other two brigades of the 1st Division were also on the road, and they were all heading upriver. The winter darkness came early, a cold nor'-wester began to blow, lashing the air with stinging drifts of snow. At eleven o'clock that evening the column halted; and all the Maine men knew was that they were in the woods somewhere north of and probably near the Rappahannock River. Fires were forbidden; they made beds of boughs and shivered in their blankets until five o'clock. A cold breakfast, and the march continued through the woods. Now they seemed to be moving directly toward the Rappahannock. At eight o'clock another halt was ordered, and strict silence was imposed on the ranks.

It was one of those winter mornings that come in cold and steel gray, with the air so quiet it seems ready to snap—a silence which was accentuated by the gloom of the deep pine forest. An order to load rifles heightened the tension. Up ahead somewhere, a crash of gunfire rolled out, deafeningly loud in the still winter air. The head of the column had struck the river near Richards Ford, where it was overwhelming a small cavalry picket. The gunfire lasted ten minutes; then word came back that the ford was cleared and ready for crossing.

While the 1st Brigade moved forward and waded the ford, the 3rd Brigade remained behind as a supporting force in the woods. From across the river, the sound of a few shots came back along with a great deal of shouting, but soon this receded and all was silent again except for the sighing of the pines. The brigade remained in the woods all day and bivouacked there. That night, the Maine men sat around their campfires and wished each other a Happy New Year as 1862 blew itself out, a whining wind driving snow clouds across the sky. Next day they marched back to Stoneman's Switch. The 1st Brigade returned after recrossing the Rappahannock farther up, at Ellis Ford. Not much had been accomplished, it seemed. The 1st Brigade had marched ten miles in enemy territory, had seized three cavalrymen, captured a mailbag, accidentally wounded a civilian—a young lady, they regretted to say, shot in the leg—and on the return march had been followed by a flock of crows, hovering and cawing in rear of the column. The whole affair had been very odd. But later this "reek-o-nuisance" to Richards Ford, as some of the men called it, would be better understood. It was a prelude to other moves that Burnside had in mind.

There followed another period of monotonous life in camp. During the sunny, dusty, wind-swept days the officers kept them busy with drills, parades and an occasional review. For the long winter evenings the men were left to their own devices. Some of the more fortunate had the ability to sleep for long periods of time. Others talked, told stories around the fireplaces or wrote letters.

Much of the letter writing, however, was done on Sunday when there were free hours and daylight to write by. The letters often began, untactfully, "I have nothing to do this afternoon, so I guess I will write to you." They usually assured the recipient that the writer was in perfect health and never felt better in his life. They asked about the folks at home. They asked for things to be sent from home in packages. They might contain a bit of news about battles, or life in the army, and sometimes they closed with a declaration of patriotic purpose or a religious reassurance, as for example, "Don't worry about me, but leave me in the hands of Him who doeth all things well."

Quite often the letters gave hints of homesickness which the soldier did not want to reveal, but which he could not quite hide. He would wish for some of his mother's buckwheat pancakes. He would wish for maple syrup. Or some spruce gum. One day a heavy snowstorm put Corporal Will Owen in mind of home. He wrote, "It began snowing early Sunday morning and snowed and blowed hard all day long. It was just like some of our N.E. Maine storms. When it stopped there was about a foot on the ground. . . . How are things in Milo now. Same as ever? How many lambs have we got? Any? I want you to tell me all about everything about the barn—even the hens. For I want to know."

When a Maine farm boy inquires for the hens it may safely be said that he is desperately homesick, for of all the creatures that inhabit a farm, the menfolk are likely to have the least regard for hens, untidy, excitable things that are always getting underfoot and flying up in a man's face.

As another resource for whiling away the hours, the 20th Maine also had a considerable talent for practical jokes which were, to say the least, strenuous. One favorite entertainment was to toss cartridges down the chimney of a neighboring hut. This made a fine puff and flash in the fireplace; and sometimes it brought the occupants dashing out in a rage and there would be a fist-fight—this capable of being re-enacted later with mockery and gestures, all exceedingly humorous.

As might be expected, with so many men crowded into quarters that were something less than sanitary, they got lousy. This was humiliating at first, but later lousiness, too, came to be humorous. A whole folklore of lousiness developed, with dozens of tall tales. Typical was a sentence in a letter written by the brigade bugler. "I would be willing to let them have what blood and meat they want to eat, but the devils amuse themselves nights by biting out chunks and throwing them away."

Through the first half of January, 1863, the days were bright and unusually cold for Virginia; and the roads, firm and dry, invited Burnside to his final adventure as commander of the Army of the Potomac. On the opposite banks of the Rappahannock, the Confederates had observers and pickets watching the river for around forty miles of its length. They had also thrown up earthworks and dug rifle pits covering all points of probable crossing, these being the various fords in most cases. Burnside's plans and preparations were admirable. Roads were cut to the river at not one, but many fords. In a similar way, areas at several points were cleared for battery positions near the banks of the river. The Confederates would be aware of these preparations, but they could not predict the exact point that Burnside would choose for his crossing. A fast march over the excellent roads, and Burnside would have the jump on his enemy. Before the Army of Northern Virginia could concentrate to meet the crossing, he might win the decisive victory that the North was clamoring for.

March orders came on Tuesday, January 20. The men of the 20th Maine lined up and heard a general order read, to the effect that the Confederates were in for a shattering surprise; the rebellion would presently be struck a deathblow and the war would be over if every man did his duty. At around two P.M. the regiment moved out with the Fifth Corps. The whole army seemed to be moving in the direction the Maine men had taken on the way to Richards Ford three weeks previously. The day had begun cool and crisp, like all the other days they had been enjoying. But as the afternoon wore on a northeast wind began to blow, and there were signs of a storm. After a march of about five miles, they bivouacked in an extensive oak woods. As the light of the short winter day faded, drops of rain were spattering on the dry leaves overhead. Burnside's luck, which was nearly always bad, was running true to form.

As they resumed the march next morning, the weather was soft and mild, like that of a morning in May. The rain had ceased temporarily. However, the sky was a mass of heavy, low-hanging clouds. The frost was coming out of the ground. Water lay in pools over the roads and fields. Soon it began raining again—a steady drizzle that increased to a downpour. The temperature climbed rapidly. Steam arose in clouds, obscuring the landscape. A dank, earthy smell was everywhere.

The bottom dropped out of the roads. Fieldpieces sank to their muzzles. The wheels of vehicles disappeared entirely. The pontoon carriages went down until the big bridge-supporting boats were resting on the mud, which was not quite fluid enough to float them, and too thick to allow them to be dragged. Double and triple teams of horses were harnessed to the pontoon wagons, in vain. Ropes were attached, and 150 men per wagon were set to pulling with loud heaving and ho-ing. No good. The artillerymen were having no better success. Twelve horses could not move a gun; it was like trying to plow with a whole cannon as a plowshare.

Avoiding the roads where all this confusion was steadily mounting, and struggling through fields and thickets, the 20th Maine moved through what amounted to a vast bog, or swamp. Men jumped from hummock to hummock, slipped, sank into mud knee-deep, often felt their shoes drawn off by the mud. By night they had made seven miles, which may have been close to the record in the Army of the Potomac that day.

Thursday morning, January 22—still rainy and warm—disclosed through the luminous mist a scene of almost incredible chaos. Along the roads supply wagons were upset, artillery almost completely submerged, and there were dozens of horses and mules dead of exhaustion. Many of the animals had been trampled completely out of sight into the mud. The 20th Maine went nowhere that day; obviously, the whole army had stalled.

On the opposite bank of the Rappahannock, the Confederates had put up huge signboards with taunting phrases. "BURNSIDE STUCK IN THE MUD" was one, and there were others equally insulting. The Confederates had also brought up a number of plows, and could be seen busily plowing up the ground near the fords in order to facilitate the production of more mud in case any of the Union troops did manage to get across the river. They could hardly have thought of a more effective way of wasting their time. Burnside's problem now was not how to get across the river, but how to get back to camp. Rations were running out, and supply trains could not get through the mud to replenish them.

It was thought that the soldiers were becoming dispirited, and so a gill of whiskey per man was issued. Or at least it was a gill officially. Many of the mud-marchers apparently got more than that, for a terrific fist-fight broke out involving four regiments of the Fifth Corps' 1st Division. There was intense excitement and there were many varying accounts of what happened. Possibly some of the historians had also had more than a gill. One account has it that the conflict ended only when a battery, shotted with canister, was trained on the combatants. Another claims that "the giants of the 2nd Maine soon cleared the field." The 2nd Maine was the one other Maine regiment in the 1st Division; they were contentious men (as will presently be seen) and if there was a fight going on they probably would have been in it and may have won it.

Next day the 20th Maine worked at cutting timber and corduroying roads. The rain stopped on Saturday, the twenty-fourth, and on that day they were able to get back to the camp at Stoneman's Switch. For the soldiers, the hardships of the Mud March had reached a point where they had become just plain ridiculous. A wonderful thing about the much-beaten and bewildered Army of the Potomac was that it could always laugh at itself, and perhaps that was one reason why it was such a durable army. "Well, it is tough," one soldier wrote home. "When Burnside got stuck in the mud, the artillery harness all broke, and the only way they could get the guns out was for the men to cut their rations of beef into strips, and make tugs out of them."

Mud, lice, bad rations, long marches to no purpose, defeat—all this was material for self-mockery. The Mud March inspired enough of this bitter but beneficent humor to make a joke book. There was one ditty going around camp in the form of a bedtime prayer.

> Now I lay me down to sleep
> In mud that's many fathoms deep;
> If I'm not here when you awake,
> Just hunt me up with an oyster rake.

In summing it all up, the man from *The New York Times* had a flash of insight into Burnside's ill-starred fortune. He wrote that Burnside's plan had been a good one, but that success had been snatched away by "some elfish fate." Immediately after the Mud March, General Burnside was relieved and Major General Joseph Hooker was named to replace him. The choice was a popular one with the 20th Maine. Hooker was to do great things for their morale. For one thing, he looked like a successful general. One of the Maine men remembered him as tall, erect and dashing, with a full red face and prominent features. The red face was sometimes ascribed to booze, but that was of no consequence as far as the soldiers were concerned. The main thing was that Hooker had a reputation for being able and willing to fight; "Fighting Joe" they called him. Furthermore, Hooker looked after his men—and right at this point the men needed looking after, for the camp at Stoneman's Switch was rapidly descending into squalor. In the muddy fields, thousands of soldiers were huddled together; it was cold; and men were reluctant to ventilate their huts. Rations were not coming through in either the proper quantity or quality, although supplies in the depots were more than adequate. Much of the cooking was being done individually, and men had scraps of food squirreled away in clothing, under bunks or in rough cupboards. Instead of going to the hospital, sick men were lying around in the huts, being cared for by comrades. Because of poor administration—which usually precedes a letdown in combat effectiveness—the army was a sickly, smelly, unhealthy mess.

Hooker quickly snapped the soldiers out of all this. He enjoined them to air out their huts, observe the Sabbath, and do other things good for body and soul. Under Hooker, the rations arrived and were properly accounted for, with orders that no food was to be retained in haversacks, huts or elsewhere. The practice of cooking by squads or individuals, which may have been necessary in the field, but which was highly unsanitary in a camp such as this, was done away with. Cookhouses were built and company cooks appointed. Bakeries were set up, and the men received fresh bread—"soft bread," they called it, to distinguish it from hard bread, or hardtack. Meats and vegetables were supplied, to provide meals that were varied, appetizing and nutritious.

Sick men had to have their names entered in a sick book, answer "sick call" and be marched off to the hospital by a "sick marcher" for examination. Even the horses and mules got better fodder and shelter. Under Hooker, the whole army spruced up, and its health and spirit improved tremendously.

Hooker did something else that was simple, but a great booster of *esprit de corps*. He ordered each man to wear a corps badge. This antecedent of the modern shoulder-patch is said to have been previously originated by General Philip Kearny; but Hooker's chief of staff, General Dan Butterfield, apparently had much to do with devising a badge system for the Army of the Potomac —the same Dan Butterfield who had already given the army Taps and the 3rd Brigade its famous "Dan, Dan, Dan, Butterfield, Butterfield" call. The plan was to assign to each corps a distinctive badge, to be worn upon the center of the top of the cap. Soldiers of the 1st Division in each corps would wear a red badge, soldiers in the 2nd Division a white badge, and those in the 3rd Division a blue badge. Thus, it would be possible to tell at a glance which division a man belonged to. The cap-badge of the Fifth Corps was a Maltese cross, measuring one and seven-eighths inches across. Being in the 1st Division, each man of the 20th Maine wore a red Maltese cross on his cap. As a means of fostering unit pride as well as quick recognition, the scheme was enormously successful. To these little pieces of colored cloth, great and lasting devotion was attached.

As another means of building morale, Hooker staged inspections and reviews. President Lincoln visited the camp. On April 7, Lincoln along with Hooker and his staff made a sort of informal inspection of the Fifth Corps and reviewed the 20th Maine and other regiments. The President, they thought, appeared even more careworn and anxious than he had looked at Antietam. And somewhat abstracted. He was clad in a suit of solemn black. They had put him on a horse that was several sizes too small for his giant frame, so that his legs looked longer than ever and his toes seemed almost to touch the ground. The President had neglected to strap down his trouser legs, which had drawn up, revealing the white legs of his drawers. As he jogged along on his little horse, with his tall silk hat jammed down over his ears, the sight was ludicrous and yet no one felt the slightest urge to laugh. For all about his gaunt figure was the sense of brooding sorrow and tragic awareness of the destiny in which they were all involved. Again, as at Antietam, the deep-shadowed eyes seemed to see all that lay ahead.

In the mind of Fighting Joe Hooker, however, Lincoln's worries were about over. Hooker's army was now in the best of condition and he was supremely confident. Immediately after Lincoln's visit, Hooker began putting into effect a plan to cross the river and attack Lee. The scheme was so good that Hooker was at first apprehensive. He was afraid that Lee would get away—would make his escape to Richmond before being caught and crushed by the Army of the Potomac. Hooker's plan, as it was finally executed toward the end of the month—after some delays and modifications caused by the April rains and other difficulties—envisioned crossing the river with part of his force near Fredericksburg, while the larger part of the army went upriver, crossing the Rappahannock and Rapidan and swooping around Lee's left flank in the vicinity of Chancellorsville. This would put the Confederate army in a frightful predicament, Hooker figured, and the outcome would be a smashing victory for the Union.

The 20th Maine, however, was not to take part in this prospective triumph. For the 20th, the medical department had another fate in store. Army regulations required that every man be vaccinated for smallpox, but Maine, along with most of the other states, had not succeeded in fulfilling this requirement before sending the troops into the field.

The practice of preventive inoculation—that is, of inducing a mild form of the disease to provide immunity against the real thing—was far from new. It had been applied to troops in the Revolution. The improved method of vaccination to induce cowpox—which provides similar immunity—had been announced in 1798. But the procedure was far from perfect. Today smallpox vaccine is derived from the blisters "raised" on heifers inoculated with cowpox. In Civil War days it was "raised" on children, aside from a small quantity of bovine vaccine manufactured by a Dr. Ephraim Cutter of Woburn, Massachusetts. In dispensaries of large northern cities, notably New York, children were vaccinated by the thousands. The harvest of vaccinia crusts and lymph taken from the pustules on their arms was then shipped off to the army camps, where the vaccine was scratched into the arms of the soldiers.

On the whole, the results were good, but with the science of bacteriology then practically unknown, a number of things could go wrong. The vaccine could lose its efficacy on its way to the army—or it might not have had any to begin with. Or it could contain another virus or become contaminated with assorted

73

bacteria. Also, by the time vaccination caught up with the soldiers in the field, many of them were in a run-down condition because of disease and hardship, and their debilitated systems reacted in peculiar ways.

So there were several possibilities for trouble, and trouble overtook the Maine men. Following vaccination at Stoneman's Switch (with what the men of the 20th Maine always believed was smallpox virus instead of vaccine), Surgeon N. P. Monroe of the 20th Maine reported on April 17 that there were eighty-four cases of smallpox in the regiment, thirty-two of them gravely serious, and that three men had died of the disease. Several other men gave every indication of coming down with smallpox. Monroe was highly alarmed. He could visualize the whole Army of the Potomac being infected by the 20th Maine and probably losing the next battle as a result, with the Union falling, and he, Monroe, being blamed for the whole disaster. That afternoon he sat down and dispatched a frantic warning to the Adjutant General of the army. "As this reg't is under marching orders, in company with other troops, they are liable to communicate the disease to others, also liable to be taken on the march themselves & left along the road, sick, or if taken along with the reg't of increasing the exposure of others—I wish it distinctly understood that it is entirely against my idea of safety to our men, as well as others. I wish also to relieve myself of the responsibility of even allowing the reg't to leave camp for the purpose of marching with other troops . . . For if they should mingle with & spread the disease through the army; with the warm weather coming on, there is no telling when, or where it would end. And somebody would be responsible. I therefore feel it my duty, as surgeon of the reg't to report, officially, to Head Quarters, in time to avert the calamity of having the Small Pox spread through our splendid army of the Potomac, thereby giving aid and comfort to the enemy. . . . Hoping this report will be in time to relieve me from any future blame, in responsibility, should the reg't move & the small pox be communicated to other portions of the army, I remain yours truly. ——N. P. Monroe, Surgeon, 20th Maine Vols."

Colonel Ames received this report from his regimental surgeon with dismay. He fervently wanted to get into the forthcoming battle. Ames did not forward the report through channels until April 19, perhaps hoping that the surgeon's alarm was ill-founded. Then he sent it on and immediately got himself detached from the regiment and assigned to the staff of General Meade, where there would be a chance of getting into the fight. Monroe's report finally got up through brigade and division and was acted on by the proper authorities five days after he had written it—anxious days, it must be supposed, for the surgeon. But the result was as he had recommended. The 20th Maine was moved apart from the army and sequestered at a place known as Quarantine Hill.

Meanwhile Lieutenant Colonel Chamberlain, who had been left in command by Ames' timely escape, was also fussing and fuming in disappointment. When he heard the booming of the first guns opening the battle of Chancellorsville, Chamberlain could stand it no longer. Mounting his horse, he galloped off to army headquarters where he entreated General Dan Butterfield to put the 20th Maine into the fight. The answer was thoroughly negative. Chamberlain had one last plea, perhaps suggested by Monroe's report and its prophecy of dire consequences attending any association with the 20th Maine; the regiment was, according to Monroe, a veritable bomb of pestilence. Addressing Butterfield, Chamberlain made what must rank as one of the most surprising statements ever coming from an ex-theologian. Cried he, "If we couldn't do anything else we would give the rebels the smallpox!"

But this particular form of germ warfare did not appeal to Butterfield. The 20th Maine received the inglorious assignment of guarding a telegraph line in rear of the combat area.

The telegraph line ran from Falmouth, headquarters of the army near Stoneman's Switch, all the way to United States Ford. Guarding the line was important because it was a main channel of communication, and telegraph wires were always getting cut if they were not watched carefully. It was just as important to guard against Union men as it was to watch for enemy agents. Union teamsters had been known to cut up the wire for use in repairing their wagons, and these patriots had also used it for tying up fodder on occasions. Back-country soldiers, who had never seen an insulated wire before, would be likely to stop and cut it with their bayonets to see what was inside.

Yet the duty was rather ignominious, because it was a known fact that skedaddlers often went to the rear with the avowed purpose of guarding the telegraph line. An officer would see a man he suspected of being a straggler and would say, "What are *you* doing back here?" And the man would say, "I'm guardin' the telegraph, sir." Sometimes there would be a man guarding every few feet of the wire—enough, in all, to withstand a regiment of enemy wire-cutters.

In this instance, however, the 20th Maine would have been glad to have some help. The regiment was strung out all the way from Falmouth to United States Ford, with orders to shoot to kill anyone seen tampering with the line. In this extended formation, the regiment itself was a sort of telegraph line; news was passed from one man to another. Up until late afternoon of May 2, the news was mostly good; Hooker had moved fast, and had indeed outflanked Lee, just as he had planned. But a sudden thunder rolled up from the west, striking the right flank of the army from an unexpected direction. Word flew along the line that Stonewall Jackson had outflanked the outflankers. One Union corps had already broken and was running for the river. And the rest were in serious danger. Next day brought reports that the boys in blue had fallen back to an entrenched line where they were holding their own, which was not particularly promising, coming from troops who had gone over the river to crush the Army of Northern Virginia like an egg shell. From then on, the news was progressively worse, until on the night of May 5-6, in a driving rainstorm, the army came streaming back across the pontoon bridges, defeated and utterly discouraged. One man in the 20th Maine believed that on that rainy night, as the troops marched through the mud back to Stoneman's Switch, the army was demoralized as it had not been since the first battle of Bull Run. And Will Owen reported that he "never saw a more tired and disheartened set of men than our troops were when they came back. It was raining hard, and they were all mud from head to foot." The 20th Maine remained on the telegraph line until about ten o'clock on the evening of the sixth, when it, too, started back for camp through pouring rain and utter darkness. On the way the regiment got lost and floundered through swamps, brooks and ditches before it finally struck the railroad and followed the tracks to the encampment. Owen wrote, "The next morning you could compare us to some hog that has been rolling in a mud hole all day. . . . And thus ends the second attempt on the capture of Fredericksburg. I have nothing to say about it in any way. I have no opinions to express about the Gen'ls or the men nor do I wish to. I leave it in the hands of God. I don't want to think of it at all."

One of the effects of the battle of Chancellorsville upon the 20th Maine was a quick change in command. Having distinguished himself in the battle, Colonel Adelbert Ames was promoted to brigadier general on May 20. He was promptly sent to command a brigade in the corps that had broken under Stonewall Jackson's attack; perhaps headquarters figured that these troops were in need of some of the Ames discipline. Chamberlain had also managed to get across the river, where he became "implicated" in a charge being made by the 1st Division, and where he'd had another unfortunate horse wounded under him. Then on the night of the withdrawal, Chamberlain had worked on the pontoon bridges, which were being swept away by a freshet, and he had otherwise rendered service over and above the duty of guarding a telegraph wire. Upon the departure of Ames, Chamberlain received a promotion to colonel and took over the command of the 20th Maine.

By then the regiment was in need of replacements. Sickness, which had swept so many men away during the previous autumn, had continued in varying degrees throughout the winter. Only three recruits had arrived from Maine, and the regiment was now down to about four hundred men present for duty. Chamberlain badly needed more soldiers. He got them under somewhat peculiar circumstances. The 2nd Maine was going home. It was decided to transfer approximately 120 soldiers from the 2nd to the 20th Maine. But many of these 120 men disagreed with the decision violently. They, too, wanted to go home.

On May 23 the transferred 2nd Mainers were marched into the regimental area of the 20th Maine under guard of the Corn Exchange Regiment. The replacements looked angry, and the Corn Exchange men evidently considered them dangerous because they were moving them along carefully, with fixed bayonets. Chamberlain was ordered to make them do duty, and to shoot them down if they refused. The story was that they were mutineers.

But the real story was not quite so short, or simple. In order to understand the refractory attitude of the men from the 2nd Maine, it is necessary to go all the way back to the beginning of the war. Although the regiment was numerically second, it was actually the first Maine regiment to reach the field in 1861, and it was remarkable in other ways. Going into the first battle of Bull Run, it carried a $1,200 flag, sent to it by a group of Maine ladies living in San Francisco. The slide, rings, and the battle-axe surmounting the staff were of solid California silver. There were thirteen silver stars on the color-bearer's belt, and a socket of silver. In the field on one side of the flag were the emblems of Maine and California; in the field on the other side, an American eagle with thirty-four stars. At the flag presentation ceremony in Centreville, on the way to the battle, a bird appeared in the sky overhead, and a congressman, peering through a spyglass, excitedly announced that it was a real bald eagle, of the largest size. This seemingly favorable omen was the occasion for much congratulation. The regimental commander, in one of those high-flown speeches so typical of the times, declared that the fair folds of the new flag would never be stained except by the blood of its defenders. His words were uncomfortably prophetic. Next day in the battle of Bull Run a bullet went through the color-bearer's throat; he fell, splashing the new flag with crimson. Another man grasped the flag, and he, too, was shot dead. The flag fell on the ground, the enemy got hold of it, and the whole 2nd Maine had to charge and fight desperately to get its $1,200 flag back.

As the war went on, the 2nd Maine fought prodigiously in eleven battles and countless skirmishes. But the eagle that had appeared at Centreville might have been—as it possibly was—a buzzard for all the luck it ever brought the 2nd Maine. The regiment had many troubles, most of them caused by various men who had come around with papers for them to sign.

The regiment came mostly from the region around Bangor and was made up of existing militia companies and other companies formed by volunteers at the very outbreak of the war. The first papers signed were for three months. At about this time the Maine legislature, meeting in extra session, authorized the raising of ten regiments to serve for *two years,* the 2nd Maine being included. So the soldiers of the 2nd Maine were presented with a second set of papers, enlisting them for two years, and the men had signed these papers too—anything to get the red tape out of the way and get on with the war. Later, in the process of being mustered into United States service, the Federal officer in charge had said he'd have to muster them in for *three years*—he had no authority to do otherwise. Some of the men had signed the three-year papers and some had not. All, however, had continued with the regiment.

In August, 1861, three months after the 2nd Maine men had left the state, they observed that a number of regiments were packing up and going home, including another Maine regiment which had signed up for two years. The men of the 2nd Maine couldn't see the justice of this; sixty-six of them refused duty, were court-martialed and sentenced to a prison island in the Dry Tortugas. This sentence was commuted to a transfer; the sixty-six men were then sent to a New York regiment, but later returned to the 2nd Maine and continued with their own regiment for the remainder of its term.

When in May, 1863, the two-year term ran out, there was more trouble. The 2nd Maine departed for home with the men who had signed for two years. But the recruits and the men who had signed for three years were told that they couldn't accompany the regiment, but would be held in service. Whereat there was another mass refusal of duty. And this was the mutinous group now being delivered to the 20th Maine. It didn't seem to these men that they had been done right by, and they weren't going to serve any longer than they thought the law should require. Chamberlain's orders were to conduct a wholesale execution if they persisted in this refusal; he was to draw up his regiment and fire on them in case of any further disobedience.

This was a real predicament for Chamberlain. Shooting the

men from the 2nd Maine would not only deprive him of his replacements, but it would make the State of Maine a highly uncomfortable place if he ever wanted to return there. Yet orders were orders, and if he, Chamberlain, wouldn't obey them, someone else would. After thinking it over a few minutes, the young officer rode to the corps commander—then Major General George Gordon Meade—and asked permission to manage the men in his own way. Permission granted. Then he rode back and confronted the sullen men who were waiting, still under guard. The men from the 2nd Maine hadn't eaten for three days, and Chamberlain decided that there was no use trying to reason with hungry people. He therefore saw to it that they were well fed, and had the guard removed to make them feel like free men again. Next he placed their names on the regular company rolls, distributed by groups, so as to break up the mass spirit of mutiny. Then he called the men together and pointed out a few of the facts: that they were on his rolls as soldiers by authority of the United States; that he could not entertain them as civilian guests, but he would be glad to treat them as soldiers should be treated; and that they would lose no rights by obeying his orders. At the same time he promised to see what could be done for their claim.

Six of the 2nd Mainers continued their refusal and were kept with the regiment as prisoners to await court-martial. All the rest yielded to Chamberlain's persuasions and returned to duty. This group, in fact, added a measure of strength to the 20th Maine that was to be decisive for the regiment, and perhaps for the country, a little more than a month later. They were also to prove that stubborn soldiers—men who won't be pushed around—are sometimes worth cultivating by means other than force, the chances being that they're the sort of men whom the *enemy* won't push around, either.

On the whole, leadership is a quality that is complex and not too well understood. Yet a great deal could be learned about the subject from a study of Chamberlain's life in the army. Leadership in military affairs is ordinarily thought of as the clarion shout, the waved sword, the "Follow me, men!" But it is also the right word, spoken quietly, at the right time. In addition, leadership is many other things, and whatever these attributes are, Chamberlain seems to have had most of them. And he would soon have ample opportunity to prove it. Within a couple of weeks the new bird-colonel was on his way—to Gettysburg and a rendezvous with destiny.

CHAPTER FIVE

Sunstroke, Sore Feet and Stuart

EARLY June on the Rappahannock. Back home in Maine, this would have been late spring; but here in Virginia it was like deep summer, hot sunlight irradiating the thick foliage with greenish fire, mockingbirds singing in the branches, strawberries ripening in the grass.

The 20th Maine was picketing the riverbank at United States Ford with the Confederate pickets on the opposite bank. "We get along with them first rate," Will Owen wrote home. "We go in swimming with them and talk and joke. It seems strange to see two armies or pickets from those armies come together with the best of feelings—shake hands and talk matters over, just as though they were the best of friends instead of enemies." There was a sort of unexpressed agreement whereby the private soldiers refrained from shooting at one another, provided that no one made any attempt to cross over.

The agreement apparently did not cover general officers. One day a Confederate soldier called across the river, "I say, you Yanks, why didn't you shoot General Hill? He stood right here half an hour ago." (The Maine men had seen an officer pass along the riverbank, but they had mistakenly thought he was an ordinary line officer.)

While guarding the various fords, the 3rd Brigade was strung out along the river for a distance of six or eight miles. There were just four regiments of them now: the 20th Maine, the 16th Michigan, the 44th New York, and the 83rd Pennsylvania. They had a new brigade commander, Colonel Strong Vincent, former CO of the 83rd. He looked almost exactly like his name, strong, erect, stalwart, with a luxuriant set of sideburns—an intelligent and resolute-looking face. The brigade had a new flag too; it was triangular-shaped, white, with a blue border, and a red Maltese cross in the center—part of General Hooker's new scheme of flags and badges for quick identification.

By June 6, the brigade had moved farther along the Rappahannock, and the 20th Maine was guarding Ellis Ford. There was a distant muttering of cannon somewhere down the river, where it was rumored that the Sixth Corps had crossed. On the ninth, news came of a cavalry fracas at Brandy Station. Army headquarters seemed highly nervous about something; they were calling for reports of everything observed across the river, every four hours, day or night. If nothing at all was observed, they wanted to know that, too; in the patchwork pattern of army intelligence, *nothing* could be as significant as *something*.

There was nervousness in the rifle pits along the riverbank at Ellis Ford, too. One night a couple of mules got into a pile of empty hardtack boxes off to the right of the 20th Maine line, and the frisky animals began kicking and banging the boxes around, which, as Corporal Livermore noted in his diary next day, "frightened the Adj. so he jumped out of bed and ran to Capt. Clark's tent and they turned the Co. out, and the Adj. ran to the guard house and asked why they did not give the alarm. They told him they had heard nothing. He said there had been more than 100 shots fired."

So there was a continuing flow of rumors and alarms, some true, some false. But as Joe Hooker studied the whole pattern at army headquarters, its meaning began to be evident. The forces of Robert E. Lee were leaving his front on the Rappahannock and moving off into the Shenandoah Valley, which was an avenue north as well as south.

Lee had begun his invasion of Pennsylvania.

It is a fashion among military historians nowadays to characterize this movement merely as a "raid." But those who had to deal with it at the time may have considered it as something more. In any state of health, the Army of Northern Virginia was a deadly antagonist. Now, with morale high following the two successive victories of Fredericksburg and Chancellorsville,

Lee's army was in top shape, both mentally and physically. Going north along the Shenandoah Valley, the gray troops were practically unopposed. They were supremely confident, stepping high, and spoiling for a fight. One more victory, won on Northern soil, might attract foreign recognition and aid . . . might bring the weary North to a negotiated peace . . . might end the war.

Fighting Joe Hooker moved fast, once he saw what was up. He started the Army of the Potomac northward on what was to become one of the hardest forced marches that ever blistered the feet of mankind. In a red sunset on June 13, the 20th Maine pulled away from Ellis Ford, joined the rest of the division at Morrisville, and marched the next day to Catlett's Station, where they took their place in the Fifth Corps column, hurrying northward. The next few days brought some of the hottest weather they experienced during the war. Under the intense heat men were gasping, staggering, falling out with sunstroke. In desperation, some of the soldiers put leaves in their caps and cut boughs to shade their heads.

On their way up past Manassas Junction, they marched through the old Bull Run battlefields, still littered with broken muskets, old shoes, canteens, and the skins of dead animals. Wind and rain had weathered away the coverings of shallow graves; partially exposed bones were bleaching in the sun—"not a cheerful or encouraging sight to behold," as one soldier noted. The much fought-over Manassas fields were now almost a desert, with soil uncultivated, the land growing up to weeds, the air stifling with dust and the pungent odor of pennyroyal, which seemed to be everywhere. Worst of all, water was scarce.

On June 17, between Manassas and Gum Spring, the regiment participated in one of the hardest marches of the war, nearly eighteen miles under a broiling sun with insufficient water—men falling from exhaustion and thirst, four soldiers in the division dying of sunstroke, and nearly every regiment leaving at least half its men lying along the roadsides.

There was a day of rest on the eighteenth, and on the following day the direction of march turned westward, toward a low range of hills—the Bull Run Mountains. Under the June heat, summer was coming in full-blown, with ripening cherries, acres of grain lightening to the paleness between green and gold, fields of daisies blazing white. Ahead there had been occasional thudding of cannon, so that the mystic presence of the enemy lay over all this landscape, making it sharp and clear and poignant. Many of them would see this country again, but it never would look quite the same, for it would not then be June, 1863, and the Army of Northern Virginia would not be just over the sky-line.

The firing they had heard came from a series of fights crackling along the mountain ridges that separated the two armies. The Army of the Potomac was moving northward along a course that was generally to the east of the Bull Run Mountains. Along the parallel Blue Ridge range, mostly to the west of it, Lee's army was also marching northward. The gaps in both mountain ranges were points to be disputed by cavalry—Union horsemen pressing toward the west in order to observe Lee's movements, Confederate riders countering these thrusts in order to screen the advance of their infantry. For the Confederates, this job was being handled by an enterprising cavalry general named J. E. B. Stuart. And Stuart was not only effectively screening the Blue Ridge route, but he appeared to be trying for an additional screen, farther to the east, by attempting to seize gaps in the Bull Run Mountains. Stuart had struck eastward to Aldie with a strong force. There'd been heavy fighting; Stuart had been repulsed; but now as the Fifth Corps approached Aldie, there was still a strong body of Confederate cavalry at an uncomfortable distance —only three or four miles to the west, around Middleburg.

It would be necessary to drive these people back toward the Blue Ridge. And it would be vitally necessary to find out whether they had any infantry behind them on the east side of the Blue Ridge. Presumably, if the Confederate cavalrymen at Middleburg were attacked and driven back, the Confederate infantry, if any were present, would come up and support them. But driving the gray cavalry would be a hard job. The country around Middleburg was broken and hilly, with an abundance of stone walls behind which dismounted men could put up a stubborn defense. Considering all this, the Union cavalry commander decided that he'd need help from the foot soldiers. The request went to army headquarters; the principal assignment, descending through channels, went to Vincent's Brigade. And so it was that the Maine soldiers, on the morning of June 21, set out with the rest of the brigade to molest the enemy force at Middleburg.

Colonel Chamberlain was down with a partial sunstroke that day. Lieutenant Colonel Freeman Conner of the 44th New York was in temporary command of the 20th Maine. They left Aldie at three o'clock; by daylight they were past Middleburg and facing the Confederate position in the fields astride the Ashby's Gap road, just west of the town. To their right, Gregg's Union cavalry was forming for the advance. In front the white roadway led up over rising ground through a patchwork of woods and green fields crisscrossed with stone walls. There were Confederate horsemen in the fields, dismounted men behind the walls, and a six-gun battery near the road.

Mysteriously, the 83rd Pennsylvania withdrew from the brigade and moved off to the left, disappearing in the woods. The remaining three regiments of Vincent's Brigade formed line of battle, colors bravely flying. A bugle sounded. The line of battle surged forward.

The six-gun battery was firing busily; patches of ground around them were flying up and there were slamming sounds, as though small iron stoves were exploding into hot, humming fragments. Puffs of smoke and little tongues of flame darted out over the stone walls; the 20th Maine heard, for the first time, the snap of carbine bullets going past. And some *not* going past. Down the line, a man fell with a clatter of canteen and musket; then another, and the file closers were yelling to never mind that, keep your eyes front, and dress that line on the colors. Tension built up . . . it was a relief to open fire, to yell.

But most of all it was a relief to see the 83rd Pennsylvania, which had gone by a roundabout way, coming out of the woods upon the Confederate flank, and the gray people getting ready to pull their traps. ("This Vincent fellow knows how to handle a brigade!") Then the field was drumming with pounding hooves, and the Union cavalry went in with a rush. As they struck the Confederates, the whole position seemed to boil up in a confusion of rearing horses, flashing sabres, and falling, running men. Out of it, somehow, the Confederate force disentangled itself and went streaming off to the west, leaving one artillery piece and a batch of prisoners behind it.

It was the first look the 20th Maine had ever had at cavalry in action, and they were tremendously impressed. Earlier in the war, Union cavalry had been generally inferior to the Southern horsemen, but now they were coming into their own. Even the Confederate prisoners, as they were being marched away, appear to have been lost in admiration. One is reported to have shouted, "You'ns will soon be as good as we'ns!"

The brigade re-formed in column and pushed forward after the cavalry. Before long they again came up with the enemy, behind another series of stone walls. Another flanking movement combined with frontal pressure, another cavalry charge, and the Confederates withdrew, like gray ghosts fading into the distance. It was like that for the rest of the day. Stuart's men were fighting a skillful delaying action—standing, forcing the Union columns into time-consuming deployment, then fading, drawing them back into column, and making another stand farther on. With the heat, the continual marching and maneuvering, and the mounting and falling nervous tension, it was an ordeal for the infantry. By late afternoon they were too exhausted to continue, but they had pushed the Confederates back toward the Blue Ridge six miles. While the tired foot soldiers rested, Union cavalry drove the Southerners on into Ashby's Gap. Stuart, they knew, would come popping out again, here or somewhere else, like a weasel from a woodpile, but the mission had been a conspicuous success. In the 20th Maine, thanks to Vincent's skillful handling of the brigade, there were only nine casualties—one killed and eight wounded.

Next day the 3rd Brigade returned to Aldie where the men camped, gratefully, for three days. But on June 26, in a drizzling rain, the northward march was resumed at a brutal pace. Wet to the skin, the Maine soldiers slogged twenty miles, crossing the Potomac at Edwards Ferry and going into bivouac at Poolesville several miles beyond.

The next day's march took them nearly to Frederick, where they rested on the twenty-eighth. By now the regiment was well stripped down. Everything not absolutely essential to human existence had been thrown away; the average soldier's extra clothing consisted of a pair of socks. When the regiment happened to halt near a stream, men would sometimes seize the opportunity to take off their sweaty, dust-caked shirts and wash them. When the march was resumed, the shirts were tied to bayonets to dry and flapped in the breeze as the column moved on.

During the halt at Frederick, there was time for more thorough laundering, and some of the adventurous soldiers who sneaked into town came back with civilian food—and the latest news. Lee was now deep into Pennsylvania, and there was a great ruffling of feathers up that way—a fear and trembling that extended even to the deepest bank vaults of Harrisburg. The whole North was scared, they reported.

Big news had been made right in camp, too. Hooker had had a falling-out with the authorities in Washington. Major General George Gordon Meade—the Fifth Corps commander—was taking over Hooker's job, and Major General George Sykes was taking the Fifth Corps.

This transfer of command made no great impression on the 20th Maine. By now, the soldiers were long past being shaken up by a change of army commanders. McClellan . . . Burnside . . . Hooker . . . now Meade. Maybe it wasn't a good idea to switch generals right on the eve of what looked like a critical battle, but after all one general was very much like another, and Meade, whom they knew to be a brave and judicious officer, was probably as good as any of them. And anyway, if the war was going to be won, it was beginning to look as though the enlisted men would have to win it. No general, so far, had produced that sudden stroke of magic that would mean victory overnight.

The chief gripe of the men in ranks at this point appears to have come from reading the newspapers they picked up at Frederick and elsewhere along the way. When Lee had crossed into Maryland, the Army of the Potomac had been soundly denounced for allowing him to get so far north. But now, as Lee was advancing into Pennsylvania, Private Theodore Gerrish noted that "this tone of abuse was changed, and from ministerial studies and editorial sanctums, there came the most frantic appeals to the army. These men felt that it was a gross violation of their rights as American citizens to have the rebels so near, and their peaceful minds disturbed by scenes of bloodshed and fears of personal danger, and they called upon the soldiers to avenge their sufferings with Spartan-like courage and sacrifice, exhorting them to shed their last drop of blood, if necessary, to hurl Lee's forces back across the Potomac."

(Later they would find that there was no possibility of satisfying the peaceful citizens of the North. Once Lee had been, as they wished, driven back across the Potomac, the army would be abused again for allowing him to get away.)

Greatly complicating Meade's assignment to deal with Lee was a consternation in Washington that even exceeded that in the more northerly cities. Washington was saying, in effect, "Don't let him go up there, but don't let him come down here, either." Meade's orders read in part: "Your army is free to act as you may deem proper under the circumstances as they arise. You will, however, keep in view the important fact that the Army of the Potomac is the covering army of Washington as well as the army of operation against the invading forces of the rebels. You will, therefore, maneuver and fight in such a manner as to cover the capital and also Baltimore, as far as circumstances will admit. Should General Lee move upon either of these places, it is expected that you will either anticipate him or arrive with him so as to give him battle."

With this requirement in mind, Meade kept to the south and east of Lee, with the several infantry corps of his army spread out like the fingers of a hand. As the fingers probed northward, they were closely controlled, moving fast, and ready to draw into a fist wherever contact with Lee's lancing divisions should first draw blood.

The men who completed that hike were infantrymen such as we may not see again. In today's motorized army, a twenty-mile march is considered an unusual hardship. Here, by way of comparison, are some days and distances from the march of the 20th Maine to Gettysburg:

June 26 — 20 miles
June 27 — 20 miles
June 29 — 18 miles
June 30 — 23 miles
July 1 — 26 miles
July 2 — fought the battle

With heel-and-toe walking like this, much of it during periods of intense heat, there was bound to be a heavy toll. Late in the afternoon, men would be falling out almost continually with foot trouble and exhaustion. Some received medical treatment; some were urged on by sundry persuasions of the Provost Guard; some got up of their own volition and struggled painfully on to join their comrades in bivouac during the night.

The procedure, when a man was compelled to leave the regiment on the march was rigid but simple. Each company commander always carried a supply of paper slips, bearing his own signature, and some such message as "The bearer has my permission to fall out of ranks, being unable to proceed with the regiment." If a man was found absent without one of these "tickets" he was in serious trouble.

For temporary absences, when, for example, a soldier had urgent business in the bushes, he would get verbal permission from the captain, take off his knapsack, and hand it along with his musket to the men of his section to be carried by them until his return. The rule operated for the good of the service in two ways. First, it left the man unencumbered and theoretically enabled to return sooner. And second, it discouraged loitering by subjecting the absentee to the extreme displeasure of his already overloaded fellow trudgers if he lingered too long away.

But men, generally, helped one another willingly. One young soldier, George Estabrook, was particularly fortunate in having his strong little uncle, Glazier Estabrook, with him in H Company. George used to play out sometimes, but when he folded toward the end of a day's march, Glazier would pick him up like a satchel and carry him along into camp.

In bivouac, upon stacking arms and breaking ranks, the first thing to do was to start fires for the evening meal. Fence rails often provided the fuel, and a farmer whose land was the bivouac area of an infantry corps could figure that something akin to one of the curses of Pharaoh had fallen on him—a plague of fence burners. There would be a rapid scattering of men into the fields, and the fences would seem to come alive and walk away, rail by rail. When the army got up into Northern territory, there was an attempt to prevent the fence burning; but the habit had been strongly formed in Virginia, and with dusk coming down over the countryside, a great number of fence rails would get up and walk into camp. A smart farmer would provide piles of wood, then put in a sizable claim to the government after the army had passed on.

Concurrent with the fuel gathering, other men searched out brooks, springs and wells, filling the canteens. Fires were lighted. Tiny columns of smoke arose by the hundreds. Soon the fragrance of cooking coffee pervaded the bivouac area. Like all the rest of the army, the men of the 20th Maine became great drinkers of coffee—one of the main items of sustenance, both physical and moral. On the march the men usually carried their coffee ready-mixed with brown sugar. The detachable lining of the haversack provided the bag. The ground coffee and the sugar made a solid ball held in the bottom under a retaining knot tied in the lining. They cooked the coffee in a battered and blackened tin can, hung over the fire on a pole, north-woods style. There was rarely milk to put in the coffee, unless an unsuspecting cow could be commandeered. But it was hot, it smelled and tasted good, and it sent a warming and refreshing glow coursing through tired bodies.

Along with coffee, the marching ration usually consisted of salt pork and hardtack. Salt pork was roasted over the coals or used for frying fat, and it was often eaten raw. Fresh beef, if any was issued, usually came from cattle that were driven along on the march and slaughtered at the end of the day. Fresh was the word for it; the meat came to them practically quivering. The men fried or broiled it and considered it a wonderful luxury.

Much has been written about hardtack, which was a dense sort of flour-and-water biscuit, or cracker, about three inches square, serving as an all-purpose ration. When hardtack got old it was really hard. As years went by and the stories were told, it got harder and harder. Ellis Spear of the 20th Maine used to wonder about the army regulation that required every recruit to have a full set of teeth. The reason given, or generally understood, was that good teeth were necessary so the soldier could bite the end of his paper cartridge. But this was a piece of dark duplicity, for when you got to thinking about it, you realized that a full set of teeth wasn't necessary for biting the cartridge; a man only needed front teeth for that. The real reason for having good solid back teeth was hardtack. Or as Spear put it, "It then appeared that the men were selected not for courage or endurance, which could not be examined into, but for good grinders, and the wonder now is that men enough to put down the rebellion could have been found with teeth equal to the task of putting down the army hardtack."

He then went on to describe hardtack. "It was not a stratified rock. It was homogeneous and amorphous, excepting when wormy. It did not resemble anything in the vegetable, animal or mineral kingdom, excepting brick. It was inflexible, inelastic, infrangible and indigestible, suited neither to the stomach nor bowels, and was adapted, except in shape, better as armor. Indeed, instances have been reported, though perhaps not in the official records, where the haversack of a soldier stopped the bullet of the enemy, and these perhaps are the only cases where it was found that the hardtack saved life. It is well known that the army mule would not eat it, and it is another proof of the high intelligence of that noble animal, without whose constant aid the rebellion never would have been put down."

The reason mules would not eat hardtack was simply that they couldn't eat it, according to another soldier-historian. This man, with no indication that he was telling anything but the solemn truth, related an incident in which a piece of hardtack proved impenetrable even to his exceptionally good teeth, so he passed it to an army mule which was standing by, looking at it longingly. The mule, he wrote, "received it joyously, and set to work; he worked away at it for awhile on one side of his mouth, then deftly transferred it to the other side and tried again. A kind of worried look came into his eyes, and, finally, laying his ears well back on his head, he made a determined effort to crush it, but finding all his efforts useless, he dropped it on the ground and paid no further attention to it."

This delightful imagery—mule with ears laid back trying to crush resistant cracker—is the picture of hardtack that has come down to us. Actually, many soldiers stated that when some hardtack was fresh it tasted pretty good. And judging by the marching and fighting that was done on this food, it must have contained a substantial amount of nourishment.

After supper, it was time to think of bedding down. If the bivouac was for one night only and the weather was good, a man usually did without shelter and made his bed on the ground with his rubber and woolen blankets. If the stay was for longer, or if the night promised rain, the men put up tents. These were quite similar to the shelter-halves used in the army today. Each man carried a piece of stout cotton cloth, and two or more of these pieces could be fastened together with buttons to make a tent. The handy little folding pole that the soldier carries nowadays was not issued; the army figured that a man could go cut his own pole. But sometimes—particularly if rain was falling—two soldiers used their rifles as tent poles by fixing the bayonets and driving them into the ground, then stringing the tent rope between the trigger guards of the two upright muskets.

However, a much better tent could be made with two forked poles driven into the ground about six feet apart, with another pole laid from fork to fork. Over this sturdy framework, the shelter cloths were buttoned in place. In the 20th Maine, three men often pitched tent together. Two of the shelter pieces made a roof, a third closed in one end, and the other end could be left open to the fire on cold nights.

Then there was the earth to receive the soldier's tired body. An infantryman gets to know the earth; here he knew it in a welcome way; the solid feel of the ground, seeming to press up and relax knotted muscles; the smell of roots and small spicy weeds; the sound of insects. The fire crackled and burned low. Distant voices faded in a hum; and the numbness of total fatigue swept him into a dreamless sleep, until reveille and another day of heat, dust and marching.

Of all these marching days, July 1 was longest remembered by the 20th Maine. The regiment was taking its turn as advance guard, with skirmishers out and flankers wide. Behind them as far as the eye could see came the Fifth Corps column, moving masses of dark and light blue, rifles glinting in the sunshine, dust rising all the way back to the horizon and far beyond. By now they had left their trains behind them, excepting ammunition wagons and ambulances and were carrying three days' rations in haversacks. The soldiers marched silently, impassively, heads sagging forward, feet moving one past the other in a rhythmic swinging slide—the seemingly slow, yet deceptively rapid, route step of veteran infantrymen.

They were now marching through a beautiful, big-barned country, rich with ripening grain, knee-high corn and lush orchards where fruit was beginning to hang heavy on the bough. The Maine soldiers feasted on ripe cherries, and one of them, impressed with the size and flavor of the fruit, sent a few of the seeds home in a letter, urging the folks to plant them. As they neared Pennsylvania, the march became livelier. Toward noon they crossed the state line and the 83rd Pennsylvania, back on its native soil, uncased its colors while the drum corps struck up "Yankee Doodle." The enthusiasm spread to other regiments; soon colors were flying and fifers and drummers were sounding off all down the column.

The initial reception in Pennsylvania, however, was disappointing. The inhabitants had set up roadside stands, and were busy selling milk at ten cents a pint and fresh buttermilk, bread, cakes and pies at prices that seemed equally high. Among the roadside merchants were several strapping young fellows who looked as though they ought to be in the column, carrying a gun. Theodore Gerrish of the 20th recalled that "we usually purchased their entire stock; and as we had no money told them to 'charge it to Uncle Sam.' They endeavored to shame us by comparing our conduct to that of the rebels, but they soon learned that words had no effect upon hungry Yankees."

But the farther north they went, and the nearer they got to the scenes of rebel depredations, the friendlier the people became, and the lower the prices. As the afternoon wore on, a chill made itself felt, even through the hot July sunlight—a sense of mystery and dread hanging in the air like a thin haze of smoke. Nearing Hanover, they came upon dead horses—and corpses of cavalrymen staring fixedly at the sky as though they had seen a wonder that words could not tell. There'd been fighting here. What had happened? They soon learned the answer. Jeb Stuart.

After the Army of the Potomac had passed, Stuart had sallied out from the passes of the Blue Ridge. During the past few days, with a large force of cavalry, he had completed an amazing gallop completely around behind the Federal army and up past its right flank. Meanwhile he had done General Meade the considerable favor of cutting all telegraph wires leading to him from higher headquarters in Washington. Nevertheless, Stuart had been ungratefully set upon by Union cavalry here at Hanover, and that explained the corpses.

As they marched through Hanover, the column was greeted with resounding cheers. A group of young ladies, clad in red, white and blue, appeared on a balcony and sang "The Star-Spangled Banner," which was most elevating. A newspaperman who was in that vicinity wrote about "rays of sun beating down through showery clouds, gilding every object with a peculiar golden light."

Off to the west there were disturbances of the atmosphere, as though someone were beating a rug, far over the horizon. Late in the afternoon they went into bivouac near Hanover, then right out of bivouac again, for a lathered horseman arrived with bad news that soon spread through the entire corps. The report said that the First Corps and the Eleventh Corps had run into Lee at a place called Gettysburg, fourteen or fifteen miles to the west and had been hurt badly. General Reynolds, the First Corps commander, had been killed; the two corps had been driven back through the town of Gettysburg and now were dug in on some hills this side of the town, waiting for the rest of the army to arrive.

This meant that the march of the Fifth Corps would continue into the night. The bugles sounded "Forward!" and they were pushing westward again. In midevening, the moon came up, illuminating the countryside with a clear blue light, and suddenly a phantom was riding ahead of them. "At a turn of the road a staff officer, with an air of authority, told each colonel as he came up that McClellan was in command again, and riding ahead of us on the road," Colonel Chamberlain reported. And Private Theodore Gerrish of the 20th Maine wrote, "Men waved their hats and cheered until they were hoarse and wild with excitement." No one knew how the false rumor got started, but for a time that evening they marched believing that their beloved McClellan was once again leading them into battle. The men were intensely keyed up. Later there would be a rumor that the spirit of George Washington was accompanying them, riding on a white horse.

It was a night that Gerrish always remembered. He wrote, "The people rushed from their homes and stood by the roadside to welcome us, men, women, and children all gazing on the strange spectacle. Bands played, the soldiers and the people cheered, banners waved, and white handkerchiefs fluttered from doors and windows, as the blue, dusty column surged on."

But as the evening wore on, excitement gave way to weariness. The cheering died away. Many of the men began to stagger, half asleep on their feet. They had now marched over twenty-five miles. Some time after midnight a halt was called and they got two or three hours' sleep, lying in the dust and the dew beside the road.

Around four-thirty the sun came up red, indicating another hot day. They arose, dazed and stiff, and continued the march. Arriving on some level, open ground, the two divisions of the Fifth Corps then present formed as though for a grand review, with colors unfurled, lines dressed, pieces at the right shoulder. Details cleared away fences in front, and they advanced in formation—great blocks of dusty blue, with the flags and the shimmer of steel over them in the morning light. There was a remarkable stillness in the ranks, broken only by low-voiced commands and the swishing of legs through growing grain, hay, and low bushes. Coming to the crest of a knoll, they saw a group of rough, wooded hills ahead, with the brown scars of earthworks on them . . . wagon and artillery parks . . . rows of stacked muskets where troops were resting . . . other evidences that they were in the rear of a battle line.

East of the hills, the Fifth Corps divisions maneuvered into a line facing generally north, and there was a lot of waiting and standing around. Officers got out in front of their regiments and read an order from General Meade. A number of phrases filtered through to tired brains . . . "enemy are on our soil . . . whole country now looks anxiously to this army to deliver it . . . homes, firesides and domestic altars are involved." It sounded pretty serious. And then came a grim and remarkable sentence that made them realize just how serious it was. "Corps and other commanders are authorized to order the instant death of any soldier who fails in his duty at this hour."

Later in the forenoon the corps moved, crossed a creek, and went into a reserve position in a field just off the Baltimore Pike near an orchard. The town and the scene of yesterday's fighting were not visible, being hidden by the hills and some woods on high ground west of them. They could see a lot of activity. Ambulances coming up. Staff officers riding furiously on mysterious errands. Wagons distributing ammunition. But aside from the occasional boom of a cannon, it seemed mighty peaceful for a battlefield.

The men stretched out and got some much-needed rest. It felt good to have the earth pressing against the back instead of the feet. They dozed off. From off behind the hills and the woods, someone began popping corn. First one kernel went *pop*. Then others, softly—pop, pop, pop, pop, p-p-p-p-p-popopopopopopo-popop—the sound of musketry, muffled by heat, distance and intervening terrain. The sound started in the northwest, then ran around to the west and finally died away. A few eyes opened, then closed. It was just skirmish firing. The men of the 20th Maine dozed and slept. The scent of trampled and crushed grass rose around them. Summer breathed hot on their upturned faces. It was quiet at Gettysburg.

CHAPTER SIX

Unhooked, Unhinged, and Almost Undone

HILE the tired soldiers of the 20th Maine slept behind Powers Hill, the stage was being set for their entrance, and various actors were moving about in the wings.

Chief of these was Major General George Gordon Meade, former Fifth Corps commander, now commanding general of the Army of the Potomac. Meade was not a spectacular leader but he was a safe one, and a man of character—not given to throwing soldiers' lives away needlessly. This seems to have been a virtue that had impressed the men of the 20th Maine. Private Theodore Gerrish described Meade thus: "He had not the dashing appearance of many other generals, but when we saw that tall, bowed form, enveloped in a great brown overcoat, riding to the front, we always felt safe." Gerrish also remembered that Meade appeared to be continually bent over by the great burdens placed upon his shoulders; as the General rode along "he always seemed to be looking upon the ground, at a point about twenty yards in advance of him."

This overborne appearance, combined with sharp eyes, a deeply lined face, and a large Roman nose, usually gave Meade the look of a tired eagle, but on this morning of July 2, somewhere between eight and nine o'clock, as he came out of the little house in the rear of Cemetery Ridge serving as his headquarters, he was wearing a cheerful face, relatively speaking. Captain George Meade, his son and aide, said that "to one who was familiar with the general's manner and tones of voice in different moods he seemed in excellent spirits, as if well pleased with affairs as far as they had proceeded."

And well he might be pleased. In falling back from their defeat west and north of the town on the previous day, the First Corps and the Eleventh Corps had occupied and held excellent ground. Arriving on the field shortly after midnight, General Meade had found them dug in and reinforced on hills south of Gettysburg. Now the rest of the army, with the exception of one corps, had arrived and had occupied more of the high ground.

The line, as planned by Meade that morning, looked like a big fishhook. The hook itself, with point to the east, lay on a group of rather steep hills just south of the village. The long shank of the hook ran south along a ridge known as Cemetery Ridge. The eye of the shank was supposed to rest upon a rough, rocky hill called Little Round Top. Opposite Cemetery Ridge, on Seminary Ridge about a mile to the west, and curving through the town of Gettysburg, lay the Confederate line. It was longer than the Union line; troops had to be moved farther in any maneuvers along it. With higher ground, with shorter interior lines, Meade had the advantage.

But things started to go wrong for him, and there were hints of trouble early in the day. The southernmost corps in line was the Third Corps, commanded by Major General Daniel E. Sickles. Sickles was a brave officer, affectionately regarded by his men, but he was a "political general," and the West Pointers were inclined to look upon him with a certain amount of suspicion. General Meade told his son, Captain Meade, to go down and see what Sickles was doing. Captain Meade rode down the Taneytown Road and came upon the temporary headquarters of the Third Corps in a patch of woods west of the road. He was told that General Sickles had been up all night and was now in his tent resting; that the Third Corps was not in position; and that General Sickles didn't know exactly where he was supposed to go.

Captain Meade thereupon galloped hastily back to army headquarters and told his father of this seeming indecision on the part of General Sickles. In Meade's mind the picture was clear; the shank of the fishhook was to run straight south; half that shank was the Second Corps; and below it, resting its left upon Little Round Top, the Third Corps. Sharply and decisively, he told Captain Meade to gallop back to Sickles again and tell him that his instructions were to go into position on the left of the Second Corps. His right was to connect with the Second Corps and he was to prolong the line of that corps, occupying the "position that General Geary had held the night before."

Back down the Taneytown Road rode Captain Meade once more. At General Sickles' headquarters, he found the tents struck, staff officers hustling about, and a movement of some sort under way. General Sickles, a thick-set man with a large head, full round face and heavy moustache, was sitting on his horse. There are good days and bad days, depending on your name, and for the name Dan Sickles July 2, 1863, wasn't going to be a good day. It was starting wrong already. The commanding general of the army had assigned his corps to an area that he, Sickles, considered completely indefensible. Cemetery Ridge was no ridge at all here. It sank away into low ground, with high ground a few hundred yards in front, where Sickles believed the enemy could plant artillery and make his own position untenable.

And now here was this young whippersnapper of an aide telling him something about getting into a position held by General Geary on the night before, and implying that he ought to be quick about it. However, it is politic to be civil to a general's aide, particularly if the aide is the general's son, and Sickles told young Meade that his troops were then moving and would be in position shortly. But he also muttered that General Geary had no battle position the night before; his troops were merely massed in that vicinity. Captain Meade rode back to army headquarters, where it was assumed that Sickles now knew where he was supposed to place his men, and was acting accordingly.

Around eleven o'clock, General Sickles appeared briefly at Meade's headquarters. He was fussing about his position. Meade went over it again with him, explaining that Sickles' corps was to prolong the line of the Second Corps down toward Little Round Top. Reference was apparently made again to the position as that held by General Geary the night before and Sickles said Geary hadn't had any position, and so on and so on. Sickles wanted to know if he couldn't use his own judgment in posting his corps and Meade said, "Certainly, within the limits of the

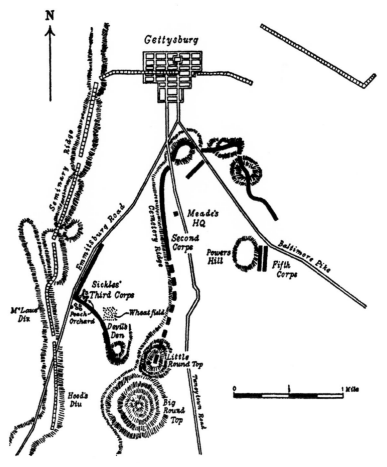

Confederate Troops

Union Troops

Position planned for, but not occupied
by Sickles' Third Corps

N

Gettysburg

Seminary Ridge

Emmitsburg Road

Cemetery Ridge

Meade's HQ

Second Corps

Powers Hill

Baltimore Pike

Fifth Corps

Sickles' Third Corps

McLaws Div

Peach Orchard

Wheatfield

Devil's Den

Little Round Top

Hood's Div

Big Round Top

Taneytown Road

0   1 Mile

Gettysburg, about 4 P.M., July 2, 1863

general instructions I have given you; any ground within those limits you choose to occupy, I leave to you."

Sickles then got General Hunt, the army chief of artillery, to accompany him back to his area to have a look at the ground. A Confederate attack would be—Sickles thought—disastrous if he remained where he was. What did Hunt think about that ridge of high ground out in front? Wouldn't that be a better position for Sickles' artillery? Shouldn't Sickles move his corps out there? Hunt advised him to wait for orders before making any such move. Later Hunt went back to army headquarters and reported that the advanced position Sickles was contemplating had some good points and some bad ones—and that if he were the commanding general he wouldn't put troops out there until he had gone and looked it over for himself. About this time there was a disturbance over to the right, and this seems to have given Meade and Hunt something else to think about.

At about the same time—farther to the south, out to the west and southwest of the Round Tops—another loose end was coming unraveled. Here General John Buford was patrolling with two brigades of cavalry. Buford and his men had brought the Confederates to their first halt on the day before and had stood them off until the Union infantry corps arrived. They had continued to fight beside the infantrymen all day, taking heavy losses. Now they were out of rations and forage. Many of the horses had thrown their shoes and were unfit for service.

Buford had sent word of all this to his superior, General Alfred Pleasonton, the cavalry chief. Pleasonton, and General Dan Butterfield, now army chief of staff, had apparently given Meade the impression that other cavalry was immediately available to replace Buford. Pleasonton now reported that Buford wanted to go to the rear and refit, since the rest of the army was nearly all up. All right, said Meade, let Buford go as a guard with the army trains back to Westminster and refit there. Meade assumed that Pleasonton would substitute other cavalry for Buford's, so that this watchful and protective screen in front of the army's left would be maintained. This Pleasonton failed to do. And Butterfield—fine composer of bugle calls, great designer of badges and banners, but right at this moment somewhat lacking in the qualities of a desirable chief of staff—failed to see that Pleasonton had slipped up.

So Buford moved back and no one went out in his place. From this area, out beyond the Round Tops, the Union left was now open to surprise and to a sudden, smashing attack of troops in mass.

The blow was on the way. It had been under consideration for several hours, and it was the first move over which Robert E. Lee exercised personal direction. The fight of the day before had been one that had boiled up from a chance encounter when advance elements of the two armies had run into one another near Gettysburg. But now General Lee was taking charge. And if one would believe Longstreet's account, Lee was like a man who saw a fateful struggle ahead of him, and who knew that he could postpone it, perhaps to a more favorable time and place, but who found further waiting intolerable. Arriving at Gettysburg at five o'clock on the afternoon of July 1, Longstreet had found his chief on Seminary Ridge, watching the Union forces taking positions on the opposite height of land after their initial defeat. Lee had pointed out the Union positions. Longstreet had raised his glasses and studied the landscape for five or ten minutes, intently, for there were questions of life and death in every patch of woods, every ridge or hollow of the ground, and if men were going to get killed out there, they had better get killed advantageously. It seemed to Longstreet that the big decision hinged on a couple of round-topped hills that stuck up starkly on the south end of what appeared to be the Union line.

Longstreet lowered his glasses and proposed a plan: Move way around those hills. Get behind the Union left. Get between Meade's army and Washington, in a strong defensive position. Then Meade would attack, and on ground of Lee's expert choosing the Union army could be badly beaten. Or if Meade did not attack immediately, they could pick another strong position nearer Washington and move to it at night. Then Meade—and Washington too—would be frantic. The Union army would be forced to attack, into some trap of the terrain that Lee could set.

But Robert E. Lee, ordinarily as composed as steel and stone, had been gripped in a fixity of purpose that, for the good gray general, seemed almost like a passion. Lee had struck the air with his clenched fist and declared, "The enemy is there, and I am going to attack him there."

Once again Longstreet had urged his scheme, pointing out that the move around the Union left would give Lee control of the roads to Washington and Baltimore. But Lee had vehemently declared, "No; they are there in position, and I am going to whip them or they are going to whip me."

And again on the following morning—July 2—Longstreet had proposed that the army move all the way around the Round Tops to Meade's left and rear. But the great commander still would not listen.

Lee's plan was to attack frontally with part of his army, while Longstreet's Corps made a concealed movement to the right, falling upon the Union left flank and driving it in. Once in position on Meade's flank, Longstreet was to attack in a northeasterly direction, guiding his left on the Emmitsburg Road.

After a long delay—Longstreet waiting for one of his brigades, Law's, to come up—the flanking move finally got under way around eleven o'clock in the forenoon. Longstreet was lacking Pickett's Division, but with the two big divisions of Hood and McLaws he still had a massive force. The corps started moving south, keeping behind Seminary Ridge and other high ground in order to avoid observation from Union signal units on Little Round Top. Longstreet was in a bad mood, deeply resenting the fact that his recommendations had been disregarded. He was further exacerbated when it began to appear that the route reconnaissance, performed by one of Lee's engineer officers, had been done badly, resulting in many halts and countermarches. And Longstreet had another grumble. Stuart, who with his cavalry was supposed to be the eyes and ears of the army, was off galloping around somewhere miles away from Gettysburg. The little cavalry that remained with the army was elsewhere on the field. Here where Longstreet was making his move, not so much as one trooper was available to precede him. In the absence of cavalry, Longstreet ordered General Hood, one of his division commanders, to send out picked scouts in advance, so that the infantry would not be walking into the area entirely blind.

With many troublesome delays, Longstreet's column moved south. It got to be one and two and three o'clock, and they still had not arrived at the attack position.

Back at the little house behind Cemetery Ridge, Meade's headquarters, a conference was called, to assemble shortly after three. The battle of Gettysburg was a great one for conferences and consultations on the Union side, and the corps commanders were arriving to talk things over. But the conference didn't last long. Major General Gouverneur K. Warren, Meade's chief of engineers, came in with a report to the effect that General Sickles had advanced his corps and was way out of position. Warren made this startling disclosure to General Meade.

It was now somewhere around three-thirty. Longstreet's sweating infantrymen were coming into position on a low ridge slanting across the Emmitsburg Road. Ahead of them on their right, they saw the Round Tops. Ahead, and much closer on their left, a peach orchard, and here there was a surprise—Yankee guns and infantry in the orchard, also extending up the Emmitsburg Road. From the peach orchard, the Union line seemed to angle back toward the Round Tops. It was Sickles' Corps, thrust out in a salient, with one arm facing generally west, the other southwest. If Sickles' move had seemed questionable to Meade's staff officers, it now seemed devilishly inconvenient for the Confederate commanders. Their orders were to attack up the Emmitsburg Road. But here was a strong force of bluecoats to overcome before they could even start.

The situation began to look more favorable, however, when reports came back from the scouts that Hood had sent out. The reports said that the Round Tops were unoccupied, and this whole area seemed to be lightly, if at all, defended. The scouts had climbed Big Round Top and, looking down, had seen Union wagon trains parked just east of the hills.

General Hood now urged Longstreet to alter the course of the attack so as to move around Big Round Top and come in on the Union left and rear. This was, substantially, what Longstreet had wanted Lee to do with the whole army. But Longstreet was now sullen—and stubborn. Lee's orders were to attack up the Emmitsburg Road. Well, then, they would attack up the Emmitsburg Road.

With McLaws' Division preparing to advance on the peach orchard, Hood took his division far to the right in order to envelop the southward-facing arm of Sickles' salient and be in position to strike at the undefended Round Tops.

At headquarters, Army of the Potomac, the conference of corps commanders had broken up with explosive suddenness. First had come Warren's report of Sickles' new and highly original position. Then from far over on the left, cannonading and a few rattles of musketry had been heard. And now to the conference came General Sickles, having previously been detained. Meade told him not to get off his horse. He told General George Sykes, the Fifth Corps commander, to go get his corps and move it over there to the left. General Sykes, a little man with a big nose and a fine suit of whiskers, flew off to rouse up the Fifth Corps, still resting in rear of Powers Hill. Meade then told General Sickles to get back to his corps and he would follow him and see just what the situation was. Even though prepared by Warren's report, Meade was shocked, when he arrived, to see how far forward Sickles had actually posted the Third Corps—entirely disconnected from the rest of the army and far out beyond the possibility of support from existing positions.

General Sickles was deeply sorry. He said that he would withdraw his troops. Meade replied, "Yes, you may as well, at once. The enemy will not let you withdraw without taking advantage of your position, but you have to come back, and you may as well do it at once as at any other time."

General Sickles turned to give the necessary orders; just then Longstreet's cannoneers pulled their lanyards and the sky smashed over the Emmitsburg Road. It was now too late to withdraw. Meade told Sickles to hold on and do the best he could and that some way or other he would be supported. A projectile shrieked past. Meade's mount reared, plunged and went crazy. Meade was carried from the scene on a runaway horse—the final touch of frustration. It was now around four o'clock.

Meanwhile, General Gouverneur K. Warren had arrived on the summit of Little Round Top to play his big part, on his Big Day in history. A slight, dark, intense officer who bore a faint resemblance to Edgar Allan Poe, Warren had come to this elevated point to see what was going on out there beyond the Round Tops to the west. The hill was unoccupied except for a few signalmen. Since he was a military engineer, Warren presumably had recognized the importance of Little Round Top long before this. But he had not realized that it was completely undefended, and this discovery was highly disturbing. He also saw that off to the west there was a long line of woods, which made an excellent concealment for the enemy. Acting on a sudden inspiration, Warren sent word down to a battery emplaced on a smaller hill below (Devil's Den) where Sickles' line ended, and asked the artillerymen to fire a shot into the woods. The projectile, flying among the trees, caused the Confederate infantrymen to look upward, and the corresponding gleam of reflected sunlight on shifting rifle barrels and bayonets revealed their position to Warren. It also gave him a nasty shock. For here was a long line of battle that would far outflank the Union left when it advanced. With a thrill of mortal danger, Warren saw what would happen. The right of Longstreet's attack would sweep over Little Round Top. With this point in their possession, the Confederates would have the key to the battlefield. Starting here they could enfilade and roll up the Union line in a wholesale disaster. Troops here would be in command of the vital Taneytown Road. And if Meade's troops were routed, Lee would be between them and Washington, a most embarrassing possibility, in the light of Meade's orders from that city.

There was only one thing to do: get some soldiers up here as soon as the Lord would let him. Warren sent an aide flying off to find Meade and request at least a division. He sent another down to Sickles asking for a brigade. Sickles had to say no. He had enough fighting to do right where he was. By now the attack had begun and Longstreet was starting to smash in his salient with an overwhelming violence that was to cost Sickles his corps and his right leg. (The Third Corps was practically destroyed. The leg, shattered by a shell, had to be amputated. General Sickles sent it to the Army Medical Museum, where the bones can be seen today. Sickles used to visit the museum and stand for minutes at a time, looking at his bones and thinking—no doubt—about the day that was not his day at Gettysburg.)

So there was no help to be expected from Sickles. But help was at hand from another source—the Fifth Corps which General Sykes had started forward at Meade's order. The reconnaissance officers and advance elements of the Fifth Corps were now appearing, passing north of Little Round Top, and going out to the support of Sickles.

The leading brigade's was Vincent's, and right near the front was the 20th Regiment Infantry, Maine Volunteers.

CHAPTER SEVEN

A Hard Day for Mother

UMMONED to support the unhooked and unhinged salient of General Sickles, the 1st Division of the Fifth Corps had marched rapidly toward the firing. The 20th Maine, near the head of the column in Vincent's Brigade, reached the edge of a wheatfield, where the brigade halted momentarily to await instructions.

The woods ahead, beyond the field and out toward the Emmitsburg Road, was roaring and smoking; tiny flashes of lightning winked over the treetops, changing instantly to lazily drifting puffballs; the ground shook, and underneath was the sound of musketry, the shrill piping of far-off yells and the almost-human screams of horses being struck in the short-range artillery duel.

But Colonel Chamberlain and his Maine soldiers didn't have long to look, or listen. Warren's call for help was being directed to Colonel Vincent, their brigade commander. A staff officer came dashing up to Vincent, and the focus of attention suddenly shifted to the left and rear. There was a great deal of shouting and pointing at Little Round Top—an ugly, rock-strewn hill with woods all over it except on the western face. Vincent turned his horse and made for the hill with an urgent squeak of saddle leather, leaving word for the brigade to follow. His standard-bearer galloped after him. Chamberlain and the others saw the two horsemen try to ride up the northwest face of Little Round Top, but it was too rough; they couldn't make it. They then skirted the northern foot of the hill and disappeared in the woods behind the crest. The triangular flag with its red Maltese cross flashed once or twice between the trees. Near it, a shellburst blossomed with a growling roar. The Confederates, too, had their eye on Little Round Top. The artillery fire intensified as the brigade, following Vincent, scrambled up the lower gradient of the hill. In this movement, the 20th Maine now came last. Three Chamberlain brothers were riding abreast: Colonel Joshua; Tom, now a lieutenant acting as adjutant; and another brother, John Chamberlain, who had arrived at Gettysburg with the Christian Commission and who had chosen to go along with the 20th Maine to help the chaplain and the ambulance men. A large, unseen object swished past their faces. Said the Colonel, "Boys, I don't like this. Another such shot might make it hard for mother. Tom, go to the rear of the regiment, and see that it is well closed up! John, pass up ahead and look out a place for our wounded."

The regiment scrambled up the northern face of the hill under a heavy artillery fire from the Confederates. Shells were bursting among the trees and on the rocks and there were miserable slashing and humming sounds in the air—fragments of iron and splintered stone flying, sliced-off branches tumbling down. Mounted officers got off their horses, sending the animals to sheltered positions in the rear. The Maine men turned south behind the summit, getting some protection from the crest, and on the southern slope of the hill they found Colonel Strong Vincent putting the brigade into line of battle.

Within the fifteen minutes or so available, Vincent was doing one of the war's best jobs of reconnaissance, selection and occupation of position. His regiments were following him in this order:

44th New York
16th Michigan
83rd Pennsylvania
20th Maine

Vincent had chosen a line of defense that would start on the west slope of Little Round Top and continue around the hill in a quarter circle—not on the crest, but well below it. As the regiments arrived, he put them into line carefully, even taking time to defer to a whim voiced by Colonel James C. Rice, commander of the 44th New York. The 44th and the 83rd Pennsylvania were known as Butterfield's Twins, and going into line in the order in which they were arriving, the two regiments would be separated by the 16th Michigan. Colonel Rice had a seizure of superstition or sentiment, and he said to Vincent, "Colonel, the 83rd and 44th have always fought side by side in every battle, and I wish that they may do the same today."

He was accommodated. The 16th marched past the 44th and took position first, on the west slope. The Twins, following, went into line side by side, curving around the hill. Coming up last in the column, the 20th Maine extended the formation to the east, and Vincent told Chamberlain, "This is the left of the Union line. You understand. You are to hold this ground at all costs!"

Chamberlain ordered his regiment in "on the right by file into line." This was a slow maneuver, made even more awkward by the rough ground, rocks and trees, but it anchored the right of the 20th firmly to the left of the 83rd, and each man was ready to commence firing as soon as he came into position. They now saw that they were on the brink of a smooth, shallow valley, lightly forested and strewn with rocks. Across this valley to the south, facing them: Big Round Top, gigantic, covered with forest and huge boulders, apparently impassable. On their right, the rest of the brigade.

On the left, nothing!

Chamberlain was looking off in that direction, studiously. To his men it afterward seemed that the Colonel had the ability to see through forests and hills and to know what was coming. This apparently magical gift of great infantry officers was something that Chamberlain had caught on to; it was merely a matter of studying the terrain closely, imagining all kinds of horrible things that might happen, and planning countermeasures in advance.

Knowing that he had no support on the left, Chamberlain sent Company B, commanded by Captain Walter G. Morrill, out in that direction to guard his exposed flank and act as the necessities of the battle would require. Chamberlain didn't know quite what these necessities would be, but he knew Morrill and he was the sort of fellow who would do something and probably do it right.

Holding the left of the entire four-or-five mile Union line, the

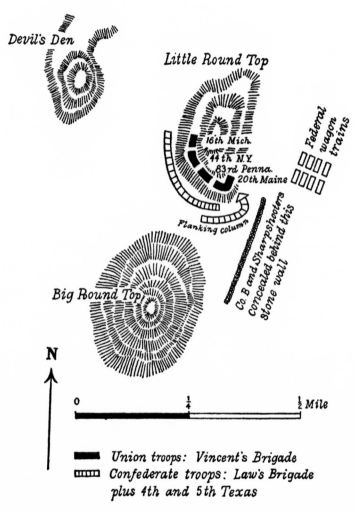

Devil's Den

Little Round Top

Federal wagon trains

16th Mich.
44th N.Y.
83rd Penna.
20th Maine

Flanking column

Co. B and Sharpshooters concealed behind this stone wall

Big Round Top

N

0   ¼   ½ Mile

Union troops: Vincent's Brigade
Confederate troops: Law's Brigade
plus 4th and 5th Texas

Infantry Positions at Little Round Top

20th Maine had stepped, all unawares, into the spotlight of history. Off to the west, Sickles' salient was caving in. Up from the south was coming the powerful right hook of Longstreet's attack. If this point failed, the Confederates would be smashing into the rear of a Union line that was already wildly confused by a massive frontal attack. Robert E. Lee and the Confederacy were never so close to victory.

So here on this hidden corner of the battlefield, one of the world's decisive small-unit military actions was about to begin. And upon this spot were converging many chains of cause and effect starting from previous events that had seemed, in their time, unimportant.

When Hood's Division swung across the Emmitsburg Road and prepared to attack, its right brigade, Law's Alabamians, had already marched twenty-eight miles since three A.M. In the 15th Alabama, canteens were empty and the men were thirsty. A detail of twenty-two men collected all the canteens and started for a well a hundred yards or so to the rear to fill them and return. But before they could get back the advance started. As the Alabama brigade approached Big Round Top, the men saw near the western foot of the hill what appeared to be a small regiment in an advanced position. These Yankees were beyond good shooting range, but puffs of smoke appeared from among them and Alabama soldiers began to fall in alarming numbers. Later they were to learn that this regiment was the 2nd U. S. Sharpshooters. Including a company of Maine marksmen, as well as sharpshooters from other states, this was a group of men who could each put ten consecutive shots into a target at six hundred feet with an average distance from the center of less than five inches. Against this deadly fire, one of Law's regiments almost broke, but they rallied and the brigade swept on, a long line of veterans in sun-bleached gray, bayonets shining, color staffs slanting forward, the flags of the Confederacy flickering above them. When they got to where they could start giving it back to the Yankees, the sharpshooters suddenly withdrew; part of them went back to a little hill on the left (Devil's Den) and the other part ran up Big Round Top and disappeared among the trees and boulders.

From this position the sharpshooters began sniping again at the right flank of the Confederate advance. On this wing in command of the 15th Alabama, with the 47th Alabama also acting under his direction, was Colonel William C. Oates, a mustachioed and bewhiskered officer who was both courageous and perceptive. Not wanting to go on and leave the hornet's nest of sharpshooters in his rear, Oates ordered the advance to extend to the right, up over Big Round Top, to clear his flank. It was a brutal climb. (It's an exhausting climb today on the smooth path the Park Service has built.) For infantrymen who had already marched twenty-eight miles, who had to climb over boulders and through brush, who were laden with arms and ammunition, and who had to fight dead-shot Yankees on the way, it was an ordeal. Several fainted in the heat. But the sharpshooters finally disappeared, and the right of the 15th Alabama reached the top, where Colonel Oates told them to stop and rest.

Here they hoped the water-carriers would catch up with them. But the canteen party was destined never to arrive; it had walked into a concealed party of sharpshooters and had been captured to a man. The men of the 15th Alabama always thought that the loss of this water detail had a lot to do with losing the battle of Gettysburg.

During the break, Colonel Oates found a place on the summit from which he could peer through the heavy July foliage and get some idea of where he was, and what was going on. He was amazed at the prospect. He could see Gettysburg in the distance. He could see the battle smoke drifting up from Devil's Den and hear the racket of the fighting that was starting around Little Round Top. He realized that he was on the highest point in the neighborhood. It was like sitting high in a box seat, overlooking the flank of the Union line.

Oates also realized that he held what could be the key of the battlefield. Drag up some artillery, cut down a few trees to clear a field of fire, and he could command not only Little Round Top, but the whole Union line all the way up Cemetery Ridge. Oates was entranced with the idea of a position here on Big Round

Top. He thought . . . "within half an hour I could convert it into a Gibraltar that I could hold against ten times the number of men that I had." A staff officer from Law, now acting division commander, came up and Oates urged a halt for the purpose of occupying Big Round Top; that, clearly, was the thing to do. The staff officer admitted that Oates was probably right, but their orders were to find and turn the left of the Union line, and the left of the Union line was not up here, it was down there on Little Round Top. And there was no time to go back and find someone with authority to change those orders. (The absence of general officers on this critical right end of the Confederate line was a deficiency that Oates was to deplore to his dying day.) But orders were orders, and so Oates told his weary men to get up and start down the slope of the hill toward Little Round Top.

As they were descending, Oates saw, only a few hundred yards away, the Federal trains, including an extensive park of ordnance wagons. If he could work his way a little farther east, he would be completely in the rear of Meade's army. By the time he reached the bottom of the hill, Oates had moved his troops by the right flank and had them in a column of fours. Rapidly, the column headed eastward through the thinly wooded valley between the Round Tops. As soon as he got past the Union flank, Oates would bring his command to a "front" and go crashing into the Yankee rear in an attack that ought to start the Union left falling like a row of tenpins.

Back on Little Round Top, the men of the 20th Maine had been waiting. These minutes of inactivity would be almost intolerable, but blind instinct would be getting their bodies ready—blood beating harder and faster through the arteries; lungs seeming to dilate deep down, reaching for more oxygen; stomach and intestines shrinking and stopping all movement; and tension rising to the point where it could shake a man like the passage of a powerful electric current. When it came, any kind of action would be a relief—and the reaction would be explosive.

The Maine men had watched Morrill's Company B disappear into the trees on their left front, walking warily, rifles held high.

Now they turned their attention to the right front, where the shallow valley opened out toward Devil's Den. There was a great commotion in that direction. Minié balls began to whistle through the branches overhead, twigs and leaves falling around them. An order ran along the line: *Come to the ready . . . take good aim. . . .* They heard volleys crash out from the rest of Vincent's Brigade on their right, followed by the frantic rattling of ramrods and the "thugging" of leaden cones being driven home in rifle barrels. They heard something else that raised the hair on the backs of their necks. It was a shrill, undulating yell—sharp and chilling as a winter wind, full of hate, exultation, and "Let's go get 'em!" It was the rebel yell, and they were coming on with a rush.

The order-in-line of the forces about to confront each other was as follows:

LAW'S BRIGADE (Plus 4th and 5th Texas)

CONFEDERATE RIGHT
15th Ala., 47th Ala., 4th Ala., 5th Tex., 4th Tex., 48th Ala., 44th Ala.

VINCENT'S BRIGADE

UNION LEFT
20th Maine, 83rd Pennsylvania, 44th New York, 16th Michigan

Neither was an actual straight line. The Union regiments were in a quarter circle around part of the hill. Of the Confederate regiments, the 15th Alabama and the 47th Alabama were behind the others, retarded by their climb over Big Round Top. The two Texas regiments didn't belong with Law's Brigade, but had got into the middle of it in a shuffle during the advance. The 44th Alabama did not come all the way to Little Round Top, but turned off and attacked Devil's Den.

The first troops the 20th Maine caught sight of were those of the 4th Alabama—fierce, lean men who were charging up the hill on their right, then drawing back as the fire of the rest of the Union brigade came out at them, then extending farther up the valley. They soon reached the right front of the 20th Maine and the regiment opened fire. Confined in the rocky valley, the noise became a continuously re-echoing roar, punctuated with the spanging of soft lead on stones and the yowling of ricochets. The attacking force gradually covered the entire front of the 20th Maine, and the smoke of the firing grew thick, hanging in the sultry air.

But this fighting had no more than started when Lieutenant James H. Nichols, commanding Company K, ran up to tell Colonel Chamberlain that something very strange was going on *behind* the attacking Confederate line. Mounting a rock, Chamberlain saw a solid gray mass advancing along the valley toward his left, partially screened by the smoke and the fighting already in progress on his front.

This was Oates and his flanking column. By itself, it was a large force, outnumbering the 20th Maine almost two to one, and the sight gave Chamberlain a real jolt. What did the book say to do, in a situation like this?

The order-in-line of the 20th Maine companies (less Company B, detached as skirmishers and now presumably cut off by the Confederate flanking column) was as represented here:

Colors

Left G C H A F D K I E

In the face of the impending flank attack, the obvious counter-move was to change front with the whole regiment, in order to face to the left and thus guard the flank of the brigade against the heavy assault that would presently be coming in from that direction. But Chamberlain quickly saw that this wouldn't work. The 20th Maine was on a spur of high ground extending out from Little Round Top. In changing front, in order to keep his right in contact with the 83rd Pennsylvania, Chamberlain would have to swing the whole regiment back. This would relinquish part of the high ground to the enemy. Also, much of the 20th Maine was already participating in the fire-fight that had involved the rest of the brigade.

Rejecting the obvious maneuver, Chamberlain called his company commanders and gave them instructions that were completely fantastic, considering the fact that the regiment was already under fire. Chamberlain decided to move the left wing (left half) of the regiment to the left and rear, facing it at right

117

angles with the original line. Meanwhile the right wing would extend itself by taking intervals to the left and forming a single rank, so that the regiment would stand thus:

F   D   K   I   E

A

H

C

G

As the left wing moved, the right wing was instructed to stay in contact with it, the men taking side steps to the left, meanwhile keeping up their fire to the front, without regard to the effect or whether or not the fire was needed. This would tend to conceal the movement.

The plan was executed in a way that never thereafter ceased to be a source of wonder to the officers of the 20th Maine. With bullets smashing into it, and the roar of gunfire making commands inaudible, the regiment writhed and twisted into the new formation like a single, living organism responding to a sense of imminent danger. Or—it was almost as though every man had been party to a quiet conference, where everything had been diagrammed and perfectly understood. On the right wing, men were firing, shouting, dodging from rock to rock and tree to tree, and gradually forming a single rank that covered the entire original front of the regiment. Chamberlain remembered that while this was going on there seemed to be no slackening of fire on that front.

Meanwhile the men of the bent-back wing were forming a solid line facing to the left, taking what concealment they could find behind rocks and undergrowth. Their presence came as a grievous surprise to the 15th Alabama.

When the Alabamians came to a front and charged up on what had been a few moments before an unguarded flank, the Maine men rose above the rocks and a volley flashed out that lighted all the fires of hell in that hot, shadowed backyard of the battle. At close range, it was a deadly blast, followed by hoarse screams, the sound of bodies falling in the bushes, the clatter of rifles dropped on the rocks by stricken men. Broken by the fire, the Alabama charge stopped momentarily. But these were hard men and they came on again, this time right up into the Maine line. Squads of them bayoneted their way through and had to be disposed of in horrid hand-to-hand grappling. The Maine men hadn't fixed bayonets; they clubbed their muskets and chopped with them like axes.

No one could ever describe this part of the fight coherently, or tell just how long it lasted. From here on everything was a medley of monstrous noises and a blur . . . muzzle-flashes blazing . . . gray forms appearing through the smoke . . . faces looming up with red, open, yelling mouths ringed with the black of cartridge biting . . . strangled animal sounds . . . and the queer-sounding resonances of skulls struck by musket butts. Chamberlain remembered that "the edge of conflict swayed to and fro, with wild whirlpools and eddies. At times I saw around me more of the enemy than of my own men; gaps opening, swallowing, closing again with sharp convulsive energy; squads of stalwart men who had cut their way through us, disappearing as if translated. All around, strange, mingled roar . . ."

Somehow, the line held, in one form or another, although the fighting was raging up and down in such a way that often no definite line could be seen. Nearly everyone but the hospital attendants of the 20th Maine were in ranks, and all were fighting like madmen. One young fellow was cut down with a ghastly wound across the forehead, and Chamberlain, thinking that he might be saved with prompt attention, sent him to the rear. Soon he saw him in the fight again with a bloody bandage around his head.

George Washington Buck, the boy who had been unjustly reduced to private at Stoneman's Switch, made sergeant again. Chamberlain came across Private Buck lying on his back, tearing his shirt away from his chest. What he saw convinced him—and the Colonel—that there wasn't much time left. Chamberlain bent over him and told him that he was promoting him to sergeant on the spot. Sergeant Buck was carried to the rear and died shortly afterward.

There were other transformations in the flame of battle. Two mutineers from the 2nd Maine, who were being held with the regiment as prisoners awaiting court-martial, chose this moment to return to duty. Picking up rifles, the two 2nd Mainers waded into the fray and laid about them so lustily that Chamberlain resolved to get the charges against them dropped if he survived.

And the Colonel saw something else he was always to remember—a grouping that could have been a model for the sort of heroic statuary that came out of the war to adorn village squares. "I saw through a sudden rift in the thick smoke our colors standing alone. I first thought some optical illusion imposed upon me. But as forms emerged through the drifting smoke, the truth came to view. The cross-fire had cut keenly; the center had been almost shot away; only two of the color guard had been left, and they fighting to fill the whole space; and in the center, wreathed in battle smoke, stood the color-sergeant, Andrew Tozier. His color staff planted in the ground at his side, the upper part clasped in his elbow, so holding the flag upright, with musket and cartridges seized from the fallen comrade at his side he was defending his sacred trust in the manner of the songs of chivalry."

The fight was seen through many eyes, but all seem to have seen it through the same red, smoky haze. Private Gerrish described the action where Company H was fighting, out on the bent-back wing. "If a rock promised shelter, down went a man behind it, and a rifle barrel gleamed and flamed above it. Every tree was also utilized, but a great majority of the troops were not thus provided for. As the moments passed the conflict thickened; the cartridge boxes were pulled around in front and left open; the cartridges were torn out and crowded into the smoking muzzles of the guns with a terrible rapidity. The steel rammers clashed and clanged in barrels heated with burning powder."

Gerrish saw the first sergeant, Charles W. Steele, stagger up to the company commander with a big hole in his chest. "I am going, Captain," the sergeant reported. In reply, Captain Joseph F. Land shouted, "My God, Sergeant!" and sprang to catch him, but too late, and Steele was dead by the time his body struck the ground. Another sergeant, Isaac N. Lathrop—a giant of a man—went crashing down with a mortal wound. Gerrish recalled that "of twenty-eight of that company, fifteen were either killed or wounded, and in other companies the slaughter had been equally as great. Not only on the crest of the hill, among the blue coats, was blood running in little rivulets and forming crimson pools, but in the gray ranks of the assailants there had also been a fearful destruction."

The 20th Maine had sixty rounds per man, and in the relatively short time of an hour or an hour and a half, they fired nearly every round. This meant that over twenty thousand bullets went out, and many more than that came back, slashing across the valley, flattening on rocks and flying in tearing ricochets.

Trees on the slope were gashed and peppered with white scars up to a height of six feet. One three- or four-inch tree in front of the left of Company F was gnawed completely off about two feet off the ground, the ragged edges of the cut showing that it had been made by bullets and not by a shell.

Everywhere, men going down. . . .

Colonel Oates of the 15th Alabama saw a bullet strike Captain J. Henry Ellison in the head. "He fell upon his left shoulder, turned upon his back, raised his arms, clenched his fists, gave one shudder, his arms fell, and he was dead."

And then more of his officers falling . . . "Captain Brainard, one of the bravest and best officers in the regiment, in leading his company forward, fell, exclaiming, 'O, God! that I could see my mother' and instantly expired. Lieutenant John A. Oates, my dear brother, succeeded to the command of the company, but was pierced through by a number of bullets, and fell mortally wounded. Lieutenant Cody fell mortally wounded, Captain Bethune and several other officers were seriously wounded, while the carnage in the ranks was appalling."

And later, "My dead and wounded were then nearly as great in number as those still on duty. They literally covered the ground. The blood stood in puddles in some places on the rocks. . . ."

There were charges and countercharges up and down the slope. Colonel Oates believed that he drove the Federals from their position five times, and each time they rallied and drove back, twice coming to the point of hand-to-hand combat. He remembered that once "a Maine man reached to grasp the staff of the colors when Ensign Archibald stepped back and Sergeant Pat O'Connor stove his bayonet through the head of the Yankee, who fell dead."

There came a lull when the Confederates drew back temporarily, and the Maine soldiers could have agreed with Oates that the scene had taken on a decidedly reddish tinge. The 20th had lost almost a third of its strength. They saw their dead and wounded out in front of them, mingled with those of the enemy. During the countercharges they had been scattered all the way down the slope to the very feet of the enemy, now rallying for another attempt.

Across the valley, a Confederate soldier saw Colonel Chamberlain standing by himself, in the open, behind the center of the 20th Maine's line. It was evident from Chamberlain's uniform and his actions that he was an important officer, well worth a careful shot. The soldier found himself a place between two big rocks, rested his rifle over one of them and looked at Chamberlain over the sights, taking steady aim. When he started to pull the trigger, a queer feeling came over him and he stopped. Ashamed of himself, he once again lined up his sights, but for some reason that he couldn't explain, he was unable to pull the trigger. Years later, he wrote to Chamberlain saying he was glad that he hadn't fired and he hoped that Chamberlain was too.

Over on the right of the 20th Maine, the rest of Vincent's Brigade had been holding its own. The right wing had almost broken once but was rallied by Colonel Vincent himself, and the 140th New York had arrived in time to hurl back the Confederate attack at this point. But Vincent had fallen with a bullet in his left groin, saying as they carried him back, "This is the fourth

or fifth time they have shot at me, and they have hit me at last."
On this western part of Little Round Top, Hazlett's Battery had
also arrived, and the men of the 20th Maine could hear Hazlett's
guns pounding, with heavy musketry also telling of desperate
fighting. There was no hope of assistance from that quarter. The
left of the 20th Maine had now been bent so far back that bullets
from the attacking Confederates were falling into the rest of the
brigade from the rear. The acting adjutant of the 83rd Pennsylvania came dodging and scrambling over to Chamberlain, wanting to know if his left had been turned.

Chamberlain sent word to Captain O. S. Woodward, commander of the 83rd, that the enemy was pushing his left back
almost double upon his right and asked for a company. Woodward replied that he couldn't spare a company, but if the 20th
Maine would pull its right companies to the left, he would move
over and fill up the gap.

This move was made and brought some relief, but the 20th
Maine had been bent back so far that it was in the rear of the
army, in rear of the brigade, and in rear of itself. Let it give way
in another Confederate charge, and Lee might be rolling up the
Army of the Potomac like a rug.

And that was not the worst. There were hoarse cries of "Ammunition!" up and down the line, and soldiers were scrambling
around looking for cartridges in the boxes of the dead and
wounded. Chamberlain saw men fire their last rounds and then
look back at him as if to say, "What now?"

The Colonel's alert brain ticked off the alternatives. The Confederates were gathering for another assault, but the 20th Maine
couldn't withdraw; its orders were to hold the ground at all costs.
He knew that they could not withstand another charge. And they
couldn't continue the fire-fight for the reason that they had run
out of ammunition. (Later Chamberlain figured that this was a
good thing, for if they had continued, the enemy with superior
numbers would have finished them off on a musket-to-musket
basis.) Chamberlain decided that there was only one thing to do:
fix bayonets and charge down into the Alabamians, hoping that
surprise and shock action would drive them.

But here, too, there was a serious difficulty. With the left of the 20th Maine bent back so far, a charge might disperse the regiment or cause it to split in two at the angle. The left wing therefore had to begin the charge and swing around abreast of the right before the whole line could move forward. Colonel Chamberlain limped along the line, giving the necessary instructions. (His right instep had been cut by a flying shell fragment or rock splinter, and his left thigh had been badly bruised when a Minié ball bent his steel scabbard against it.)

As Chamberlain was returning to the center, Lieutenant Holman S. Melcher of Company F came up to him and asked permission to go out and get some of his wounded who lay between the 20th and the enemy line. To Melcher's surprise, the Colonel said, "Yes, sir. Take your place with your company. I am about to order a right wheel forward of the whole regiment."

Chamberlain stepped to the colors and his voice rang out. "Bayonet!" There was a moment of hesitation along the line, an intaking of breath like that of a man about to plunge into a cold, dark river. But along with it there was a rattling of bayonet shanks on steel. Intent on his wounded, Lieutenant Melcher sprang out in front of the line with his sword flashing, and this seems to have been the spark. The colors rose in front. A few men got up. Then a few more. They began to shout. The left wing, which was fighting off an attack at the time, suddenly charged, drove off its opponents and kept on until it had swung around abreast of the right wing. Then the regiment plunged down the slope in a great right wheel, Captain A. W. Clark's Company E holding the pivot against the 83rd Pennsylvania. To an officer of the 83rd, the 20th Maine looked as though it were moving "like a great gate upon a post."

The Confederate troops at the bottom of the slope were taken completely off guard. There were, perhaps, physical as well as psychological reasons to explain the apparent miracle that followed. The Confederates had been weakened by their strenuous approach march, thirst, and their efforts during the fighting. There was no time to fire a decisive volley and the Maine bayonets were shining in their faces almost before they knew what had happened. For a moment they fought in a daze. Then, before this roaring, downward-lunging assault, they gave backward and the affair took on the qualities of a dream. With one hand an Alabama officer fired a big revolver in Colonel Chamberlain's face, missed, and promptly handed over his sword with the other hand. Men were running, tripping, falling. The Confederate line broke up in confusion.

Farther on, the Alabamians made a stand with squads of the formidable 4th and 5th Texas, and it might have gone badly with the 20th Maine had there not been a fortuitous intervention. Even as the 20th Maine had been saving the army's left flank, so now it was itself about to be aided by one of its own fragments. This was Captain Morrill's Company B. After moving out as a skirmish party, Company B had not been heard from. Supposedly it had been cut off or captured by the sudden advance of the Alabamians. But the men of Company B had been very much alive all the while, hidden behind a stone wall. Now, having been joined by some of the sharpshooters that Oates had driven over Big Round Top, they rose up and fired a volley into the Confederate rear, at the same time making a loud demonstration.

The exhausted and staggered Alabamians were being pressed back by the charging Maine regiment in front—back so far that they were also receiving fire from the rest of the Yankee brigade on their left. And now, suddenly, bullets were coming from their right and rear. Morrill and his men had unleashed one of the most fearsome weapons of war—surprise, which explodes in the brain and destroys the power to reason. Oates saw a dreadful thing: men being shot in the face, while others beside them were being shot in the back, and still others were being struck by bullets coming simultaneously from two or three different directions. The growing panic that set in is traceable in the reports coming to Oates from his company commanders. In one of these reports Morrill's little band was magnified into two regiments. Another report had it that there was a line of dismounted Union cavalrymen in the Confederate rear, although there is no record of cavalrymen in the Little Round Top fight, either mounted or dismounted. Oates believed that he was completely surrounded, and his regiment would have to cut its way out. "I

. . . had the officers and men advised the best I could that when the signal was given that we would not try to retreat in order, but every one should run in the direction from whence we came. . . . When the signal was given we ran like a herd of wild cattle, right through the line of dismounted cavalrymen. . . . As we ran, a man named Keils, of Company H, from Henry County, who was to my right and rear, had his throat cut by a bullet, and he ran past me breathing at his throat and the blood spattering."

In spite of their numbers, their courage, and their almost super-human exertions, the Confederate troops had suffered a baffling defeat.

Part of the reason had been superb handling of a regiment by a college professor who had been in the army less than a year. And part had been—well, everything going against them, events combining in a way that might not happen again in a thousand years.

To find any parallel, it would almost be necessary to go back to Second Kings, 7, wherein the four leprous men had said to one another, "Why sit we here until we die?" and had then risen up and advanced into the camp of the Syrians, the Lord at the proper moment causing the Syrians to hear "a noise of chariots, and a noise of horses, even the noise of a great host," so that they all fled for their lives.

After sweeping the front of the brigade clear and rounding up an estimated four hundred prisoners, the 20th Maine returned to its original position on Little Round Top, and it was a triumphant but a sobering walk. The slaughter had been sudden, prodigious —and sickening, now that there was time to look at the results. As Oates had noted, the ground was literally covered with bodies. Some moaning and moving and bleeding. Others silent, lying in the ridiculous, rag-doll postures of the dead. They were scattered everywhere, among rocks, behind trees. The 20th Maine had suffered 130 casualties, including forty killed or mortally wounded. Mingled with these were around 150 dead and wounded Confederates.

In his official report Colonel Chamberlain stated, "We went

A HARD DAY FOR MOTHER

into the fight with 386, all told—358 guns. Every pioneer and
musician who could carry a musket went into the ranks. Even the
sick and footsore, who could not keep up in the march, came up
as soon as they could find their regiments, and took their places
in line of battle, while it was battle, indeed."

Now that there was time to stop and think about what had
happened, it was enough to give a man the shakes.

The thing that was most frightening about it was how the
weight of a momentous battle could have come to rest so dispro-
portionately upon just a few ordinary men—farmers, fishermen
and woodsmen. Seldom if ever before had one small regiment
been in such a fantastic spot.

And seldom had a regiment fought so fantastically. The maneuver whereby the double line of battle had stretched itself out
into a single line, extending and bending back under fire with
the noise making ordinary commands impossible, was something
out of a dream.

The charge, the swinging and straightening of the left wing
back into line, the plunge down the slope had succeeded simply
because it had been so improbable.

And if the Maine men had been in any mood to reflect, they
might have mused upon the workings of a Providence that had
brought them past Antietam, Fredericksburg and Chancellorsville to arrive at this spot with the unfit weeded out, but with
the lean fighting muscle of the regiment largely unimpaired.

It was immediately clear to a lot of people that one of the
most important actions of the war had just been fought. Corporal
William T. Livermore recorded the day's events in his diary.
"The Regiment we fought and captured was the 15th Alabama.
They fought like demons and said they never were whipped before and never wanted to meet the 20th Maine again. . . . Ours
was an important position, and had we been driven from it, the
tide of battle would have been turned against us and what the
result would have been we cannot tell."

But the man who had seen the Confederacy's lost opportunity
more clearly than anyone else was Colonel Oates. Roll call that

night revealed that less than half of his once-great regiment remained. In later years he would reflect, "There never were harder fighters than the Twentieth Maine men and their gallant Colonel. His skill and persistency and the great bravery of his men saved Little Round Top and the Army of the Potomac from defeat. Great events sometimes turn on comparatively small affairs."

And later, for this day's work, would come the Congressional Medal of Honor for Joshua Chamberlain.

It was, as Maine men would say, *"a caution!"* But right now, with nostrils filled with the sulphurous, sickish-sweet smell of burned gunpowder, heads dazed, and ears ringing, they weren't saying or thinking much of anything.

The smoke settled and the shadows deepened in the little valley. Westward, trees turned black against a sultry purple sunset. To the west and north, the roar of battle died away in a slow, rumbling diminuendo. Darkness came, and in barns and other buildings where the wounded had been taken, the surgeons were working desperately by candlelight.

CHAPTER EIGHT

So Nobly Advanced

ITH the fall of Colonel Vincent, Colonel James C. Rice of the 44th New York took over the command of the brigade. Writing home about him a week or so later, one of the soldiers said that he was known as "Old Crazy" because in battle he was too excitable to do anything right. But no one ever had occasion to doubt Rice's bravery; when he was later mortally wounded at Spotsylvania—by then having been made brigadier general—he told the attendants to roll him over on his side so that he could die with his face toward the enemy.

Also, the soldier may have been wrong about Rice's inability to do anything right when excited. During the battle on Little Round Top, which was crammed with excitement of the highest voltage, he did a number of things right. He was instrumental in getting up ammunition for part of the brigade; sent promptly to corps for reinforcements; and apparently handled the brigade capably enough. Now that the fight was over and darkness was deepening, Colonel Rice started thinking about Big Round Top, the large rocky hill towering over them against the southern sky. The Confederates were still in possession of this commanding height. If they retained it and were reinforced during the night, there might be bad trouble in the morning.

In response to Rice's call for reinforcements, Fisher's Brigade of the 3rd Division had come up. This brigade was now massed in the rear, supporting Rice close by, and it was expected that Fisher would advance and seize Big Round Top. For some reason, this move did not take place. So Rice ordered Colonel Chamberlain to give it a try.

129

The 20th Maine had expended 130 men and all of its cartridges. But it hadn't run out of courage. At nine o'clock that evening the regiment began an advance up Big Round Top which was, in its way, almost as audacious as the charge on the Alabamians. In the words of Colonel Chamberlain, "Without waiting to get ammunition, but trusting in part to the very circumstances of not exposing our movement or our small front by firing, and with bayonets fixed, the little handful of 200 men pressed up the mountainside in very extended order, as the steep and jagged surface of the ground compelled."

They could hear scattered squads of the enemy falling back before them in the darkness. Now and then there was a flash of light up ahead, a loud report and a bullet snapping through the brush. But they pushed on and grabbed seven or eight prisoners, including a couple of officers. Arriving at the summit, Chamberlain drew his regiment together in a solid front, then sent back for reinforcements and ammunition. It was a dangerous, isolated position. They had ample reason for nervousness.

A couple of Fisher's regiments now tried to come up the mountain on Chamberlain's right, making a good deal of noise in the darkness. The 20th Maine, thinking that they were Confederates, prepared to fight for its life. At the same time the enemy fired a volley into the groping regiments; there was shouting and confusion; then the voices faded away down the mountain as Fisher's regiments withdrew, leaving the 20th isolated again.

Chamberlain wanted no more of *that* nonsense. He hastily threw a picket line across the upper part of Big Round Top, then pulled his main body back down the hill to a position nearer the foot. He sent word to Colonel Rice that he wanted the 83rd Pennsylvania to come up on his right, a request that was promptly answered, along with a partial supply of ammunition. With the reliable Pennsylvanians on his right, followed shortly afterward by the 44th New York, Chamberlain once again advanced his line up Big Round Top, and the men rested on their arms.

But the picket line was busy for the rest of the night. The pickets stole down the southwest slope of the mountain until they could see the enemy campfires and hear the Confederates talking; then they withdrew to a prudent distance. A squad from the 4th Texas came up to investigate.

"Halt! Who goes there?" a picket challenged softly.

"Friends," said the Texans.

"Advance and be recognized."

The Texans advanced and were quietly and efficiently gathered in. The process was later repeated until twenty-five of the Texans had been captured. Then firing broke out farther down the line, and no more prisoners were taken.

During the night Fisher's regiments managed to get up into position, and by morning there was a solid Union line covering both Little Round Top and Big Round Top. From the higher summit just a few hours before, Colonel Oates had looked down upon the Promised Land of military opportunity. Now that opportunity would not come again. Out over the Peach Orchard, Wheatfield and Devil's Den (the names had a special meaning now) the gray light disclosed a litter of death, the hundreds of dark, scattered bundles that were the bodies of horses and men. Morning also disclosed that Lee's army was still there in full strength. He would be coming again, they figured. But not here, against the Round Tops.

At nine o'clock that morning, the Maine regiment, along with the rest of the brigade, was relieved, withdrawn from Big Round Top, and sent to a position near the left center of the Union line. On the way they marched back over the ground around Little Round Top where they had fought on the preceding evening. Corporal William T. Livermore noted in his diary that the dead Confederates were still there, but the Union dead had been gathered up and taken away somewhere for burial. Of his dead comrades, he wrote that "nothing but the blood was to be seen."

During the night the story of the 20th Maine's accomplishment had apparently spread all over the battlefield. At their new position, the Maine men received a complimentary call from their former commander General Ames, who was now in command of a division of the Eleventh Corps. This made another entry in the Livermore diary. "He said he was proud of the 20th," wrote the corporal—and this was something well worth recording, for it was Ames who had once advised them all to desert and go home.

They knew now, of course, he hadn't really meant it, but, from the beginning, had been deliberately lashing them into a "we'll show him!" attitude. For certainly it had not been a group of amateurs that had turned the Confederates back at Little Round Top, but a well-trained and highly effective regiment of infantry. And who could they thank most for that, if not General Ames?

For the remainder of the day, the regiment lay in reserve, but there was little rest. The thunderous artillery bombardment preceding Pickett's charge harassed them severely. It was a cannonade that also taxed the vocabularies of the brigade historians. One of them wrote, "The earth shook like an earthquake, and the air was filled with missiles of death, screaming, hissing and whirling in every direction over the field. Hundreds of the enemy's shells which failed to explode flew shrieking through the skies, for half and three quarters of a mile to the rear of our lines of battle. Those striking nearer would plough a huge furrow in the ground, and then ricocheting and leaping upward to a height of a hundred feet, could be seen whirling away for a quarter of a mile in the distance, before again falling to the earth. Hundreds burst over and around us, hurling their fragments in every direction. . . ."

They were still within sight of Little Round Top, and they noted with pleasure that Union artillerymen had batteries up there and were giving it back to the Confederates with great vigor. By now they had a sort of proprietary pride in Little Round Top.

The same historian who had described the Confederate artillery fire was carried away by the activity on Little Round Top. "Mount Sinai in all its glory never thundered, nor belched forth such volumes of smoke and lightning, as did that grand little citadel upon this memorable day." The solid shot of the Confederates, he noted, "struck savagely against the rocky walls of this little Gibraltar and then bounded off harmlessly in another direction." The day before, the rocky little hill had been one corner of a house of cards; today it was Mount Sinai, Gibraltar, a roaring fortress as Pickett's charge rushed to its noisy and foredoomed conclusion and Lee's hopes of invading the North went down forever.

Lee's complete failure, however, was not immediately apparent to the soldiers or the generals at Gettysburg. There were careful reconnaissances on the fourth and early on the fifth to determine whether or not Lee was withdrawing, and these revealed a degree of widespread destruction and death that was staggering to the men who participated.

In the vicinity of the Round Tops and Devil's Den, the dead lay practically in windrows. In many places there was still a ghostly verisimilitude of battle, as though the action had suddenly stopped short; leaving each man frozen in posture and attitude. A man in the Corn Exchange Regiment who had occasion to move over the area on reconnaissance with his brigade wrote that "the progress of the advance was much impeded in the effort to tread without stepping upon the bodies. Some kneeling behind the rocks had met their death where they dropped for shelter. The men gave way at times instinctively from the muzzles of muskets resting upon rocks and stones, down the barrels of which the sightless glassy eyes still gazed and the guards of which were grasped by hands convulsed in death. Seeking shelter in kneeling, to aim, they had fallen in the act of firing. Numbers of the enemy lay in a shallow trench they had dug, evidently to avoid the unerring fire of some expert skirmishers. They had torn and twisted leaves and grass in their agonies and their mouths filled with soil—they had literally bitten the dust."

Early on the morning of July 5, the 20th Maine moved out across the fields on a reconnaissance with the 3rd Brigade, through the Peach Orchard and on to the westward. En route they made one prolonged halt to throw up breastworks near the site of a barn that had burned in the course of the battle, and the Maine men found themselves in the midst of extensive and odorous horrors. The barn, which had been used as a hospital at one time or another by both sides, was full of dead. Some had burned to skeletons, other were half burned. On the ground in that vicinity were thirty or forty dead Zouaves of a Pennsylvania regiment, who had been lying there three days in the hot July weather. Corporal William T. Livermore had been one of the two members of the color guard who had escaped the slaughter on Little Round Top, so he had seen corpses aplenty, and he noted in a letter to his brother Charles that it was nothing to look at freshly killed men, but this aftermath of battle was a sight he hoped he might never see again.

While pioneers and detailed men began the job of burial, the Maine soldiers busied themselves with gathering up guns, and Livermore remembered that they collected about six mule-loads of rifles. "To see the piles of extra rifles," he wrote, "one would think the whole army was killed." The 20th Maine had been armed with Enfields, which Livermore said would shoot well but were considered hard to take care of, and he related that the men of the regiment took this opportunity to exchange the Enfields for Springfields, figuring that they would have about half the work in keeping them clean.

Ranging around the field in a wider circuit, Corporal Livermore found other ghastly sights. "To speak safely there was a thousand dead horses that were all swolen and the smell of the horses & men was dreadful. That whole field as far as we went was as I might say covered with dead of our own & Rebels. Where we were there were more of our men that lay there than there was of the Rebels but we know they took a great many back farther to the rear & buried them. But to our right where they advanced on our Artillery the ground was covered with them. The ground every foot of it was covered with men, horses clothing cartridge boxes canteen guns bayonets scattered cartridges cannon balls everywhere. Caissons stood where the horses were instantly killed by a cannon ball and they piled up on the pole just as they were killed. In some places on the bigness of your house there would be 8 or 10 horses & from 3 to 8 men."

Livermore also found mysterious horrors he was unable to explain completely. There were dead Confederates with their hands tied behind their backs—Livermore did not know why, unless the bonds had been tied to keep them from deserting. And there was one dead Confederate with a handkerchief tied over his mouth. From the nature of his wound, the corporal thought he might have been gagged to smother his screams.

The result of this and other reconnaissances was to confirm that Lee was in full retreat. The spear he had thrust at the heart of the North had been blunted by an impenetrable shield. For the time being, anyway, the Union had been saved. And the Army of the Potomac had at last had the heart-lifting experience of winning a victory!

But there was still some dying to do, the hard way. For the wounded the sky over Gettysburg would continue to be blazing red with pain for many days.

Following the fight on July 2, the wounded of the 20th Maine, along with those from other units of the Fifth Corps, were placed in farm buildings just east of Little Round Top. On July 3, the day of Pickett's charge, these buildings became untenable because of artillery fire, and the hospital was moved a couple of miles to the southeast. Much equipment was lacking. During the last stage of the march to Gettysburg, trains had been restricted to ammunition wagons and ambulances. Medicines had moved with the ambulances, so that the medical officers were well provided with chloroform, dressings and other supplies, but tents had been left behind, and shelter was insufficient. In his travels about the hospital area administering Christian consolations during the battle, John Chamberlain had noted that the heat and glare of the sun were causing extreme suffering among the wounded men—had thought, in fact, that "their bleeding, neglected wounds were not half so tormenting to them."

Using a little Maine ingenuity, plus sticks, stones and blankets, John rigged up temporary sun-shades for some of the wounded men. The idea spread quickly, and soon all the men in this hospital area were sheltered from the torturing sun by these improvised umbrellas.

But soon the lack of adequate shelter brought another kind of discomfort. On July 4 rain began to fall, and the rain continued, off and on, throughout the next few days. The tents arrived on the 5th, but there was canvas enough to cover only a small part of the wounded, preference being given to the severely wounded and to those who had undergone operations. The rest had to be covered with dog tents. Under the intermittent rain, straw used for bedding got wet, and the sun did not shine long enough to get it dry.

Here on these soggy fields of pain the fight continued, and death was a subtle antagonist, not always in a hurry. In the 20th

Maine as a whole, two-thirds of the wounds were in the face, hands, arms or legs—reflecting the partial shelter the men had had behind rocks and trees. Practically all of the wounds were caused by musketry, but these were not the neat holes made by modern steel-jacketed bullets. The soft lead Minié ball, around six-tenths of an inch in diameter, traveling at relatively low velocity, was likely to spread upon impact, shatter bones, and leave a dreadful hole in a man. Where an arm or a leg was badly smashed, the accepted remedy was amputation, and this led to a wholesale butchering operation at Gettysburg.

A bandsman who was serving temporarily as a surgeon's assistant back of Little Round Top reported that "frequently the severed arms and legs reached level with the tables, in ghastly heaps, when a detail of men would dig long trenches and bury them. . . . All this, too, taking place under the intense heat of a July sun! The second day around the tables, the peculiar stench became unbearable. At night we had some opportunity for lying down, in the hope of having rest, but sleep was impossible, for the pleading cry for water came from the wounded in every direction. When daylight broke upon the scene, the very foliage of the beautiful hillsides and the verdure of the valley seemed to add a sombre tinge to the mournful picture. Even the dawn was draped in misery."

But if all this was unpleasant to see and smell, it was infinitely worse for those who had to contribute their arms and legs to the piles of slaughterhouse remnants. A man who was carried to a field hospital for surgery at Gettysburg was in for a bad time. If he had a mortal wound—for example a bullet in the small intestine—for which there was no hope at all—he would be immediately passed over. If his wound justified surgical attention he underwent an experience as frightening as anything that would ever happen to him. He was taken in charge by surgeons who had their bare arms and aprons smeared with blood, their knives, often as not, held between their teeth while they helped the victim to the table. If the head surgeon decided on a major operation, ether or chloroform was administered, and the wounded soldier mercifully buzzed off into unconsciousness.

The surgeon then wiped his knife a couple of times across his blood-stained apron, and went to work. He was not, as may have been gathered, particularly fussy about cleanliness—for the principles of asepsis were then practically unknown. And the tools he had to work with were few, compared to the modern surgeon's array of specialized instruments. For example, the Civil War surgeon had no hemostatic forceps, no retractors, no hypodermic syringes until late in the war, not even a clinical thermometer; his only means of estimating fever was by touching the patient. And at Gettysburg surgeons worked under conditions that were atrocious even for those days—on tables made from saw horses and boards, barn doors, or anything that was handy—often with poor light—hour after exhausting hour without relief or rest.

If a soldier were lucky, he might have a fairly good job done on him, but even so, things could go wrong—very badly wrong within a few days. For example, a man who had lost an arm or leg would come out of the operation with from five to thirty silk strings hanging out of the stump. These were the ends of ligatures—some with knots tied in them to identify ligatures of large blood vessels. After a few days the plain strings were pulled to see whether or not the tissues had rotted away sufficiently to allow them to come loose. After a longer period the knotted strings were pulled, and often a gush of blood followed, indicating that the vessel had not healed. Then the wound had to be reopened, or the vessel had to be tied higher up, and there might even have to be another amputation. There was an unusual number of these "secondary hemorrhages," as they were called, after the battle of Gettysburg, perhaps because of the haste with which so many of the operations were performed.

Because of the almost complete lack of antiseptic precautions, the amputee faced many other dangers. For example, a man who had undergone an operation might seem to be gradually improving with his wound freely discharging "laudable pus"—a good sign, doctors thought in those days. Suddenly the wound would dry up, the man would become more feverish, his pain and restlessness increasing, his cheeks flushed. He might hear the doctors who examined him whispering a word he did not understand—"pyemia." And he might not know that his chances for recovery were then only three out of a hundred, for the word, signifying blood poisoning or infection, was virtually a death sentence. The perishability of human flesh without the safeguards we enjoy today was also underlined by a dread disease now practically banished—hospital gangrene. As one of the surgeons recalled, "Often did I see a simple gunshot wound, scarcely larger than the bullet which made it, become larger and larger until a hand would scarcely cover it, and extend from the skin downward into the tissues until one could put half his fist into the sloughing wound."

This was the nature of the battle that continued at Gettysburg, much of it waged against microscopic killers man could not see or strike back at—a vast, hidden army which was the greatest enemy of both sides in the Civil War. For many of the 20th Maine soldiers, the fight would go on a long while; for several the battle of Gettysburg would never end. The smash of a Minié ball might cause a wound that would put its victim away in an army hospital for years, while a grateful nation would be gratefully forgetting.

Somewhat typical was the experience of Private Byron Hilt of the 20th Maine. Shortly before five o'clock on July 2, 1863, Private Hilt was in the fullness of youth and health, age nineteen, a farmer boy from Presque Isle, Maine. Sometime between five and six-thirty a bullet went through his left shoulder. It made a small wound where it went in, but in smashing through the bones of his shoulder it spread and tore a tremendous hole where it came out, partially exposing the left shoulder blade.

Hilt was a rugged youngster, and he was still in good shape when they put him on a hospital train, even though his wound had had very little treatment. After the long train ride to Philadelphia and his admission to Satterlee Hospital he was still strong —pulse a little fast—but on the whole condition good. They put him on a special diet and bandaged his arm to his chest to keep it quiet.

On July 18, Private Hilt seemed to be failing. He could sleep only sitting up, and the arm felt enormously heavy. There was a quick operation, and pieces of bone were removed. Next day Hilt was feeling better, and with three-eighths of a grain of morphia at night was able to sleep. But on July 22 there was another operation to remove pus and shattered bone, and on August 1 they had to dig into the shoulder again to take out more fragments.

Hilt was in the hospital there almost a year, then transferred to Cony Hospital in Augusta, Maine. Time crept on, and in January, 1865, a medical examiner in Augusta wrote down, "Complete ankylosis of the shoulder joint; wound still open and discharging freely; arm at present entirely useless. . . ." And ten years after Gettysburg, another examiner in Presque Isle would report, "General weakness of the entire joint and much atrophy of muscles." For Hilt and several others, the train of disability and suffering would go on far into the future.

Perhaps hardest of all, however, was the lot of those who remained at Gettysburg to await death, while relatives tried vainly to get to see them. Among these was Captain Charles W. Billings of the 20th Maine's Company C. Badly wounded, the Captain was carried into an old barn where sixty-five of the worst cases in the Fifth Corps were lying on the floor. Billings saw some of his own men near him, and as these soldiers died, one after another, the sight so affected the Maine officer that he became temporarily deranged and it took four or five attendants to hold him. With great difficulty—for he was raving and struggling like a maniac—they got him away from the dying men and into a room by himself. There his mind cleared and he lay quietly.

A surgeon went into see him. He came out shaking his head and saying that if Captain Billings had had a primary amputation—that is, an amputation on the field—he might have had a chance, but there was no chance now. The Reverend Robert J. Parvin of the Christian Commission went in, and Captain Billings asked him what the surgeon had said.

"Why, Captain," Parvin replied, "you are a critical case."

Billings said, "I know that, Chaplain, but does the surgeon think I can live?"

And Parvin had to answer, "He thinks it is hardly possible that you will live, Captain."

The Captain's wife had been sent for. He asked Parvin if there had been any word from her, in reply to a message the minister had sent. Parvin told him there had been no answer, and that the telegraph lines were being used by the government, which was probably the reason why. Parvin said, "We hope she will be here."

Billings began to have his doubts. He asked Parvin to give Mrs. Billings his sword, knapsack and other personal possessions. He asked, "Could you have my body embalmed and sent home? I lost my money on the field." Parvin agreed to do this. Then he knelt and prayed with him.

Captain Billings died at eleven o'clock on the forenoon of July 15. At five o'clock that afternoon, his body was sent to the embalmer's. These gentlemen, by now, were doing a thriving business in Gettysburg and environs, setting up shop in tents and pumping their preservative fluids into the veins of dead soldiers whose relatives or friends wished them sent home.

Along toward the end of the long summer evening, a man in civilian clothes sought out the Reverend Parvin and asked him the whereabouts of Captain Billings. The man was Billings' brother. He had just arrived after coming all the way down from Maine, bringing the Captain's wife with him, and keeping her buoyed up during the long journey with the hope that her husband would be still alive. "Where is he, sir?" he asked anxiously.

The Reverend Parvin was distressed. "You have not brought the Captain's wife out here with you tonight?" The corps hospital area was three or four miles from Gettysburg.

"No, I left her in town until the morning."

Parvin then told him the bad news, and the man from Maine began to cry. It may be supposed that he was not used to crying, and so did not do it very well, and that it was a bad thing for the Reverend to watch, along with all the other hard sights he had seen that day. Finally the brother was able to say, "I cannot tell her! I cannot trust myself to try to tell her, or even to see her again tonight! I have brought her on all the way to Gettysburg for this, and now you must . . . you must tell her. . . ."

And so Captain Billings went home to Maine. But the majority of the fallen remained at Gettysburg. The 20th Maine—in keeping with a compelling tradition—looked after its own dead. Before leaving Gettysburg, the men went back to the Little Round Top area, gathered the bodies and buried them on the southern side of the crest behind their former line of battle. They marked the graves with crude headboards made of ammunition boxes, carving names and home towns into the boards.

Summer passed into fall, and in October the work of exhuming the bodies and taking them to the newly established Soldiers National Cemetery on the slopes of Cemetery Hill began—a contractor handling the job at a cost of $1.59 per body, placing the remains, as one official report put it, "in substantial coffins generously furnished by the United States Government." Most of the dead of the 20th Maine were buried in sections C, D, E and F. Private Gerrish later wrote, ". . . somehow I wish they had been left where they fell, on the rugged brow of Round Top."

It was on Little Round Top, where these men had left their bloodstains on the rocks, that their presence remained, to a degree that was almost physically perceptible to the veterans of the 20th Maine who visited the place after the war. Nearly half a century later Joshua Chamberlain went back to the rocky hill and sat down on its summit at sunset, just the time of day when the full violence of the fight had been subsiding on that July evening in 1863, and as he sat there he became so emotionally wrought up that it seemed to him that all the soldiers who had fallen there were rising around him in the dusk. Chamberlain reflected, "They did not know it themselves—those boys of ours . . . what were their lofty deeds of body, mind, heart, soul on that tremendous day."

In October of 1863, as workmen dug busily in the Soldiers' National Cemetery, there were many others who did not know, or were on the way to forgetting the full significance of the battle. The deeper meaning of Gettysburg had not crystallized. October, too, passed on—the red maple leaves, the brown oak leaves, the first of many autumns falling on the graves. The 20th Maine by then was far away—back on the Rappahannock. The sorrows and passions of that bloody July had already begun to grow more and more remote, and what more was there to do or say at Gettysburg?

In November the President came to the battlefield to participate in the dedication of the cemetery. At the review on the field at Antietam the Maine soldiers had looked into his eyes and seen "the sufferings and the thousand deaths" that the mere sight of the soldiers in mass had called into his mind. Again in the camp near Falmouth they had seen him, sad and abstracted. On this third visit, those of the 20th Maine who had remained here would not see him, but he had something to say about and for them.

Today, Lincoln's Gettysburg Address is usually surrounded by an aura quite different—the softness of spring weather on Memorial Day, the serenity of events past and gone, forever unchangeable. But Lincoln spoke here in November of 1863, with another bleak winter coming on and victory nowhere in sight. And some of his urgent meaning, as it applied to that day, has been lost in the music of the words.

About a fifth of the short speech was framed to state the basic issue of the war. Only the part embodied in the next two-fifths was in any way dedicatory, and this pointed out the futility of trying to dedicate a field already hallowed by the brave. The remaining two-fifths contained an exhortation to prosecute the war and was, in its intent and effect, perhaps as powerful and important as any charge made by Union infantry at Gettysburg. This was a fighting speech, in a sense a continuation of the Gettysburg battle effort, using as its motivating emotional force the inspiration of the deeds and sacrifices of Union soldiers on a field where their presence could still be felt. "It is for us, the living, rather to be dedicated here to the unfinished work which they have, thus far, so nobly carried on."

The issue was still to be decided. The war was far from won. Let's push on with it, said Abraham Lincoln. It was just about what the 20th Maine would have wanted him to say.

CHAPTER NINE

Living in Awful Times

FOR the 20th Maine, the remainder of the year 1863 was not a period to be remembered with any special pleasure. The trek south from Gettysburg began on the afternoon of July 5 in a heavy downpour. It had been raining, the men might have recalled, after Fredericksburg. And they could all remember the rain and the mud and the hog-wallow following Chancellorsville. Now the battle of Gettysburg had also come to a watery conclusion, and if it were true, as some thought, that battles caused rain, this was another reason why war ought to be outlawed. But then, maybe it was marching that caused rain. Water always seemed to be coming down on them when they marched, and a man couldn't really tell.

The long column ahead wound off into the haze of falling rain, fading from sight more and more as night came on, until the individual soldier was all alone in absolute blackness—unable to see the man ahead of him, only feeling, now and then, someone lurching against him from the side. Troops ahead were churning up the Emmitsburg Road mightily, and the mud—this was the worst part of marching in the rain—was recorded by Corporal Livermore as being from two to sixteen inches deep. A man's feet would be traveling up and down about as far as they went forward. With the mud dragging at him and the blackness shutting him in, the soldier fell into a stupid trance after a while and lurched on mechanically, losing all sense of time.

Along in the night—it was around twelve, someone said—a distant sound like the barking of foxes started coming back along the column. It was the command, "Company, halt!" being repeated by successive captains, until finally it got back to the 20th Maine, and the regiment staggered and slid to a stop. The men fixed bayonets, drove the points into the ground, and used their upended rifles as poles for pitching shelter tents. This not only kept the falling rain out of the rifle bores, but it saved a lot of time in going into bivouac—and if a company commander wasn't fussy about having his weapons all tangled up in tent ropes, the procedure worked fine. Lying on the muddy ground (and whatever else you might say about it, at least the mud was soft), the Maine soldiers sank into a soggy slumber.

Next day, another short march, another bivouac, and the 20th Maine heard a congratulatory order read, the gist of which was that the enemy had been utterly confounded; that history would always remember them; and that they were gallant heroes. The Maine men could hardly picture themselves in this glamorous role. They had been on the road almost a month, ruining their intestines with atrocious hand-to-mouth cooking, getting thinner and dirtier by the day. And, also, lousier. Body lice, which infested their clothing, would be eliminated only if the clothing could be boiled. And for weeks, of course, there had been no opportunity for boiling. One soldier in the brigade wrote home about this time, "I believe I state a fact when I say that not twenty men (who carried their clothing) in any regiment but were swarming with vermin. They are the pest of the army, and though you hear but little about it, they are always here. More clothing is thrown away on that very account than is worn out." Both inside and outside, many of the Maine men were in bad shape. Bowel disorders were prevalent. Clothing was in tatters, shoes worn out, hair long, beards untrimmed, bodies unbathed. They neither looked, nor felt, nor smelled, like heroes.

The men in ranks were, at the same time, conscious of the fact that the victory, if it had indeed been one didn't *feel* quite like a victory. To their right—off to the west—was the long misty-blue wall of the South Mountain range. And behind that wall, they heard, the Army of Northern Virginia, still largely intact, was moving southward. So it would be the old story, they supposed —marching, marching—the two armies on parallel courses with a mountain range between, and somewhere they would meet again.

Actually, the Army of Northern Virginia, with Union cavalry snapping at its heels, was not parallel with them at all, but a long way ahead. Lee's army was battered and bruised, but it could still move, and move rapidly. In less than three days Lee had reached the Potomac in the vicinity of Williamsport, where he discovered that heavy rains had swollen the river to a degree that would make a crossing next to impossible. There was nothing left for the Confederate commander to do but dig in and await an attack. At Williamsport the Potomac takes a sharp bend and runs generally southward for a few miles. In front of this southerly trending portion of the river, Lee dug field fortifications and made a long, entrenched line facing east. He would have almost a week before the Army of the Potomac caught up with him. For an experienced engineer like Robert E. Lee, that would be more than enough time to construct earthworks of the most formidable kind. In fact, if the Yankees came on with sufficient rashness, great quantities of them might be done away with at a highly favorable rate of exchange. Or, as Lee put it, with his customary felicity, in a letter to Jefferson Davis, "With the blessing of Heaven, I trust that the courage and fortitude of the army will be found sufficient to relieve us from the embarrassment caused by the unlooked-for natural difficulties of our situation, if not to secure more valuable and substantial results."

Meanwhile, as the 20th Maine plodded southward on the route they were taking—through Emmitsburg and toward Frederick, almost due south—distance and geography would be working against them. Along with rain and mud and scanty rations, one of the horrors of war, the 20th Maine had discovered, was that the campaigns were planned by officers who rode horses and fought by enlisted men who walked. Consequently there was a prodigious amount of walking to do, and anyone today who does not believe it was prodigious can rectify his impression by getting in an automobile and simply driving from the Rappahannock up to Gettysburg and back again. For the men who did it on foot the road back was much harder than the road up. In his plan for the pursuit, Meade had decided against following directly behind Lee. Instead, he would march east of the South Mountain range, then swing across it and try to cut the Confederates off, if and when he could get slightly ahead of them. This plan, whatever it may have had to recommend it tactically, was exceedingly hard on the feet. The Union soldiers would have to march almost twice as far as the enemy—and they would have not one, but two heights of land to cross in order to get at the Confederates around Williamsport, for another range of hills, the Catoctins, would interpose as they moved southward. In other words, the way they were headed, they would have to climb the Catoctins, and *then* the South Mountain range.

On July 7, the Fifth Corps finally started moving as though it were going somewhere. The 20th Maine marched nearly twenty miles through the rain, with the sky dark overhead and heavy mud underfoot. That night they went into bivouac near Frederick. Next day the column turned to the west, toward the hills, and this looked like business. With weary bodies sagging forward against the slopes, they pushed up over the Catoctins through one of the heaviest thunderstorms in the memory of man. At ten o'clock, on the summit of the hills, it was as dark as night, with clouds all around them, thunder rolling, lightning flashing incessantly. Going down into the valley on the other side, the sun came out and the country began to look familiar. It was the gardenlike valley they had crossed on the way to Antietam almost a year before. Then it had been approaching autumn; now the fields were fresh and green in the richness of deep summer. But ahead was the South Mountain range they remembered. Ahead also, the now-familiar thumping of guns somewhere over the horizon, where Union cavalry was skirmishing with Lee's rear guard. Since that September day seemingly so long ago, the sound had lost its former power to make the heart beat faster. But it was there, and they remembered.

The men found a strange fascination in retracing the old route to the Antietam. On the night of the eighth they camped close to South Mountain, in the same field where the regiment had bivouacked on its march to that memorable battle of the previous September. The men drank out of the same spring, washed in the same ditch, and many of them went to the trouble of finding the same strawstack to get bedding. Tomorrow they would be going over the same mountain to attack Lee again. Seemingly, they had tramped around in a dreamlike circle through time and space.

Next morning they crossed South Mountain near the place where they had seen their first Confederate dead. The weather was continuing to clear; waves of sunshine and shadow swept across the landscape. On July 10 they crossed the Antietam, and the Army of the Potomac spread itself out in a long line of battle facing Lee's entrenchments. Skirmishers went out, the 20th Maine among them. Dozens of little fights flared up and then sputtered out as the two armies felt for each other. In one of these affairs Company E of the 20th was handled roughly, which so provoked one of the mutinous prisoners from the 2nd Maine that he forgot the old army precept, "Never volunteer for anything." The 2nd Mainer caught up a rifle, returned to duty on the spot and got himself killed. Colonel Chamberlain wrote a report clearing his record of all shame or reproach, and the name of this place, appropriately enough, was Fair Play.

(Of the six men from the 2nd Maine that Chamberlain had been marching along as prisoners, only three by now had failed to return to the ranks. But these three were hard cases. They would continue their refusal of duty and would finally have to be turned over to the Provost Guard.)

On the same day there was another and more notable instance of military recognition coming a little late to do the recipient any substantial good. On this morning, the whole 3rd Brigade was formed on dress parade and an order was read, followed by a mounting wave of cheering, for it announced a promotion to brigadier general for Strong Vincent. The brigade was unaware of the fact that it was cheering a dead man. Vincent had died of his wound five days after the battle of Little Round Top.

For the next two days, the Army of the Potomac marched slowly forward toward Lee's position. Approaching Williamsport, the army moved in a long line of battle, and none of the Maine men who saw that sight would ever forget it. The advance was through country of open, cultivated fields for the most part. Many of the wheat fields had been cut; but the farmers had been interrupted in the harvesting, and shocks of grain stood in regular ranks across the stubbled fields. Out across these yellow fields moved the skirmishers, a thin line of blue against the gold. And behind them came the army in full battle-array, each corps in line, each brigade in columns of regimental front, with colors flashing in the breeze and the gleaming of sunlight on thousands of rifle barrels. It was one of those rare moments when a man could be deluded into thinking that war is wonderful—or at least wonderful until the killing begins. It seemed, also, that this ponderous mass was moving toward the final overthrow of the enemy. With the swollen river at his back, Lee was in a precarious position; as a Confederate prisoner put it, they had Yankees on three sides of them and the Almighty on the fourth, and with all this they had begun to think that the last days of the Confederacy had come. There is evidence that the enlisted men of the 20th Maine also saw the situation clearly and understood that a defeat here would be a complete disaster for Lee. William Livermore wrote home saying that he hoped there'd be a battle, pointing out that they would be better off fighting here than later on, somewhere in Virginia.

But Meade was a prudent general, and the sight of Lee's earthworks gave him pause. The advance was halted. Consultations were held. It began to rain again. Among the wheat stacks, Confederate and Union pickets stood wrapped in blankets, taking the slow soaking of the rain and staring at each other dismally. They looked, one man thought, more like scarecrows than soldiers. And so great expectations faded. On the night of July 13 the rain fell in blinding sheets, and next morning the Confederates were gone. Under cover of darkness, the Army of Northern Virginia had made a successful crossing of the river.

The rest of the month was equally disappointing and discouraging to the Maine men. They moved down the Potomac, crossed at Berlin, and from there on, a mountain range separated the two armies as before. The Confederates were moving west of the Blue Ridge range, the Union army east of it, with skirmishing through the gaps.

On July 23 they nearly caught up with the Confederates at Manassas Gap, meanwhile outmarching their rations. There were a couple of extraordinarily hungry places that the Maine men remembered from the war; one was Appomattox; the other was

National Archive

Joshua L. Chamberlain, wearing the brigadier general's star
he won on the battlefield at Petersburg

National Archives

Adelbert Ames, Brevet Major General, U.S.A.

Harold M. Owen

A sergeant of the 20th Maine, William H. Owen

Carrie B. Hamlin

A corporal of the 20th Maine, William T. Livermore
(Later a sergeant)

Emma L. Jones

A private of the 20th Maine, John F. Linnekin

Company C of the 20th Maine at a little more than a third of its full strength. The captain, Thomas D. Chamberlain, stands front and center. The first sergeant, James C. Rundlett, is third from the left. The photograph is believed to have been taken late in 1863 or in 1864.

National Archives

The 2nd Maine Regiment on Christmas Day, 1861. Part of this regiment was transferred to the 20th Maine in May, 1863.

Above—Marye's Heights as seen from Fredericksburg. The 20th Maine advanced over the ground at the extreme left.

Below—Fredericksburg, as seen across the Rappahannock, overlooking the part of the river where the 20th Maine crossed on a pontoon bridge.

Library of Congress

Library of Congress

A few of the dead at Little Round Top

Library of Congress

Woods of the Wilderness

Library of Congress

Typical fieldworks, near the North Anna

Library of Congress

Bombproof shelters at Petersburg

Library of Congress

13-inch mortar, "Dictator," at Petersburg

Library of Congress

Part of the Union line at Petersburg where the 20th Maine occupied positions in November, 1864. Fort Conahey in center. (*Photograph taken from top of a signal tower*)

National Archives

Gouverneur K. Warren, Brevet Major General, U.S.A.

National Archives

Charles Griffin, Brevet Major General, U.S.A.

here at "Molasses Gap," as they called it, a natural passageway that runs through the Blue Ridge in a series of knolls and depressions. The enemy was defending the gaps with a covering force and there seemed to be some idea of pushing these people back through the mountains so that the Army of the Potomac could get over into the Shenandoah Valley and cut off the tail of Lee's retreating column. What was left of the Third Corps—which had been badly beaten up at Gettysburg under Sickles—was elected to spearhead the push, and the 20th Maine had the unique pleasure of watching the battle without being in it. Standing with its division of the Fifth Corps on one of the high knolls in the gap, the Maine regiment saw the Third Corps move out across a valley against the Confederates defending the opposite slope. As seen from a distance, it was a picture-book battle. Union skirmishers went out; Union artillery fired over them, shellbursts lazily puffing and thundering on the ridge ahead. The heavy battle lines of the Third Corps moved through the skirmishers, gave out windrows of smoke, and then moved back again. Aside from providing an entertaining spectacle, the Third Corps didn't seem to be accomplishing anything. With stomachs rumbling, the 20th Maine watched all this impatiently.

At sunset the 1st Division of the Fifth Corps moved ahead to relieve the attackers and continue the advance on the following day. There was much foraging in fields and gardens. Ellis Spear remembered that the purveyor for his mess captured a lean old duck. "A few fragments of beet leaves from a trampled garden, and a half handful of cracker dust from his inverted haversack, water, the fragments of duck, and no salt, the whole imperfectly boiled, was offered for our dinner. It was several years before my stomach would accept duck again."

Hunger delayed the attack next morning. The Maine men were ordered out as skirmishers, but there was a long wait before this movement could get under way; the soldiers were out in the fields hunting for vegetables. And by the time the advance started the Confederates in front of them had vanished. The 3rd brigade was then given the mission of climbing and occupying Wapping Heights, a lofty ridge that shoulders up out of the gap on its southern side. This was the most difficult terrain over which the

20th Maine ever advanced in line of battle, slopes almost per-
pendicular in places—woods, tangled brush and boulders blocking the way. There was a profusion of blackberries on the
heights, shiny-ripe and plump with juice. The ravenous men
stopped to pick berries, and officers had hard work to keep them
moving. Crawling and stumbling, crashing through brush, picking berries, the regiment finally reached the summit. The climb-
ers were rewarded with a magnificent view of the Shenandoah
Valley, lying all rich and green and golden in the sun, with the
scars of war still unnoticeable.

The beauty of the scene inspired Private Gerrish to a biblical
comparison . . . "as we looked over on its fertile fields, smiling
so sweetly in the sunshine, we were reminded of Moses, when,
from the heights of Pisgah, he surveyed the promised land, but
like him, were not permitted to go over and enjoy it."

The reason they were not permitted to go over was that the
valley was empty of any enemy force. On the previous afternoon
the Confederates guarding the gap had stood off the Third Corps
long enough to allow the rear of Lee's column to pass the threatened point before the blackberry pickers could arrive. The climb
up the mountain had not been entirely wasted. The view from
the top had indeed been stupendous. And it was thought by one
of the men that the blackberries had helped their diarrhea. (This
was a new idea; the standard theory had it that rain water from
the hollow of a white oak stump was the best remedy.) But all
in all, "the blackberry affair," as it came to be remembered, had
done little to advance the prosecution of the war. The officer
who had led the advance had got lost, so there was no one to
say what to do, and the Maine soldiers stayed on the mountain
summit most of the afternoon eating berries.

Before sunset they scrambled back down to rejoin the corps.
Ellis Spear recorded further items of nourishment . . . "a lean,
wayworn steer was sacrificed, speedily dissected, and passed
around while still warm to be broiled in the smoke. . . . Too tough
for chewing, it could be cut small and swallowed. In the night,
on picket, there was a shower, by advantage of which some of
my men stole a hive of honey. I ate, in the rage of hunger, I
think a couple of pounds, comb, grubs and all, and then an op-

pressive doubt struck me that perhaps beeswax was not digestible. But I slept well, though wet, after a day in which the fare, scanty but diversified, was blueberries, blackberries, tough beef and honey, served in succession."

Once out of Manassas Gap, the regiment continued its southward march. On August 7, the 20th Maine was back on the Rappahannock, where it went into camp guarding Beverly Ford, and where further exertions were distasteful, the weather having turned hotter than Tophet.

Meanwhile, the strength of the regiment had declined to a new low. The 20th Maine had been badly shot up at Gettysburg. Sickness and exhaustion had further depleted the ranks. They heard that the Enrollment Act had gone into effect, but not enough draftees were arriving for the 20th.

The chief reason could be found in the Act itself. It contained a provision whereby a drafted man could send a substitute. Or, instead, in the words of the Act, "he may pay to such person as the Secretary of War may authorize to receive it, such sum, not exceeding three hundred dollars, as the Secretary may determine, for the procuration of such substitute. . . ." At the time, this provision probably did not seem so remarkable as it appears in retrospect today. There had been a precedent in the militia laws, which allowed a drafted or detailed man to send a substitute or pay a fine. But it was ill adapted to the exigencies of the Civil War.

Paying the money in lieu of providing a substitute, or paying commutation as it was called, proved to be immediately popular in Maine, as it was everywhere else. The government received a great many dollars, but the 20th and other Maine regiments received very few men. For the year 1863, only around twenty-five hundred men entered service from Maine as draftees or substitutes—which was an inconsiderable number when compared to a total of around seventy thousand men that Maine sent to the war as a whole.

Aside from sending a substitute or paying commutation, another way of escaping the draft in Maine—reprehensible but effective—was to remove across the border into neighboring Canada. Aroostook County, since it was right on the border and somewhat isolated from the rest of the state, became a popular place to visit. Traffic on the stage line up into Aroostook was extremely heavy in 1863, and one observer wrote, "I suppose Aroostook County has had within her borders more deserters than any other section of the country in either this or the old world." The common meaning of the word "skedaddler" in the Civil War generally was "one who flees in battle." But in Aroostook the meaning was, and still is among the older folk, "one who went over the line." Confederate sympathizers in Maine, or "Copperheads," speeded this exodus by circulating the false rumor that a provost marshal had twenty-five hundred pairs of handcuffs secreted and was ready to snap them on to men as soon as they appeared for examination in answer to the draft. Curious items appeared in the papers. For example, this one: "Those drafted persons who have knocked out their front teeth to procure exemption are informed that they will be accepted in the Cavalry, where front teeth are not needed to bite off cartridges."

Another factor working against the draft was an understandable feeling of resentment on the part of the poor, directed at the substitute and commutation provisions. These meant, they pointed out, that a rich man could stay home, while the poor man had to go. In order to equalize the situation, there were efforts in citizens' meetings to vote the sum of $300 to *every* drafted man, so that he could procure a substitute or pay commutation if he so desired. The effect of this, of course, would be to defeat the very purpose of the draft, and there were accusations of disloyalty. There was much contention and bitterness raised by the draft in Maine, but no great quantity of troops in 1863.

So as far as the 20th Maine was concerned, the results were low on the positive side. In its negative aspects, over the country as a whole, the draft was prolific of much evil in a new kind of business venture—trading in substitutes. And this, too, had an unpleasant consequence for the 20th Maine and other volunteer regiments.

In the early stages of the draft, the commutation price of $300 also established the price of a substitute, for it was thought that both commutation payment and substitute provided the same exemption. On this point, the Enrollment Act as passed by Congress and approved by the President, had been somewhat vague. A section of the Act said that a person providing a substitute got an exemption for the time for which he was drafted—which might be for as much as three years. But the term of exemption of a man paying commutation was not clearly stated by the Act. Later came this clarification: A man paying commutation would be guaranteed exemption only under the current draft. Another draft might come along within a month or so, and he would have to fork over another $300.

When this information became known, the price of a substitute immediately went up. There had been bounty shenanigans in Maine in 1862, but these were as nothing compared to financial maneuvers that took place in 1863. For example, if a man were content to be drafted, he could do this: For $300 he could pay commutation and get his name off the draft list; then he could accept $500 from some well-heeled citizen to go as a substitute, making a profit of $200 on the deal.

But this was only a minor, and relatively honest way to deal in the draft—the kind of deal any Yankee horse trader might make. Over the line that separates horse trading from criminality, there were many more profitable opportunities. A man could take money to go as a substitute, then desert, change his name, go to another state and take money again, and keep repeating the process. He was then what was known as a bounty jumper. If he got away with it, he could make a considerable sum of money. If not, they could do nothing worse than shoot him, and thousands of men were getting shot for $13 a month, a private's pay. Bounty jumping quickly became a nation-wide business. Many Confederates, even, deserted and came north to participate in it.

An allied type of rascal was the substitute broker, who raked up the scum of every large city in the country—and then met the boats to rake in dollar-hungry and ignorant immigrants from Europe—in order to reap the harvest of substitute payments.

In this particular aspect of the draft, the 20th Maine was fortunate. The few draftees it received in 1863 were several cuts above the average, coming from the predominantly rural area of

Maine. But sister regiments had their troubles. The 83rd Pennsylvania got a mob of draftees of which Captain A. M. Judson wrote, "These were the cream and flower, the very head and front of the New York rioters, gamblers, thieves, pickpockets and blacklegs, many of whom, it was said, had fled to escape punishment for the crimes of arson, robbery and homicide. . . . They fought, gambled and stole after they got to the regiment. The company streets of the once-peaceful Eighty-Third became uproarious at times with their midnight broils and battles. They were always spoiling for a fight except when in the presence of the enemy. One would have supposed that when men would wake up at midnight and fall to pummeling each other in bed, as they often did, they would have become transported at the prospect of battle; but it was at such times that they skulked and seized the opportunity to desert. They would get each other drunk and pick each other's pockets while asleep. They would decoy each other out of camp after dark, on pretense of going out to get something good to drink, and then knock their deluded victims down and rob them of their money. In short, these men would have disgraced the regiment beyond all recovery had they remained three months in it; but thanks to a kind Providence, or to some other invisible power of redemption, they kept deserting, a dozen at a time, until they were nearly all gone."

The 118th Pennsylvania, Corn Exchange Regiment, also had a hard time with the draftees. A couple of Corn Exchange officers went to Philadelphia and picked up a quota of 159 draftees and substitutes. By the time they got back to the regiment in the field, fifty had eluded the guards and escaped.

In similar incidents escaping men had been shot by the guards, and there had also been many single executions as a result of court-martial sentences for desertion. The army now decided that a wholesale shooting would be most beneficial in curbing bounty jumping and the swarms of desertions. This led to one of the most horribly impressive spectacles the 20th Maine witnessed during the war.

The victims were bounty jumpers—five of the fifty men who had deserted on their way from Philadelphia to join the Corn Exchange Regiment. They had been collared while trying to recross the Potomac and had been brought to the camp at Beverly Ford. Here they had been court-martialed and sentenced to death. There had been an appeal to President Lincoln, but Lincoln had told Meade to go ahead and shoot them. It was announced that the entire Fifth Corps would be drawn up to witness the execution. Newspapermen arrived to record the event. Sketch artists from the leading illustrated publications of the day —*Harper's Weekly* and *Frank Leslie's Illustrated Newspaper*— came to make pictures. The shooting would be a warning not only to the troops, but to desertion-minded men all over the nation.

The gruesome affair took place in an immense field on August 29, a bright, cool day with the air clear and still. The 20th Maine arrived on the field with the 1st Division and stood uneasily, watching the other two divisions of the corps march into place. The formation when completed made a vast and silent array around three sides of a hollow square. On the open side were five newly dug graves. Standing on the sloping plain, every man could see everything that took place. The Maine men stood and looked at the graves, while the silence over the field grew deeper and deeper. Now and then someone coughed, or a fly-bitten horse jerked and rattled a bridle, or a flag stirred softly in a wandering wisp of air, but aside from these little sounds and movements, the corps stood still as death. It was all very much like an elaborate funeral, with the added depression of realizing that the corpses were to be manufactured on the spot.

Presently they heard sad music—a dirge—and the procession of doomed men came into view. If the army had wanted to make an impression, it was succeeding admirably. The cavalcade was as scary as anything a producer of horror movies would devise. First came the band, playing its doleful music, marching with a slow, measured pace. Then the Provost Marshal with his firing party of fifty men, with reversed arms, keeping time to the slow beat of the dead march. Then the procession of coffins, each borne by four men and followed by a manacled prisoner. Another party from the Provost Guard brought up the rear.

Slowly, the procession moved around three sides of the hollow square and then halted by the graves. The five coffins were placed beside the five graves. The five deserters sat upon the coffins. From the standpoint of public relations, the group was admirably constituted. Two of them were Protestants; two Catholics; and one a Jew. Someone who was overly indoctrinated with army regulations had seriously made a grotesque suggestion, which had been carried out in the procession and formation. According to regulations, brigades and regiments in line were supposed to be posted from right to left in the order of their numbers. The suggestion was that the Jew, who represented the most ancient of creeds, should be given the right of the line.

The firing party now separated into five groups, ten men to a deserter. The Provost Marshal read the order of execution. The rabbi, priest and minister stepped forward to administer their final consolations. The Maine men watched with a feeling of mounting dread, the tension rising almost intolerably. It was one thing, they now learned, to watch men die in the heat of battle—and quite another experience to watch men done to death methodically, with their hands tied behind their backs. The scene seems to have impressed itself upon the minds of the soldiers with almost photographic clarity and uniformity. Normally, the several accounts of any Civil War happening come to us with variations in many details. But the accounts of the execution at Beverly Ford are remarkably alike. Nearly all of them, for example, record that the shirts of the doomed men were white and their trousers were blue.

The rabbi, priest and minister were praying earnestly. Their ghostly ministrations were taking too long. The shirts of the doomed men were becoming too terribly white, the trousers too horribly blue. Yet it was impossible not to look at them. The Maine men heard a shrill voice rising in protest in front of their division. It was General Charles Griffin, the division commander, who was mindful of the fact that the order for the men's execution had fixed the time between 12 noon and 4 P.M., and it was now after 3:45. "Shoot those men," he yelled, "or after ten minutes it will be murder!"

The clergy stood aside. The deserters' eyes were bandaged. The Provost Marshal called, "Attention, guard! Shoulder arms! Forward! Guide right—march!" The firing party moved to within six paces of the condemned men. "Halt! Ready . . . aim . . . fire!"

The volley shocked the still air, and was followed by a note of insupportable horror. Four of the five men had fallen back upon their coffins. But the fifth man remained sitting! Frantically, the Provost Marshal called, "Inspection arms!" All fifty ramrods, when dropped into the bores and "sprung," rang with tones showing that the muskets had all been fired. The Provost Marshal drew his pistol and moved to the side of the figure still sitting erect on the coffin, where it was discovered that there was no need of a final shot. A surgeon had ascertained that the man was sufficiently dead.

The band struck up a lively air—"The Girl I Left Behind Me." The 20th Maine marched briskly away, but march as far as it would, it would never forget. Wrote one of the Maine men . . . "it is a very solemn thing to see human beings led forth to be shot like dogs, and those who witness such scenes receive an impression that can never be shaken off."

And Will Owen wrote home to his sister Abbie, "It was the most affecting sight I have ever seen. I have seen men shot on the battlefield, men with their heads shot off, men with arms and legs gone and passed them all without a thought but to see five men sitting on their own coffins facing 50 loaded rifles that were to be fired at them is a sight that me thinks no one can stand and look calmly at no matter what they have been through, no matter how much misery they have seen. . . ." But Owen then went on to write that he was all in favor of the execution. "It will doubtless save 500 men to this Corps. Desertions have become very frequent and if it is not stopped t'will be in vain to try and recruit this army, and every battle be lost and thousands of noble lives lost with it. It is an awful thing, but we are living in awful times."

On the whole, August of 1863 was not a pleasant month to remember. It was oppressively hot. Swarms of insects arose from the lowlands along the river. Malarial fevers were prevalent. The disease had some element of popularity, because to combat it there were issues of quinine steeped in whiskey. But it was an unfamiliar and distressing ailment for the men from Maine.

Among those on the sick list for part of the month was Colonel Chamberlain, but he returned to duty in late August and found that he had moved up another rung on the military ladder. Colonel Rice had been promoted to brigadier general; Chamberlain took his place as commander of the 3rd Brigade. Various general officers were suggested for the brigade, but the division commander, Griffin, would have none of them. Ever since Little Round Top, he had had his eye on Joshua Chamberlain.

For the 20th Maine, the promotion of Chamberlain was a matter of considerable pride. They had not lost him; he would still be their brigade commander. And in the subsequent history of the regiment, Chamberlain would always be closely associated with the 20th Maine. During the months when he had commanded the 20th, Chamberlain had risen steadily in the esteem of the regiment as well as in the eyes of higher headquarters. "Uniform kindness and courtesy . . . skill . . . brilliant courage" . . . these are some of the words with which one of the Maine men characterized him. In the ranks of sister regiments in the 3rd Brigade he was not so well known. A soldier of the 83rd Pennsylvania, writing home at this time, recorded his impression thus: "Our new commander is Colonel Chamberlain of the Twentieth Maine, a very fine man (formerly professor in college), but not much of a military man." This was an impression that Chamberlain was to correct very quickly. He immediately brought the brigade to a high point in drill and discipline.

But there was little opportunity in the campaign that followed for Chamberlain to advance his reputation in that most military matter of all—and the one in which he excelled—fighting. This was a succession of maneuvers, completely bewildering to the private soldiers, along what the men came to call the "Centreville and Culpeper Express."

Centreville, near Washington, was one of the defense keys of that city. Passing near Centreville and trending off to the southwest ran one of the main lines of communication to the South—the Orange & Alexandria Railroad. Along this line went the supply trains, chuffing to the support of the various unsuccessful movements into Lee's territory. Along it, also, much fighting had been done, and railroad names like Fairfax Station, Manassas

Junction, and Warrenton Junction had become familiar in military reports. In fact, the armies had been tramping up and down the railroad so much that the country around it in many places was beginning to look like a desert—much of the woods cut down, fences demolished, roads rutted, farmlands torn up and laid waste, plantations burned, houses pock-marked by bullets and punctured by artillery projectiles. Threading through this dismal region, the railroad crossed the Rappahannock River at Rappahannock Station. After passing Culpeper, it crossed the Rapidan. If Federal forces followed it much beyond that point, they would be likely to run into trouble.

In the middle of September, the Army of the Potomac marched down into the vicinity of Culpeper, remaining there, more or less inactive, about a month. But on the night of October 12-13 there was a sudden panic. Meade discovered that Lee had whipped out around his right flank and was apparently starting north again. If Lee got around behind him, that worst of all possible things would have taken place—Lee would be between the Army of the Potomac and Washington. The two armies began racing north; the Union forces along the line of the railroad, with Centreville as their goal; Lee off to the west somewhere; no one knew exactly where.

The 20th Maine turned out at one o'clock on that nervous morning of October 13. By night they had made twenty-five miles up the railroad, camping at Catlett's Station. The next day was one of alarms and confusions. Around noon they arrived at Bristoe Station. The day was quiet; there was no hint of Confederate activity anywhere within miles. A halt for a noonday meal was ordered. Soon the spiraling smokes of hundreds of little campfires were climbing steadily toward the sky, and the fragrance of boiling coffee arose. And suddenly the sky fell on them. There were flashes, crashes, and bursts of smoke among the coffee drinkers—shells falling from somewhere. From a woods off to the west of the railroad, where no Confederates had a right to be, gray skirmishers were coming across the fields in a long line that indicated a heavy force behind them. It looked as though Lee were winning the race, and the Fifth Corps were about to be taken in the flank.

159

The Fifth Corps took off from Bristoe Station in a northward march that was both earnest and rapid. In the 20th Maine, it was recalled that "the ranks were well closed up." At Manassas the corps swung out into a line of battle facing south, with batteries in position, waiting. They waited until an hour before sundown. Meanwhile, the roar of heavy fighting came up from Bristoe Station. General Warren, their old friend from Little Round Top, who now commanded the Second Corps, had come upon the field at about the time they had been leaving it. Warren had engaged the Confederates.

"All the while," remembered one of the Maine men, "we were wondering why we had hurried away from them." General Sykes, the Fifth Corps commander, finally got to wondering, too. Late in the day he double-quicked the Fifth Corps back down to Bristoe, but before he arrived, Warren had won a brilliant victory. At about nine o'clock in the evening, the Fifth Corps turned north again. When the 20th Maine crossed Bull Run early next morning, the regiment had been on foot twenty-four hours and had marched thirty-two miles.

On the fifteenth, they pushed on to Fairfax Court House, camped, broke camp at night, and marched to Centreville in a pouring rain and knee-deep mud. The next four days, which were equally disgusting, included the following marches:

> To Fairfax.
> Back to Centreville.
> To Fairfax again.
> Back to Centreville.

"We oscillated," one of the Maine men wrote. And while they were oscillating, Robert Lee was tearing up the Orange & Alexandria Railroad. After which, he retired to a position below the Rappahannock, leaving a covering force north of the river.

The Federal army followed slowly, rebuilding the railroad. On November 7 it was approaching the Rappahannock, and just at sundown part of the 20th Maine gave vent to some of its frustration by participating in an astonishing attack on the defenders of the river line. On the Rappahannock, General Lee had planned to administer a solid check to the advancing Union forces. The strong point of his line was at Rappahannock Station. Here, on a hill commanding the northern approaches, there were a couple of earthwork redoubts, flanked by rifle trenches and pits. There was a battery of artillery. And there were a couple of thousand of Lee's best infantrymen in the redoubts and rifle pits, standing with leveled rifles resting on the parapets, waiting for the Yankees to come on. In front of the earthworks were other discouragements for any attacking force—a dry moat; a ditch fourteen feet wide and six feet deep with three feet of mud and water in it; and a rough piece of ground all snagged up with stumps and spiky bushes. All in all it was a position where, the Southerners felt with reason, they could stand off the whole Army of the Potomac. If Meade acted the way he had at Williamsport, there would be some artillery dueling, perhaps a little skirmishing, and then the Union general would very wisely back off.

The Union Fifth and Sixth Corps, as they neared Rappahannock Station, were coming down the railroad side by side. The Fifth was on the left of the tracks; ahead of it was mostly open ground, covered with a heavy growth of thick, dry grass, where the Confederates were waiting in their rifle pits covering the river. The men of the Sixth Corps, advancing on the right of the railroad, faced a much more dismal prospect, for in their sector lay the fortified strong point with its artillery and heavy concentration of entrenched infantry.

Coming in sight of this forbidding position, the Union commanders paused for a season of meditation and prayer. What Lee had arranged for them here was obviously going to be a hard, if not impossible, nut to crack. The two corps got control of a couple of commanding ridges, brought up artillery, and started hammering at the Confederate works with the fieldpieces. The only accomplishment was a great deal of noise, much dirt thrown into the air and a temporary cessation of Confederate fire, followed by a quick resumption when the Union artillery let up. An hour or so of this only served to prove what the Sixth Corps commander probably already knew, that he couldn't get enemy infantry out of fieldworks with artillery fire. Someone would have to go there personally and drive them out.

The one who offered to go, finally, was an enterprising brig-

adier general named David A. Russell, who was that day acting
as a division commander, although he had been commanding a
brigade. Russell had an idea for carrying the earthworks. He
was, more than likely, thinking back to something that had happened on May 3 of the previous spring. While the battle of
Chancellorsville had been going on, the Sixth Corps had been
attacking the old Confederate works on Marye's Heights, at
Fredericksburg. Marye's Heights was still, at that time, strongly
defended by infantry behind the famous stone wall, and by artillery and intrenched riflemen on the slopes behind the wall.
A couple of regiments—the 6th Maine and the 5th Wisconsin—
had spearheaded the attack. Charging with fixed bayonets and
not stopping to fire a shot, the two regiments had gone right over
the stone wall and up the hill, leading an attack that had sent
the Confederates into retreat toward Chancellorsville. In the
general confusion and dismay attending the Union defeat at
Chancellorsville, this tremendous achievement had been largely
overlooked.

But now Russell was wondering if he could not stage a repeat
show for the benefit of those who had not been present at the
original performance. He had the same two regiments—the 6th
Maine and the 5th Wisconsin—here at Rappahannock Station.
Half of the 6th Maine was out on the skirmish line, within a few
hundred yards of the enemy redoubts. The other half could be
sent out to double the weight of the skirmish line. Then, if the
6th Maine could make a sudden dash into the Confederate earthworks, followed quickly by the 5th Wisconsin, a foothold might
be gained, and supporting troops could come on to widen the
breach and carry the whole position by storm. The whole trick,
of course, would be to keep the initial charge moving fast; if the
men halted to return enemy fire, they could be destroyed. The
attack would have to depend on the bayonet, but the 6th Maine
—composed largely of muscular lumbermen from the Penobscot
Valley and eastern Maine—had already proved that it had the
resolution necessary for the use of this fearsome and unpopular
tool of war. Russell's arrangements having been completed, the
6th Maine found itself receiving the order to uncap rifles and

prepare to charge the enemy works in its front, all by its lonesome self.

However, the 6th Maine was about to receive some unauthorized and unexpected help. Over on the extreme right of the Fifth Corps skirmish line, the 20th Maine had worked up into a position abreast of the 6th Maine. At this point the railroad took a bend to the left, so that part of the 20th had been crowded over the tracks and was in direct contact with the 6th Maine. Soldiers on adjacent flanks of the two Maine regiments were neighboring back and forth, and the officer in charge of the 20th Maine skirmishers, Captain Walter G. Morrill, went over to see some friends in the 6th Maine. Here Morrill got word of the proposed assault, and presently he came running back along the skirmish line shouting, "Boys, the 6th Maine is on our right; let's go in with them!"

Considering that the attack was strictly a Sixth Corps affair—in which no troops of the Fifth Corps were called upon to participate—the response to Morrill's suggestion was surprisingly favorable. Perhaps it was because there was a bright challenge and promise of glory in the Confederate earthworks, incomprehensible to anyone who was not actually there in the deepening shadows of that late autumn afternoon. Or perhaps it was because the 6th Maine men were about to tackle a brutally hard job, and it didn't seem right for other Maine men to "lay back." But beyond a doubt, their chief encouragement was that they were going to be led by Captain Walter G. Morrill in person. Morrill was one of those men whom war reveals in their highest statures—men who are terrifically and truly great while a war is on and perhaps afterward, but who try a lot of things in later years without achieving any comparable eminence. Although only twenty-two, Morrill had seen more than his share of fighting. He had carried a gun as an enlisted man in the battles of 1861 and 1862, before joining the 20th Maine as a second lieutenant. When the trials and tribulations of warfare had weeded out less durable officers, Morrill had quickly risen to the command of Company B—this promotion being hailed with great enthusiasm by the troops. At Gettysburg, as we have seen, he had saved his company from capture in an isolated position, and had then struck the enemy from the rear in a surprise attack that had done much to turn the tide of battle. Morrill was not exactly the West Point kind of officer when it came to conducting himself with the proper snap, precision and attention to details; in fact, Colonel Ames had taken a dim view of his prospects at one point. But the private soldiers considered him a real man and a remarkable fighter when the going got tough. And if Captain Morrill was willing to attack the fortifications, they were willing to go with him. Around eighty of the soldiers in this portion of the 20th Maine's line prepared to move out with the 6th Maine.

It was almost sundown when the attack started. Ahead, the Confederate earthworks loomed up grimly, the black muzzles of cannon showing in the embrasures. A man who was behind in the Corn Exchange Regiment described the action. "The skirmishers, the 20th Maine, rising from the tall grass, began their advance with a vigorous volley, to which the enemy lost no time in replying. It was a glorious pageant of real war. Rarely is the sight seen of an advancing line so extended, all in view, and under fire at the same time. . . . The setting sun flung a mellow glow over the landscape, and the mica dust covering the uniforms sparkled in its golden hues, and the gentle beauty of the scene made it impossible, for the moment, to believe that a battle was beginning."

Among the assaulting skirmishers of the 20th Maine, there was no such impression of serenity. The Confederate battery was firing spherical case shot. Over the parapets of the earthworks and from the pits rifles were flashing, and there seemed to be a peculiar humming and resonance in the air. In front of them, patches of ground were being ripped up, as though torn by an invisible spring-tooth harrow. Private Seth McGuire went down with a shattered leg. Private Edmund Morrison, although a giant of a man, flew spinning across a pile of rocks. A projectile had struck his knapsack, tearing it off his back, and throwing him violently to the ground. Morrison jumped up and rushed on in a frenzy, leaping into the earthworks ahead of the others. Seeing that he was alone, he pretended to fall dead, later arising as the assaulting Union troops poured over the parapet into the works.

The fight was brief. Before the Confederate defenders could bring sufficient fire to bear, the Maine men—followed soon afterward by the 5th Wisconsin—were in among them stabbing and clubbing. There was a confused uproar of screaming and smashing, Confederate infantrymen trying desperately to shoot foe instead of friend in the tangled brawl, cannoneers battling hand-to-hand around their guns. Then the Confederates were departing. One little Louisiana artillery lieutenant, a smooth-faced youth who looked to be in his early teens, lingered in an attempt to fire a shotted cannon at troops who were still approaching the earthworks. "Drop that lanyard!" shouted an officer from the 6th Maine. The boy refused and was instantly killed before he could fire. (A soldier who came into the works afterward saw him lying pathetically by the trail of the piece and wrote sadly, "Some rude creature had promptly removed his boots." The army was short of footwear that summer.) The fleeing Confederates were running for the river and also taking cover in adjoining rifle pits. From these still unbroken sections of the enemy line there now came an enfilading fire that gave the Maine and Wisconsin men a very hard time for several minutes. But they hung on, and presently Russell's supporting troops came pouring through the gap to fan out and trap the Confederates between their entrenchments and the river. The total bag was four pieces of artillery, 1,700 prisoners, eight battle flags and a bridge train. For the Confederates it had been a surprising and disheartening defeat.

For the Army of the Potomac, the victory at Rappahannock Station had been like four ounces of whiskey on an empty stomach—a tremendous, if temporary, booster of morale. There was a flurry of congratulatory orders from headquarters. General Russell—who had planned the assault and led it personally, and who had been slightly wounded—was specially designated to deliver in person the captured colors to the War Department. The 6th Maine had suffered 139 casualties but added immeasurably to its fame.

The 20th Maine, by way of comparison, had lost only one man killed and seven wounded, but had reaped a lion's share of the honors. The spectacular and uncalled-for dash of the skirmishers had taken place within the sight of thousands of officers and men, and to many of these it seemed that there could be only one word to describe it—valor. Formal recognition would be slow in coming, but in 1898 Walter Morrill would be awarded the Medal of Honor. This would make three Medals of Honor earned by the 20th Maine up to this point, the others to be received by Chamberlain and Andrew Tozier for actions at Gettysburg.

As commander of the 3rd Brigade, Joshua Chamberlain had also participated in the battle to some extent in the Fifth Corps sector on the left of the tracks. While making a reconnaissance the Colonel—it becomes almost monotonous to record—had another horse shot under him. Chamberlain had been a sick man during the battle. A malarial fever was gnawing at him, and one night shortly afterward he made the mistake of sleeping on the ground in a snowstorm, without shelter or a fire. The disease flared up, and Chamberlain was shipped off to a hospital in Washington, lying unconscious on the floor of a cattle car. Recovering, he was assigned to serve on a court-martial sitting in Washington, and he would not return to the 3rd Brigade until the following spring.

In late November the army moved south still farther, following up Lee's withdrawal from the line of the Rappahannock, which had become untenable for the Confederates after their defeat at Rappahannock Station and a Union crossing farther down the river. Lee had taken a defensive position behind the Rapidan—leaving the lower fords undefended, but protecting his right flank with entrenchments on a small tributary of the Rapidan called Mine Run. Meade now devised a plan for getting at his opponent by crossing the lower Rapidan and turning the Confederate defenses on Mine Run.

This plan going into effect, the 20th Maine found itself over the Rapidan and moving through a densely wooded and dismal country known as the Wilderness. (Later the name would be written in fire and smoke and blood, but not yet; not until another spring had come and the dry winter branches of the dogwood trees had blossomed into pink and white.) On November 29, they came up against Mine Run, relieving pickets of the Second Corps, and going into position along the stream.

It was, they all agreed, a miserable sight. Banks on the opposite shore were high and covered with brush and briars. Along the brow was a line of Confederate rifle pits, with two or three pickets in every pit. From the Confederate picket line back to their main entrenchments, the distance looked to be about a quarter of a mile, over ground that was open and gradually sloping upward—ideal for sweeping with grape and canister from the fortified batteries. Many of the Maine men thought that it was even more miserable looking than Marye's Heights had been, at Fredericksburg.

Also, the pickets across the stream seemed bitter about something, and bullets kept whizzing into the 20th Maine's position, so that the men had to keep under cover. The weather turned so cold that water froze in canteens. To keep from perishing, both Union and Confederate pickets lighted small fires in their rifle pits. Living with a smoking fire in a pit is a dangerous, choky business. But the alternative was lighting a fire outside and getting shot.

Soon there was yelling back and forth across the stream.

"Why don't you stop firing?" bellowed a man in the 3rd Brigade.

"You began it!" was the answer, shouted back.

"No, we didn't; we came here yesterday, and you commenced firing at us."

This exchange cleared up the whole matter, although hardly in the interests of military security. The Confederates were unaware of the fact that the brigade had relieved Second Corps pickets. Apparently, Second Corps pickets had, indeed, started the shooting, and the Confederates assumed that these criminals were still there. This regrettable misunderstanding having been corrected, the firing ceased; the pickets came out of their holes, stretched, yawned, and lighted good fires to ward off the intense cold.

Yet rumors still had it that the attack was going to be made, and looking across the icy stream, the Maine men didn't see how a man could survive. First they would have to cross the stream under heavy fire; then it would be necessary to climb the bank and advance up the slope through a storm of shot, shell and canister; and after that, the earthworks, where the Confederate infantry would be awaiting them. In the penetrating cold, a man who was wounded would be sure to die.

On the morning of November 30, the ominous sound of artillery firing began. Men wrote their names and addresses on little tags, which they fastened inside their uniforms; some of the more pessimistic added the words, "Killed in action, Nov. 30, 1863." But presently the firing died away, and welcome news arrived. General Warren, who had been supposed to launch the attack, had on his own initiative called it off. There were loud sighs of relief all up and down Mine Run. It had been a notable year for Warren. First there had been his direction of the defense of Little Round Top, then his brilliant victory at Bristoe Station; and now—and not the least of his accomplishments in the eyes of the 20th Maine—came this courageous decision that quite possibly averted a disaster at Mine Run.

On the night of December 1, the regiment began its withdrawal northward, and the men, at least, were under the impression that this was a retreat attended by considerable danger as the army extricated itself from the gloomy forests. The men of the 20th Maine always pointed to the retreat from Mine Run as one of the fastest marches they made during their three years of service. Dog-tired though they were, the soldiers needed no urging to keep the column closed up as they pushed over the frozen roads. Theodore Gerrish, without vouching for the veracity of the story, recalled that "One fellow in our regiment always declared that he was so sleepy that he could not possibly keep his eyes open, and that with head fallen back upon his knapsack, he had actually marched five miles through the woods, sound asleep. . . ."

It was the last march of 1863. On the site of the battle of Rappahannock Station, the 20th Maine went into winter quarters, leveling off the old Confederate earthworks and building large and comfortable log-walled huts. It was a pleasant place for a camp—the ground high, wood and water easily available. Duty was light. Officers went on leaves, or sent for their wives. General Meade, in order to build up morale and encourage enlistments, issued orders that ten-day furloughs would be granted to a limited number of worthy soldiers in each regiment who could present good reasons for going home. Since no exact reasons were specified, this soon resulted in a gigantic letter-writing contest on the subject of "Why I ought to go home." A soldier's letter first went to the colonel of his regiment, who either endorsed it or threw it in the wastebasket; then, if successful, it went on up through brigade and division to corps headquarters, where the corps commander himself, General Sykes, was the final judge. There was a premium, of course, on literary skill and imagination. Approximately a hundred letters a day were getting through to Sykes, who soon grew weary of reading about so many pathetic cases of death, suffering and misery at home. He therefore turned the job over to his adjutant general, who was so saddened and upset by the harrowing tales that he assigned the letter-reading task on a confidential basis to the clerks in corps headquarters. These enlisted men, after enjoying the various fictions and fabrications, very sensibly settled the whole thing by drawing lots. So some of the men in the 20th Maine who were both talented and lucky got a chance to go home. And the rest settled down for what was the happiest and healthiest of their three winter encampments, although the weather of a Virginia winter was something the Maine men could never get used to. Will Owen wrote home on December 27, "Yesterday the old Rappahannock was froze clear across and tonight it banks are overflowing with the flood of water that is pouring into it on every side, and thus it is here—day after day. Cold as Greenland today while tomorrow may be warm and pleasant or perhaps darkened by a terrible rain or snow-storm."

Again there was time for robust practical jokes. Four men in Company H, by switching kettles of frying fat with those normally used for water and then raising the alarm of a chimney fire in the cookhouse, tricked the company cook into literally throwing the fat into the fire. There was an immense column of black smoke, and the cookhouse burned down, the humor of this occurrence being only slightly tempered by an order which compelled the four men to build it back up again.

The 20th Maine completed an exchange of compliments. A letter had arrived some time before from their old commander,

General Adelbert Ames, in response to a gift of a sword sash and belt. Ames had written, "Coming as it does from a regiment which knows no superior either on the battlefield or elsewhere—from one towards which I entertain the most profound sentiments of pride and affection—it causes greater pleasure than I can express. It will ever remind me of the noble deeds of the donors and will recall the battles in which they have borne so prominent parts."

Thinking this over, it hardly seemed possible to the 20th Maine that it could be the object of such an accolade from General Ames. Only a little more than a year before, Ames had been saying in deep disgust, "This is a *hell* of a regiment." Now he could say, with a different accent, "This is a hell of a *regiment!*"

They received a new battle flag. The old one was now stained, tattered, torn, riddled with bullets. Yet, as such it was a symbol so charged with emotions and memories that it could only be delivered into the hands of someone who would understand.

The 20th Maine sent the old flag to General Ames.

CHAPTER TEN

River of No-Return

HERE was a piece of band music called "Hell on the Rappahannock." A lively number, performed with blaring brasses and a tricky flourishing of drumsticks, it was a favorite in the Army of the Potomac. But from now on, the title would be slightly dated. Hell was about finished on the Rappahannock. It was moving to new locations below the Rapidan—the first of which would be infinitely better, for hellish purposes, than any previous battlefield.

This was the forest area known as the Wilderness. It would be hard to assign it any definite boundaries, except to say that the thickest part of the forest extended from Chancellorsville west to Mine Run, and from the Rapidan south to the vicinity of Spotsylvania Court House. It was a mineral-bearing region, and in colonial days the original forest had been almost completely cut down to provide fuel for the iron furnaces. Out of the ravaged soil a thick second growth had arisen. Much of it was pine—the trees springing up so close together that their lower limbs had reached out and strangled one another to death, meshing in a dry, scratchy, spiky tangle that would madden a man trying to force his way through it. There were also scrub oak, occasional cedars and various kinds of dense underbrush. In swampy places, willow and alder saplings stood as close together as the bars of a cage, the whole mass laced together with strong, bright green vines. There were many dead trees—some standing desolately, others fallen to make bristling barriers with their dry limbs. The ground underneath was gullied by erosion, and in many places covered with dry stuff that could easily catch fire. Through the

171

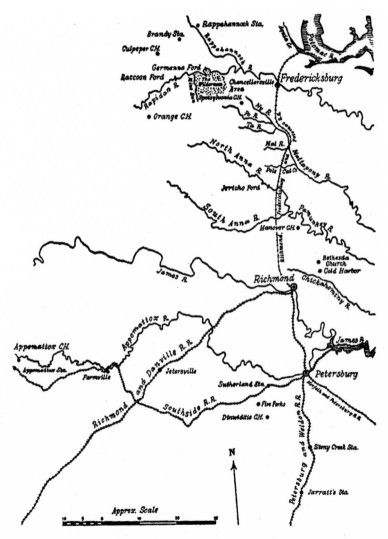

Theater of War for the 20th Maine in 1864 and 1865

area ran serpentine woods-trails that forked senselessly and often ended without apparent reason, and there were a few small farms and abandoned clearings grown up to briars, sassafras, dwarf pines and broom grass. This being the month of May, there were a few touches of beauty shining through the wildness and gloom: scattered dogwoods, now in bloom; swamp honey-suckle and great purple violets in the swales; and now and then a wild rose. But although a naturalist might find matters of inter-est in the Wilderness, no one but the devil would choose it for a battlefield.

Troops moving into this forest maze, now dense with its spring foliage, would disappear as though they had marched into the sea, once they moved off the roads. The road network, in general, featured two east-west highways, intersected by a linkage of north-south roads running from Germanna Ford down to Spot-sylvania Court House. The more northerly of the east-west roads was known as the Orange Court House and Fredericksburg Turn-pike, or more briefly as the Orange Turnpike. Once it had been a famous post road, but by the spring of 1864 it was a ghost highway—the stables and taverns along it sinking into lonesome ruins, the forest hugging ever closer, the pike itself just a com-mon dirt road. Generally parallel to the turnpike and just south of it was the Orange and Fredericksburg Plank Road, in about the same state of decay. These forest-walled avenues and a few other short connecting roads formed only thin shafts of light through an area that was one of tactical darkness. It would be hard to imagine a worse place to fight; and yet the fortunes of war would put the 20th Maine right in the middle of it.

There was a new general in charge now; he had made a big name in the West, and the name was Ulysses Simpson Grant. The name suited him perfectly. Ulysses had a heroic ring, bal-anced by Simpson, which suggested a plain ordinary Yankee, and tempered by Grant, which had a feeling of the granitic hardness that was in the man. To the soldiers of the 20th Maine, this small, hands-in-the-pocket, cigar-smoking officer would not resemble other generals they had known. Grant looked more like a small-town businessman who was about to make a deal on a hundred tons of hay.

As he gazed south with his reflective squint, Grant was thinking about war in a businesslike way. He knew that he would have a marked superiority in manpower and resources. His idea was to close with Lee and destroy him by a process of continuous hammering. From now on there would be no far-flung fancy maneuvers, no withdrawals to reorganize, no holding of large bodies of troops in reserve. Grant was going in with everything he had.

In preparation for the spring campaign there was a tactical massing of Union forces. The Army of the Potomac was consolidated into three large corps—the Second, Fifth and Sixth Corps. General Warren, who had done so well in '63, was placed in command of the Fifth Corps, much to the satisfaction of the Maine men. The old 3rd Brigade of the Fifth Corps' 1st Division —which had included the 20th Maine, 83rd Pennsylvania, 44th New York and 16th Michigan—was now increased by the addition of the 1st Michigan, 18th Massachusetts and 118th Pennsylvania. Toward the 118th Pennsylvania, the Maine regiment felt a special kinship. The 118th, the Corn Exchange Regiment, had joined the army in early September of 1862, along with the 20th Maine and the two regiments had since then served in the 1st Division. Along with the 20th, the Pennsylvania regiment had had its nose bloodied at Shepherdstown Ford, following which wags in the army with more wit than compassion sometimes referred to it as the Cob Exchange Regiment; all the kernels had been shelled off at Shepherdstown Ford, they would point out. But in spite of its early reverse, the Corn Exchange Regiment had developed into a good outfit and the Maine soldiers would be glad to have it alongside.

As for the 20th Maine, it too had come a long way since autumn of 1862. Since Little Round Top the 20th had been well and favorably known throughout the army. During the first four months of the year the regiment had received over a hundred recruits, including the expected number of substitutes and bounty jumpers. But on the whole, the 20th Maine was a seasoned and battle wise regiment. In appraising its numerical strength, there were two figures to look at—*Enlisted Men Present,* and *Enlisted Men Present for Duty.* Higher headquarters always seemed to be looking at the first, or larger number when it came to detailing men from the regiment for extra duty. Men were snatched away to serve in brigade and division headquarters; on brigade, division and provost guard; as division messengers and corps mail carriers; as pioneers, teamsters, cattle guards, orderlies, ambulancemen and hospital attendants; even as cannoneers in the batteries. Typically, on May 1, there were 510 men *Present* in the 20th Maine, but only 405 available for service with the regiment. Many of the men who made up the difference were off somewhere, performing guard, administrative and other duties for which the Civil War corps organization apparently made no other provision. This difference of 105 between *Present* and *Present for Duty* was about the average that would prevail for all the rest of 1864.

On the whole, the 20th Maine had spent a quiet winter—drilling, standing inspections, firing on the target range, doing picket duty, washing clothing, reading, writing letters and—for entertainment—attending an occasional prayer meeting. It was too quiet in some ways, and there had been evidences of restlessness. One sergeant had been reduced to ranks for forging the major's name on a whiskey order and getting drunk. Captain Walter G. Morrill had been involved in a scuffle with the Quartermaster, injuring himself so badly that he'd been laid up for days. A private had been shot through the head by a tentmate who had pointed an "unloaded" rifle at him and pulled the trigger. Even William Livermore, usually a model of soldierly deportment, had been arraigned before the regimental commander for making grimaces at the musicians during a formation.

In its command, the 20th Maine was still fortunate. In the absence of its two higher-ranking officers, Chamberlain and Gilmore both being in Washington serving as members of courts-martial, the top place was being ably filled by Major Ellis Spear. Judged merely by his physical appearance, Spear had turned out to be one of the surprise packages of the regiment. A slender man, of a constitution described in those days as "delicate," Spear hadn't been expected by the folks back home in Maine to last long in the war. But he had since had the satisfaction of telling them, while home on leave, that he had "enjoyed perfect

175

health, except for a bad cold caused by sleeping one night in a house," instead of on the tented field.

This was the regiment on May 1, 1864, and it would never be the same again. For although Grant's brutally simple strategy was a good one for winning a war, the cost would be high at the regimental level.

Preparations for a major campaign had begun to be apparent early in April. The men were hopeful—but they had a few misgivings, for there had been plans for big campaigns before, and these had all come to nothing. Will Owen wrote to his sister, "We have men enough and they will *fight* if our leading men will do what is right. It is no use for men to say that it has been impossible to settle this up before. I know that there has been men and money enough and *now* with this Grand Army of Volunteers if we are defeated it will be with mismanagement, nothing else. The Army is now most old and tried soldiers and veterans. They know how to fight and expect to. What will then defeat us? Mismanagement?"

By April 16, the regiment had packed up its overcoats and other extra clothing to be shipped back to Washington for storage. Sutlers and civilians were ordered to leave, and a few days later all the sick were sent away.

On May Day they broke camp at Rappahannock Station and crossed the Rappahannock River, marching to a bivouac near Brandy Station. Next day the brigade attempted to hold a dress parade. It was interrupted by a bad omen. A black cloud rushed in from the west, darkening the sky. Roaring winds came with it, and the air was filled with blinding clouds of fine sand. Torrents of rain followed, and the dress parade broke up as the men rushed for shelter.

After a wet, miserable night, May 3 was clear and pleasant. They moved to the vicinity of Culpeper Court House and went into bivouac again. Now they were near the Rapidan and some sort of monkey business was clearly afoot. Near midnight they were turned out and set in motion again, toward the river. Ahead they could see fires burning to mark a route toward Raccoon Ford; but this, they decided, was a fakery to indicate a crossing at that point that was never intended, for suddenly they turned

to the left and headed down river, in the darkness. By morning
they were at Germanna Ford, several miles below. Here Union
cavalry had cleared away a light screen of Confederate vedettes,
pontoon bridges had been placed, and the army was crossing.
In his strategy, Grant had not completely abandoned fast foot-
work. He was attempting to get on the right flank of the Army
of Northern Virginia, which could not well be assaulted frontally,
since it lay behind extensive entrenchments along the upper
Rapidan. Grant's plan was to move swiftly across the Rapidan
at a point well to the east of the heavily defended stretch of the
river, turn Lee's right flank, and force him to come out of his
entrenchments and fight, or else be attacked from the rear.

The movement over the Rapidan that day was an event long
remembered by the survivors of the 20th Maine. It marked the
opening of a big campaign of the army, and at the same time
they seemed to sense that it marked the ending of an era in the
life of the regiment. The day was bright and clear, white clouds
floating in a sky of luminous blue, yellow primroses glowing in
the fields beside the road. A springlike bloom was on the army,
too; it marched down to the ford with colors waving over the
columns of blue and the bands playing lively airs. In the 20th
Maine, it was remembered that Grant's presence with the army,
after his successes in the West, gave them a feeling of enthusiasm
they had not had for many months. But it was somehow like the
sailing of a great ship that would never return, or a closing of a
door that would never again be opened—this crossing of the
Rapidan. An officer who watched the men of the 20th Maine and
other units march over the pontoon bridges noted the bright
youthfulness of many of their faces. Thirty days later he looked
at them again and was struck with the impression that the youthfulness had all been left behind. A little more than a year later,
when everything was all over, the 20th Maine, going north on its
homeward march, passed over most of the rivers the war had
made familiar. But it never recrossed, never saw the Rapidan
again. Both geographically and historically the river marked a
line of no-return.

By midafternoon they had reached a crossroads clearing in the
northern part of the Wilderness, and here the corps made a vast

encampment—more than twenty-five thousand men spread out through meadow and forest, rows of stacked rifles like shocks of dark corn, tents and headquarters flags, parks of artillery and white-topped wagons, thousands of fires sending up tiny columns of smoke. After the long stay in winter camp, the activity in the fine spring weather had been invigorating and the men felt good. Bands got out their instruments, and there was music as the sun went down, with the fluffy spring clouds slowly changing from soft crimson to purple above the dark green of the pine forest to the westward.

With the coming of night, the mood changed. A breeze was blowing, and the tops of the pine trees, dark against the sky, began to sway and sigh. It grew ominously quiet. Off in the dark forest the whippoorwills were crying. An owl hooted. There was something sinister about this wild and wooded region by night and something disquieting about the fact that their advance thus far had been unopposed.

To General Warren (now the Fifth Corps commander) the danger could be seen in more specific terms as he studied his maps and orders by the flickering lantern light at corps headquarters. The plan was that the corps would move south through the Wilderness in the morning, thence out into the open country where Grant hoped to meet Lee and give him battle. But the period during which they would be moving through the forest area would offer special hazards. The Army of Northern Virginia was somewhere off to the west, and there were two main roads leading in from that direction. If the Confederates came driving in along these roads, striking the Union column at right angles tomorrow just when it would be strung out in its southward march, a disaster would be highly possible.

The danger was recognized in orders from Army for the following day's movements. Paragraph three said that Warren was to move his Fifth Corps south starting at five A.M. Paragraph four said that the Sixth Corps would follow him.

But paragraph nine said ". . . the commanders of the Fifth and Sixth corps will keep out detachments on the roads on their right flank. . . . These flankers and pickets will be thrown well out and their troops be held ready to meet the enemy at any moment."

General Warren had already made certain dispositions with this in mind. Griffin's 1st Division—which included the 20th Maine in its 3rd Brigade—had already gone out on the Orange Turnpike about a mile. There they had formed a line of battle and were resting for the night on the line, while outposts had been established farther out.

The job of the division was to guard this approach firmly, and yet not be stampeded into a fruitless battle by firecracker fights that Lee's reconnaissance raids might set off in the morning. And for this job, the division was admirably chosen. It had a hard core of Regulars, along with its seasoned volunteer regiments. And it was commanded by a cool, tough and aggressive officer, Brigadier General Charles Griffin. A West Point graduate who prior to the war had served in Mexico and on the western frontier, Griffin was a combination of strict disciplinarian and ardent scrapper—the two do not always go together. There were many stories about him in the 3rd Brigade.

One concerned a dress parade at which the General had been present. An adjutant, dressed in unorthodox corduroys, with brightly polished top boots outside his pants, had just reported, "Sir, the parade is formed," when General Griffin interrupted him. "No, it is not, sir! Nor will it be until you return from your quarters clothed in the uniform of your rank; and, recollect, sir, with your pants outside of your boots." He had then turned and chewed the Colonel. "I had hoped, sir, this would have received attention before I was compelled to notice it. You will bring your command to an order and await the adjutant's return." And the regiment had to stand at attention until the discomfited adjutant returned from his quarters in proper uniform.

And another story: Griffin one time had noticed a battery firing too high; their shots were knocking the branches off trees over a body of enemy cavalry. Griffin, who was an old artilleryman, had rushed in and showed the gunners just how it should be done, shouting, "You are firing too high; just roll the shot along the ground like a tenpin ball and knock their damned trotters from under them."

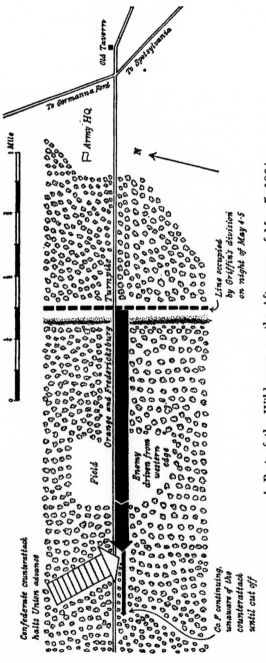

A Part of the Wilderness on the Afternoon of May 5, 1864

Black arrow shows the advance of the 20th Maine until halted by Confederate counterattack

So there was a great deal of respect for Griffin in the ranks of the 20th Maine, and the men were well satisfied to be under his command as they rested on what they hoped would be a temporary line across the Orange Turnpike. The night passed quietly, and dawn of May 5 brought in another beautiful morning, with sunlight coming in through the pines in sharp, slanting rays, and the birds cheerfully active in the branches overhead. Out on the turnpike ahead of them, the outpost commander soon discovered that more than birds were stirring. He sent a rider galloping back to headquarters with a message:

> THE REBEL INFANTRY HAVE APPEARED ON THE ORANGE COURT HOUSE TURNPIKE AND ARE FORMING A LINE OF BATTLE, THREE-QUARTERS OF A MILE IN FRONT OF GENERAL GRIFFIN'S LINE OF BATTLE. I HAVE MY SKIRMISHERS OUT, AND PREPARATIONS ARE BEING MADE TO MEET THEM. THERE IS A LARGE CLOUD OF DUST IN THAT DIRECTION.

General Warren was not greatly disturbed and was still of a mind to start the Fifth Corps south on its march as ordered. But more messages were soon flying. At six A.M., Warren sent one to Army.

> GENERAL GRIFFIN HAS JUST SENT IN WORD THAT A FORCE OF THE ENEMY HAS BEEN REPORTED TO HIM COMING DOWN THE TURNPIKE. THE FOUNDATION OF THE REPORT IS NOT GIVEN. UNTIL IT IS MORE DEFINITELY ASCERTAINED NO CHANGE WILL TAKE PLACE IN THE MOVEMENTS ORDERED. SUCH DEMONSTRATIONS ARE TO BE EXPECTED, AND SHOW THE NECESSITY FOR KEEPING WELL CLOSED AND PREPARED TO FACE TOWARD MINE RUN AND MEET AN ATTACK AT A MOMENT'S NOTICE.

There was a serious flaw in this supposition; Lee was making the "demonstration" with an entire corps of infantry, and more were on the way. Warren started his Fifth Corps south as planned. However, he left Griffin's division on the Orange Turnpike with orders to push out and find out what force the enemy had.

As the morning wore on, the reports coming back through channels sounded worse and worse, until Meade was sending this to Grant:

> THE ENEMY HAVE APPEARED IN FORCE ON THE ORANGE PIKE, AND ARE NOW REPORTED FORMING LINE OF BATTLE IN FRONT OF GRIFFIN'S DIVISION, FIFTH CORPS. I HAVE DIRECTED GENERAL WARREN TO ATTACK THEM AT ONCE WITH HIS WHOLE FORCE. UNTIL THIS MOVEMENT OF THE ENEMY IS DEVELOPED, THE MARCH OF THE CORPS MUST BE SUSPENDED. . . .

And there was a passage in the reply from Grant which set the tone for the entire campaign that followed:

> . . . IF ANY OPPORTUNITY PRESENTS ITSELF FOR PITCHING INTO A PART OF LEE'S ARMY, DO SO WITHOUT GIVING TIME FOR DISPOSITION.

Out on the Orange Turnpike with Griffin's Division, where the "pitching in" would have to be done, there was a smell of cool morning on the forest floor, the scent of fresh earth dug up for trenches, of crushed pine needles, wood smoke from the breakfast fires, coffee fragrance. And soon, the smell of danger. Orders came to throw up breastworks. Trees were chopped down—familiar work for the woodsmen of the 20th—for a distance of ten rods in front of the position in order to gain a clear field of fire. The logs were brought in and piled up to make the breastworks.

This work was soon over and then there was time to think—always a bad practice for the private soldier, there being no rational process whereby he can bring himself to a suitable state of mind for getting shot. For example, he could consider that with personal existence gone, it would not matter to him whether the Union stood or fell—nor would anything else matter at all. And so the process of reasoning would have to be suppressed by a self-imposed censorship, or else it might very logically lead to the conclusion that the soldier ought to get himself out of there while the going was good. And that, obviously, would not be the right thing to do.

One of the men in the 20th observed the different ways in which his comrades were reacting. Some were laughing and joking, nervously excited. But the thinkers were having a bad time of it. He noticed that the more thoughtful class was lying on the ground, silent, with lips compressed, seeming not to notice what went on around them.

Captain A. M. Judson of the 83rd Pennsylvania, who saw the 20th Maine in action many times during the war, and who did a lot of fighting alongside them, and whose own regiment lost more men killed in the war than any other Union regiment but one, had some interesting speculations on the qualities that keep a man going in battle. For some men, he thought, it was the fear of punishment and disgrace; for others who were desirous of rank —ambition; but for most, he thought, it was moral principle or a sense of duty. The brawlers and fighters in civilian life, in his opinion, did not usually have an equal appetite for fighting in battle, because war required a different kind of courage which he identified as moral courage. He believed that "men of the most reliable principles in private life make the best and bravest soldiers in the field. Therefore you will always find that quarrelsome bullies, thieves, cheats, sneaks and liars, or to sum it all up in one word, unprincipled men in private life, are, without exception, cowards and poltroons in the army. A bad man may not fear his inferior in strength, but he dreads a death grapple with the King of Terrors."

Judson also thought that courage was very much a matter of stomach condition. "I have seen men fight well one day, when their stomachs were in good order, and give evidences of timidity the next, when their stomachs were out of order. A fit of indigestion makes a coward, for the time, of many a supposed hero."

The 20th Maine knew the importance of the stomach, and in this period of waiting the veterans were boiling coffee and eating hard tack. Around noon General Warren came riding down the line of breastworks, and they stood up to give him a cheer, remembering his famous day at Gettysburg.

Then it was time. Griffin was moving out to see what the Confederates had to offer. The 3rd Brigade, with its right on the turnpike, had the center of the advance, with a brigade on either side. In keeping with his aggressive ideas on the employment of field artillery, General Griffin had pushed a couple of guns out on the road, but there was little the gunners could see to shoot at except the road itself.

So it would all be up to the infantry. In the 3rd Brigade, the attacking regiments were advancing in the following arrangement:

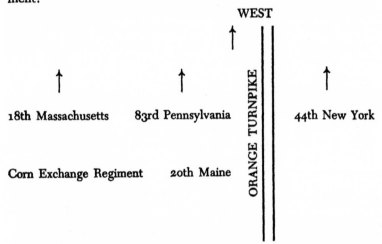

On the turnpike, the two fieldpieces were firing bravely, their projectiles swishing off down the road. In the woods, a far-spreading crackling and snapping of branches as the infantry advanced. Before long—still not able to see what was ahead of them—they began to run into rifle fire. And very soon the heavy jungle growth swallowed up and began to disorganize the lines. The brush was tearing at men's clothing, slapping them in the eyes, catching at their feet. Through the tangle a man could see only a few friends on either side, and of the enemy he could see nothing at all. Yet bullets were coming from somewhere, snapping through the leaves and occasionally cutting off a branch. Ahead the firing was developing into what a soldier in the Corn Exchange Regiment described as "a wild, wicked roar of musketry, reverberating through the forests with a deep and hollow sound." With vision so limited, and units becoming separated, every regiment had a horror of pushing out too far and being flanked; the possibilities for panic were very great. Men began shouting—perhaps at first to let each other know where they were—but later using the shout as an offensive weapon. The Confederates had always been famous for their yelling in battles, but here in the Wilderness there would be a Yankee yell, also. The yellers could not be seen, and a company could make itself sound like a regiment if it shouted loud enough. Men spoke later of various units on both sides being "yelled" out of their positions.

The 20th Maine, which was moving in the second line of battle with the Corn Exchange Regiment, came to the edge of a field and re-formed its lines to charge across the open area. The main Confederate line was apparently on the other side of the field. The fire coming across at them was the heaviest they had ever seen. Lieutenant Holman S. Melcher, twenty-two-year-old six-footer who had sparked the charge at Little Round Top, described the visible effect . . . "The bugles sounded the 'Charge' and advancing to the edge of the field, we saw the first line of battle about half way across it, receiving a terribly fatal fire from an enemy in the woods on the farther side. This field was less than a quarter of a mile across, had been planted with corn the year before, and was now dry and dusty. We could see the spurts of dust started up all over the field by the bullets of the enemy, as they spattered on it like the big drops of a coming shower you have so often seen along a dusty road."

For the Wilderness, the field was a large one—one of the few open areas. Extending on both sides of the pike, it was about eight hundred yards north and south. East and west it was about four hundred yards, and this was the distance the 20th Maine would have to traverse. The ground sloped down to a gully in the middle—the dry bed of a stream—and then ascended to the Confederate works on the west side.

The brigade commander, now General Joseph J. Bartlett, led the charge across the field. A dark, handsome man, Bartlett was exceedingly fond of dress; once when he had appeared in a uniform brilliant with gold lace, General Griffin—a plain sort himself—had inquired, "Well, Bartlett, when will the rest of the circus arrive?" Bartlett was too brave for his own good on this afternoon, and with his circus-pony trappings, too conspicuous. But he had a charmed life, and he would be seen performing heroics and acrobatics all over the field as the enemy tried vainly to shoot him.

They went across the field at a run—a scattered, irregular blue line, thinning as it went, with men stopping, staggering, falling as though they were continually running into invisible wires. To Private Gerrish, the shadows of the trees on the enemy side of the field stood out in conscious memory. He recalled dashing up a little swell of ground and into the shadows, and then a red volcano seeming to erupt in front of him as the Confederates poured out a volley. The 20th was in good stomach that day; it went right in until the two sides were firing in each other's faces with rifle barrels almost touching. There was a high-pitched medley of musketry, yelling, cursing and screaming and then this Confederate line also gave way, and the Maine men went farther on into the woods. Here, too, the enemy fire was intense.

Will Owen recalled that "the balls were cutting the little limbs of the trees so they fell like leaves in Autumn." Owen got about four rods into the woods when one of the balls went through the calf of his right leg and he was through for the day—and the summer. Owen fell, got up, and went hobbling to the rear while the regiment crushed onward. The growth they were now in was just as thick and tangled as the first stretch had been. The 83rd Pennsylvania, which had charged ahead of them in the first line of battle, had been badly cut up and was now further disorganized by the jungle. So the 20th Maine moved through it and pushed on in the forefront of the attack. All around them the clatter of musketry was growing and it had an unfamiliar sound, because it was not accompanied by the deeper bellowing of massed artillery that had always been present in other battles. One soldier described it as the noise of a boy running with a stick pressed against a paling fence, faster and faster until it swelled into a continuous rattling roar. Smoke from the firing hung under the branches and added its gray haze to the already impossible obscurity. And soon there was smoke from another

186

source. From the hot muzzle blasts of the muskets (the men might just as safely have been carrying blowtorches), little flames caught and flew away through the tinderlike dry stuff. A strong breeze was blowing and fanned the flames higher. Before long, forest fires were starting and the smoke went up to dim the sky.

Crashing on through the underbrush, still driving the Confederates, the 20th Maine, with its right on the turnpike, came out into a second field. This clearing was smaller than the first one, so that the right of the regiment was in the clearing, while its left was still buried in the forest. Major Spear ordered the colors out into the field and was just forming the regiment on them when a deadly volley came in from the right and rear. The worst had come to pass. The 20th Maine was flanked.

What had happened was this: while the 20th Maine and other regiments on the left of the pike had been making good progress, troops on the right of the road had run into serious trouble and hadn't been able to keep up. Unaware of this fact, in the obscurity of the forest and the noise of battle, the 3rd Brigade had been moving forward with its right flank in the air. At the same time, the Confederates were launching a powerful counterattack. When the first blast of killing fire came in from the right, the Maine men were indignant as well as alarmed; they thought Federal troops were firing on them. Not so, they soon discovered. These were Confederate bullets, and enemy infantrymen were swarming into their right and rear in frightening numbers.

The regiment tried a maneuver that had worked at Little Round Top, but it didn't work here. Captain Walter G. Morrill took what he had left of his Company B and, with fragments of other regiments, formed a bent-back line facing the turnpike. For a few minutes they held the Confederates in check. Then a Minié ball crashed through Morrill's face, knocking him down. Morrill got up, tied a handkerchief around his face and went on fighting, but soon he was blinded and gargling in his own blood, and his men took him to the rear.

By now the attack was all over and the brigade was retreating to avoid capture. Most of the men got into the woods and made their way back to the Union breastworks. But a few who had been advancing through the thick woods on the left did not learn that the brigade had been flanked. Lieutenant Holman Melcher, pushing on with a remnant of his command, Company F, noticed after a while that the firing had died away and there were no Confederates in front of him. Furthermore, he couldn't find the rest of the 20th Maine anywhere. While he was pondering this mystery, one of his men came up and said, "Lieutenant, come this way and let me show you something." The man led Melcher over to the Orange Turnpike and pointed back along it toward the Union lines. "See that!"

Looking down the straight, level road Melcher saw something that, as he said later, froze the blood in his veins. A strong column of Confederate infantry was moving across the road into his rear, completely cutting off the way of retreat. Surmising what had happened to the rest of the brigade, Melcher held a brief council of war with his first sergeant, Ammi M. Smith. They had two choices: submit to capture, or cut their way back through the enemy lines. Counting noses they found that they had eighteen including Melcher. The young officer and his first sergeant decided that it would be worth while to try to cut their way back; in the uproar of a battle like this anything could happen and they might be successful. Melcher called the men together, explained the situation, and declared that he, for one, would rather die making the attempt than rot in a rebel prison. Would they stand by him? The answer was yes.

Melcher ordered, "Every man load his rifle, fix bayonet and follow me." He then attempted to lead his little band around the right of the Confederate line, which had formed between them and the Union forces. This proved to be impossible. The Confederates, by now, had extended too far. The only chance was to drive through them. Melcher formed an eighteen-man "line of battle," with Smith on the left while he took the right. As silently as they could, the Maine men approached the Confederate infantrymen, who fortunately were so intent on the Yankees in their front that they were not aware of the eighteen coming from the rear. The character of the Wilderness battle was all in Melcher's favor. When an assault was made through the smoke and dense underbrush, there was no way of telling whether it was being made by a squad or a regiment. Within fifteen paces of the Confederate line, each of Melcher's soldiers picked his man, fired, and charged, yelling, "Surrender!" This was the sort of thing that was happening all the time in the battle of the Wilderness—groups of Confederates and Federals alike thinking they were outflanked or surrounded and giving way to sudden panics. There were a few seconds of wild confusion and a series of nightmarish incidents. A Confederate turned, pointed his rifle at one of Melcher's soldiers who was only a boy, and pulled the trigger with the muzzle only a few inches from the lad's face. There was a click; the gun did not go off. The look of imminent death in the boy's face was replaced with one of tearful rage as he lunged forward and pinned the gray infantryman horribly to the ground with his bayonet, crying, "I'll teach you, old Reb, how to snap your gun in my face!"

In another incident, Melcher saw a tall, lank Confederate raising his musket to fire on a Maine man, and realized that he was the only one near enough to help. Melcher sprang forward, swinging his sword in a mighty downward stroke, but he was so anxious to connect before the man could fire that he struck before he got quite near enough. The point of the blade nicked the scalp of the Confederate and split his coat all the way down the back. That was near enough for the Southerner. He dropped his gun without firing and surrendered.

By now this portion of the Confederate line, astonished and terrified by the unexpected attack, was completely demoralized, many fleeing through the woods, and thirty-two surrendering. Melcher had lost two killed, with several wounded, but all the wounded were moving under their own power. By spreading his little company thin, the young officer was able to surround his captives and start them moving toward the Union lines ahead. A few of the prisoners, seeing the smallness of his force for the first time, hesitated, but Melcher drew a revolver (which he had completely forgotten to use in the excitement of the fray) and with this he persuaded them to keep moving.

Weird incidents continued. One of Melcher's men suddenly took fright and dived behind a log, where he huddled in abject terror. Melcher shouted, "Come on, come along with us, George, or you'll be captured." Childishly and nonsensically, the man cried, "Don't let them know I am here!" Melcher later learned that he was captured and starved to death in Andersonville Prison.

Herding his prisoners along, Melcher struck the main Union line some distance from the point to which the rest of the regiment had returned. He passed through, delivered his prisoners to division headquarters in the rear, then returned, coming up behind the 20th Maine, now safe behind the breastworks. Here the final incident took place. Seeing Melcher approaching from the rear, Captain W. W. Morrell (not to be confused with Captain W. G. Morrill) shouted "Well, Lieutenant, how did things look down at Rappahannock Station?" The inference—that Melcher and his men had skedaddled all the way back to their old winter quarters—was painfully clear, and Melcher recalled that the remark stung him like a viper. So there were hard feelings, and the two young officers never had the opportunity to clear up the misunderstanding. Three days later Morrell was dead and Melcher was on a stretcher, headed for the hospital.

Some of the wounded had a harder time getting back to the Union breastworks, and many did not get back at all. One soldier of the 20th Maine described the experience of being struck by a bullet. The first sensation he had was that of falling heavily on the ground with his leg numb to the hip. He at first thought that his foot had been shot off but discovered that it was a bullet through the ankle. The trees around him were on fire and the Confederates were coming. Fear brought him to his feet and he found that he could walk. But for some reason, if he bent his knee the ankle gave way, and he would fall, so after a few hard falls he kept the leg stiff and made surprisingly good speed. Crossing the field over which they had previously advanced, he paused to watch an awesome spectacle.

It was General Bartlett, dashing out of the woods on horseback with the enemy yelling and shooting behind him. Bartlett was alone; his fancy uniform was torn; blood was trickling down his face. The horse, with rider perfectly erect, went across the field at a tremendous gait, with hundreds of bullets flying in pursuit. Halfway across there was a ditch, six feet deep and ten or twelve feet across. The horse gathered itself for the fearful leap and flew into the air—nostrils dilated, ears pointed forward, eyes flashing. A bullet caught the animal in midflight; it turned a complete somersault and fell dead, the rider underneath. Surprisingly, Bartlett crawled out from under the dead horse and made his escape into the woods beyond. The soldier ran, stiff-legged, after him.

Counting up his casualties after this first day's fighting, Major Ellis Spear could report that the regiment had lost heavily: eleven killed, fifty-eight wounded and sixteen missing. And the night that followed was worse, in many ways, than the day had been. This was the night when hell went into high gear below the Rapidan. Nerves on both sides had been badly shaken by the confusions and terrors of the day. There was uneasy, frantic firing most of the night, with bullets sweeping low through the bushes. The forest fires were making a reddish glow through the trees and on the sky. Thick smoke covered the ground. Underneath all this lay the wounded, where no one could get at them. And the wounded cried for help.

The progress of some of their tragedies could be heard in the voices. A wounded man would see the fire approaching and would start calling, his voice changing to insane terror and finally to screams of pain. If the hurt man could manage it, a shot might end the matter. So it was a bad night, and yet as a man in the Corn Exchange Regiment put it, the soldiers behind the breastworks "did not seem to have such conception of its horrors as they had upon reflection in after years. . . ."

On the next day, May 6, there was no significant action on the front of Griffin's division, but the rest of the army was heavily engaged on the right and left, along an irregular line five or six miles long through the Wilderness. Beginning soon after dawn, the tumult of battle on the left rolled up to a high-pitched, throbbing roar, louder, more continuous than ever. The 20th Maine, with the rest of the division, moved out to a position in front of the breastworks and lay on the defense most of the day. The Confederates opposite them had somehow got some artillery into action, and the Maine men lost two killed and ten wounded under artillery and sniper fire.

Toward night, the Sixth Corps on their right was heavily attacked and "yelled out" of its entrenchments by the Confederates. A few of Griffin's regiments, fearful of being flanked again, withdrew; but the 20th Maine and most of the 3rd Brigade held fast. And the Sixth Corps, much to their relief, regained its position and once again covered their right flank.

Dawn of May 7 was foggy and smoky; visibility zero; smell terrible, with the Wilderness reeking of sulphurous gunpowder fumes, burned bodies, burning forest. It was hard to tell where sounds were coming from, but all around there seemed to be less firing. In front of Griffin's division, however, there was action at six A.M. Confederates came in suddenly out of the gray murk, broke up the picket line and got within rifle range of the breastworks. Driven back by repeated volleys, they nevertheless left a swarm of sharpshooters in the woods and these began to be highly annoying to General Griffin. So there was an advance to clear out the snipers, and stories to the effect that some of them were shot out of the trees, while others leaped from branch to branch like squirrels and got away.

Then later in the day, the 20th Maine and the Corn Exchange Regiment went out to make a brief demonstration which came to nothing in particular. There was skirmishing and incoming artillery fire that knocked off a good many treetops, but did little damage.

In this action there was a human incident, strangely enough not recorded by any member of the 20th Maine, or even by a member of their brigade, but by a soldier of the 155th Pennsylvania. He wrote of how the 20th Maine came out to relieve them on a skirmish line, and of how they went back to the position vacated by the 20th Maine and found good cooking fires burning behind the breastworks. A group of men from the 155th promptly began boiling coffee, and a solid shot came down and scattered fire, cups and coffee in all directions, which "induced strong language from some of the boys." At about this time a sergeant of the 20th Maine, who had remained behind to gather up some of his gear, quickly followed the regiment out to the skirmish line. Ten minutes later he was carried back dead, a bullet having gone straight through his chest. The Pennsylvanian wrote that "the grief of his brother, who helped carry him back, was pitiable."

It was a sorrowful day in other ways. One of the wounded of the 20th Maine who was back at a field hospital a few hundred yards behind the lines reported that there were scores of rumors flying, all different in their portrayal of disaster—but all agreeing that the army had been defeated. He was in a good position to observe that the losses had been frightful. (The army had actually lost between 17,000 and 18,000 men.)

They had expected great things of General Grant, but he had brought them only another harvest of death. The soldier wrote that many of the wounded forgot their wounds and wept. There would be now, they expected, another retreat across the Rapidan and the Rappahannock, another general, another period of waiting, and the war going on its weary way forever.

In the course of the afternoon, the 20th Maine discovered that it would share in the duty of covering the Fifth Corps withdrawal. What amounted to a picket brigade was made up: the 20th Maine, 16th Michigan, the Corn Exchange Regiment, and detachments from the 9th and 22nd Massachusetts. The little force would be under the command of a good officer, Colonel Charles P. Herring of the Corn Exchange Regiment, and it had a responsible job to do.

Herring got his command lined up in late afternoon, and in order to keep the withdrawal of the corps from being observed, he ordered an advance to push the enemy back. The 20th Maine and the 16th Michigan led in the push. Moving, as one of the Pennsylvanians noted, "with its usual vigor," the 20th Maine struck the enemy pickets and ran them back about five hundred yards, right into the Confederate breastworks. Then the 20th, under heavy musketry and artillery fire, pulled back, and Herring's little picket brigade formed an advance line. For the 20th Maine, fifteen casualties was the price of this affair.

At dark, the corps started fading away behind them. It appeared that the Confederates were fading from their front, too. An officer of the 83rd Pennsylvania remembered that "they yelled as they went, and as their voices kept going further and further away, this was the first evidence we had that they were also on the move. They even got started in advance of us."

As the exhausted men of the 20th Maine began their rear-guard vigil on the smoky wreckage of the battlefield, they might have reflected upon the past three days with a certain bitterness. The regiment had lost well over one hundred men in killed, wounded and missing—the worst since Gettysburg. Yet there had been no victory—or if there had been one, the Army of the Potomac certainly had not won it. If there was any consolation, it was in knowing that the losses of the Confederates must have been equally heavy.

So it might have been an occasion for gloom and grief, but behind them, where the army was presumably withdrawing, something was happening that would give the tired regiment an electrifying shot in the arm. Word came that the army was not going back across the Rapidan. It was moving south! The Fifth Corps had turned and gone down the road toward Spotsylvania Court House.

That little fellow, Grant! He hadn't won, but he was *acting like a winner.* Here at last was a general who was going to get this thing over with. In three days he had taken them straight into hell and it looked like there would be more of the same. But even hell was hopeful if there was a manifest determination to come out on the other side.

CHAPTER ELEVEN

On the Grinding Wheel

HE war up until now had been a fire-and-fall-back affair, with plenty of time between battles—time in which a man could get some rest, wash his shirt, clean his equipment, read the papers and think about things, so that the fighting could be seen in some sort of rational perspective. But from now on everything would be badly mixed up—the battles, and even the days and nights, all running together with a sort of desperate urgency, like the episodes of a feverish hallucination.

And for the man who came out of the Wilderness on a stretcher or slung blanket, there would be delirium in reality. The flow of wounded from Griffin's Division had begun about noon on May 5, and by nine that evening over twelve hundred had been received at the hospitals in their rear—an average of better than two a minute. The doctors had been prepared for business, but not for any like this. When the stream of wounded continued at a similar rate throughout the army for the next two days, it began to be apparent that there would be a serious transportation problem. It had first been planned to take the wounded back by the way the army had come, over the Rapidan. But that line of communication had now been abandoned, so it became necessary to haul them across country to Fredericksburg.

For this purpose, all the wagons that could be spared by the army were taken over, but even these were insufficient and ill-adapted to the need. The wagons normally used for hauling baggage, ammunition and other supplies did not have the springs necessary for an easy ride. The medical people tried to provide some cushioning effect by placing boughs in the beds of the

195

wagons and placing blankets or shelter tents over the boughs. But comfort was out of the question. One wounded soldier from the 20th Maine, shot through the arm, was placed in a wagon with nine companions; he got on his knees and held his painfully throbbing arm in his uninjured hand to guard it against the jar and vibration, little realizing how long his journey would be. Another man from the 20th Maine stated that he was jammed into a baggage wagon with twelve others. All vehicles were similarly packed, and the work of loading them took a long time. Then the long train started off. The roads were rough; the wagons rocked and jolted; the wounded cried out; after a while, blood began to run through the wagon beds and drip on the road. With all the swaying and jolting, arteries that had been secured by the surgeons were breaking open, and men were bleeding to death.

The Maine soldiers believed that the wagons in which they were riding were on the road from Saturday night, May 7, until noon Monday. And when the flood of wounded finally came pouring into Fredericksburg, little relief awaited them except the merciful conclusion of the wagon ride. The authorities in Washington had had no advance warning of this diversion of the wounded to Fredericksburg; food and medical supplies were on the way but hadn't arrived. The citizens of Fredericksburg, aghast at this sudden torrent of misery into their town, had not been well conditioned to act as ministering angels. The army's public relations with Fredericksburg were about as bad as they could be. In December of 1862 Burnside had knocked the town to pieces with his cannon, and his soldiers had ransacked it from one end to the other. The more cruel and unfeeling of the citizenry must have taken a savage delight at this turn of events, if they hadn't already seen a sufficient number of dead Yankees on the slopes of Marye's Heights. The more charitable, who were by far in the majority, lacked the facilities even to begin to care for the thousands of suffering men who were dumped into every yard, square and vacant building.

Mrs. Charles A. L. Sampson, a worker from the Maine Soldiers' Relief Association, who had arrived in Fredericksburg, learned that there were some Maine soldiers in the stores on one of the downtown streets. She described what followed: "As yet our supplies had not arrived, but we went down, and by the light of one solitary candle in each store, beheld such wretchedness and suffering as we had never before seen. On every counter and shelf, abreast the counters, under the counters and on the floor before them, without blankets even were our noble boys, officers and soldiers sharing the same hard fate, each seriously wounded; and not only were they suffering from wounds, but from hunger and thirst; and though the weather was warm, many were suffering with chills. We could do little for their comfort that night, but to assure them of care on the morrow; that we had come with tokens of love from their friends who were thinking of and praying for them, and that this was surely the darkest hour of their lives. It encouraged them to feel that some friends from their own State had come to their relief; some of them cried for joy, and we cried with them."

And this was not the end, but only the beginning. More wounded men were pouring in from the south. Grant's new war policies were, in operation, producing casualties at a rate that had never been equaled. One of the Maine wounded in Fredericksburg heard "the growling of a distant cannonade" and he wondered how the 20th was doing.

The 20th Maine was doing well, but it wasn't too happy.

At about one o'clock on the morning of the eighth the Maine soldiers left their rear-guard position on the Orange Turnpike and marched, along with the rest of Colonel Charles P. Herring's little picket brigade, along the route the corps had taken. Even before daylight it was hot and sultry; the marching corps had left an immense cloud of dust; the forest fires were still burning; smoke and dust hung in the windless air to blind and choke them. They had had very little sleep for the past three days; red-eyed, exhausted and out of temper, the 20th Maine went plodding along after the Fifth Corps to see what would be coming up next.

With daylight, a roar of gunfire came up from the south and they knew the corps had run into something. By midmorning they had caught up with what seemed to be a full-scale battle, near a place called Spotsylvania Court House. There was a strategic crossing of roads here; Grant had been headed for it, but Lee had got there before him. So there was a big fight blazing up and spreading out through the fields, and it didn't appear to be going too well. Their own 3rd Brigade, they heard, had already taken a mauling. They wanted to rejoin the brigade, but the plan seemed to be for them to stay with Herring's group for the day, and there was no clear idea of what Herring was supposed to do. They were moved here and there and several times formed for a charge, only to be withdrawn. This was hard on the nerves; and the men of the 20th Maine were hungry, tired and on edge.

By late afternoon they had been separated still farther from their own brigade. Now they were not even with their own 1st Division, but were attached to General Crawford's 3rd Division. Toward evening Crawford's troops went up to assault a wooded rise of ground called Laurel Hill, with Herring's little force—the 20th Maine, 118th Pennsylvania, 16th Michigan and the few companies of the 22nd and 9th Massachusetts—making a supporting line in the rear. It was getting dark; in the shadows of the dense cedar and pine thickets, nothing could be seen distinctly.

The whole thing happened with disgusting suddenness. They came upon Crawford's line halted, and firing. There was a red glare of gunfire in reply, and a Confederate charge came whooping in out of the darkness. Crawford's troops disappeared, and Herring's found themselves alone and about to be swept off the hill. The 20th Maine was carried backwards for several yards. Then it returned to fight—out of pure cussedness—one of its greatest actions.

There was no particular reason for them to stay here. In fact, they had to be withdrawn later in the night. There was apparently no sense of pride involved, because it was dark and the rest of the army was too far behind to know and applaud what they were doing. And there was no feeling of special responsibility such as they had at Little Round Top. At Laurel Hill the 20th Maine fought simply because it was tired, hungry and mad. And the rest of the picket brigade fought beside it.

There were Confederates to the front, on the flanks and in the rear. It was, as Private Theodore Gerrish noted, "an easy task to find a rebel anywhere." He described the resulting conflict as a hand-to-hand mob fight at close quarters. Gerrish had become a minister by the time he set it all down, and he regretfully wrote that for a time the 20th Maine forgot "all the noble and refined elements of manhood, and for that hour on Laurel Hill they were brutes, made wild with passion and blood, engaged in a conflict as deadly and fierce as ever raged upon the continent."

It was an extremely noisy fight, with officers roaring orders, men yelling and cursing, guns going off in deafening proximity to ears, the thuds of clubbed muskets, the groans and screams of the wounded. Men dropped their guns and grappled; sometimes two would circle each other for a moment, peering warily through the darkness to determine whether they were friends or foes, then clinching and rolling on the ground in a death struggle. It was one of the few infantry engagements of the war where sword fighting took place; officers drew their swords and plunged into the fracas, slashing and stabbing. Three of them went down: Captain William W. Morrell killed, Lieutenants Holman S. Melcher and Howard L. Prince wounded.

The Confederates made a final lunge down a ravine on the flank but were met and checked by the 16th Michigan. Then their commanders decided to call the whole thing off. Judging by the amount of hollering, fighting and people getting hurt, there was a powerful force of Yankees in front of them, and it would be best not to get too far involved in the darkness. Actually, there were only these three and a half regiments and it was a good example of what a relatively few men can do if they are angry enough.

So the fighting ceased, and Colonel Herring wondered what he ought to do next. He had won and held the crest of the hill. The 20th Maine had captured one hundred prisoners; Herring's group as a whole had taken around two hundred prisoners. But the cost had been high. The 20th Maine had lost twenty-three men; the other regiments had also suffered heavily. Out in front there was a cracking of bushes and a lot of tramping around, as though the Confederates were forming for another attack. Herring feared that they were beginning to find out that the Union force was not as strong as it had seemed. He finally sent Lieutenant James H.

Stanwood of the 20th Maine and two other officers to the rear
to see if they could find General Crawford and get instructions.
These officers returned around midnight, after much wandering
in the woods, and reported that they had not been able to find
Crawford, but they had found another general, and he said to
hang on until three A.M. and then withdraw. They had another
nervous three hours on Laurel Hill, with the enemy restless on
their front; then at the appointed hour they began a silent withdrawal, men holding canteens and other gear to prevent rattling.
A detail had to go back to warn the pickets of the main line;
otherwise they could have expected a volley from their own
troops. The pickets greeted them with some amazement; they
had supposed there was nothing in front but the enemy; now
here came this straggling column of stooped, slow-moving forms
out of the night. A lot of men were being carried, and the pickets
could make out that the heads and arms of some of these hung
inertly. The 20th Maine was carrying in its dead along with the
wounded.

On this day the 20th rejoined the 3rd Brigade, and they began
to get a better idea of the kind of warfare that now awaited them.
The country here had patches of woods that were akin to the
Wilderness in character, but generally it was more open. Around
Spotsylvania Court House the Confederates dug miles of
trenches. The Maine men knew that General Lee had been a
famous officer of the engineer corps; the skill with which these
fieldworks were prepared seemed to bear out his reputation. The
trenches ran with many angles and traverses providing opportunity for protective fires; and there were communications
trenches wherein troops could move from one part of the line to
another without exposure. Artillery covered the approaches. In
places there were felled trees with butts implanted in the earthworks and sharpened branches pointing at the attackers. Behind
all this stood the Confederate rifleman in his deep trench; in front
of him there was a solid parapet of packed earth and logs; he
could shoot through small openings and never show himself.
Armed with an accurate rifle, he might kill three or four Yankees
before one Yankee could get up to the trench and jump in on
him.

A couple of weeks later Grant was reporting, "Lee's army is really whipped. The prisoners we now take show it, and the action of his army shows it unmistakably. A battle with them outside of entrenchments cannot be had."

To the soldiers of the 20th Maine it was never quite so evident that Lee was whipped. Instead, one of the facts of the war was becoming increasingly apparent: specifically that troops in field-works such as these could be driven out only with a highly unfavorable proportion of losses to the attackers. The accuracy of rifled muskets had given the defenders an advantage that was to make the Civil War, in its emphasis on trenches, somewhat similar from then on to World War I. And of course the infantryman in ranks was the first to discover this. "We found," wrote one of the Maine men, "that it was much more to our advantage to have them charge upon our lines than it was for us to charge upon theirs." But Lee was letting Grant do the charging; this was one way to cut his bigger army down to size.

The Confederate line was entrenched around Spotsylvania Court House generally in a half circle. Warren's Fifth Corps was on the Union right, facing this curve. On the evening of May 10, Griffin's division of the corps got ready to launch an attack. The 3rd Brigade moved out a short distance and the men lay down. Orders were for the 3rd to guide its movements on those of a brigade composed largely of U. S. Regulars. When they saw the Confederate works facing them, it was noticed by one of the officers in the 83rd Pennsylvania that every man in ranks was taking a dim view of the project, and the colonels were wearing the longest faces he had ever seen. Fortunately the Regulars were equally impressed and did not push the attack, so the 3rd Brigade did not feel obliged to move. The Pennsylvanian wrote, with a combination of irony and appreciation, "If I ever had reason to thank God for the regular army, it was on that occasion. . . . By their prudent and judicious behavior they not only saved the Division from a bloody repulse, but laid us under a debt of gratitude which I, for one, shall never forget to my dying day."

On May 11, the rain began to fall heavily. On the twelfth there was a big attack that broke in an angle of the Confederate line and left the ground literally covered with piles of dead, but it all came to nothing in the end. Meanwhile the 20th Maine was digging rifle pits in the mud, moving here and there, losing a few men to sniper and shellfire, but thankfully having no major part in these slaughters at the breastworks. It continued to rain. On the night of May 13 they pulled away, with the Fifth Corps, from the right of the Union line and moved all the way around to the extreme left, floundering through the mud and darkness, over forest trails and through streams.

This type of movement came to be so characteristic of the campaign that Private Charles H. Mero of Company E later wrote a poem about it. As a poem, it left something to be desired, but it contained a good description of Grant's strategy.

> Down in the wilderness we met—
> The brush was awful thick,
> But the Johnny Rebs were thicker still,
> And seemed inclined to stick;
> We fought them and we flanked them, too,
> And voted Grant a brick
> At changing corps from right to left
> Upon the double quick.

For all this marching, in the morning they found that they were still not far from Spotsylvania Court House. They had simply circled around and were now to the east of it. It was one of many similar moves that would follow. The soldiers invented a name for the maneuver. They called it a "jug handle."

After their jug-handle move, there were a few days near Spotsylvania Court House when their spirits lifted slightly; they were out of the gloomy forest region at last; the rains ceased; a breeze blew away the mists; the colors of spring were bright; and as a man in the Corn Exchange Regiment put it, "the land was all aglow with sunlight." The 20th Maine occupied rifle pits and lost only four men killed. And Colonel Joshua L. Chamberlain returned to command the regiment for a brief period (he would soon be given command of the division's 1st Brigade).

On May 20 the army began another of its flanking moves, pushing relentlessly south. They were in a region of streams and rivers that meandered southeastward toward the sea. Around Spotsylvania there were the Mat, the Ta, the Po and the Ny, flowing together to form the Mattapony—a remarkable confluence of names as well as waters. Then would come the North Anna and the South Anna, flowing into the Pamunkey. And after that the Chickahominy, last river between them and Richmond.

As the Army of the Potomac tried to move south it would, like the rivers, roll to the southeast. For as fast as it could move, Lee could somehow or other move faster, and they would find his troops solidly entrenched in front of them, barring the roads to Richmond. At these points there would be a series of bloody collisions, with the names of obscure little towns, road crossings, fords and streams flaring up to glow redly in the news and the history of the 20th Maine.

Some were memorable for reasons having little to do with high strategy. There was, for example, the affair at Pole Cat Creek on May 22. General Bartlett was sick. Colonel Chamberlain had the brigade, which was leading the advance of the Fifth Corps. Alert as usual, Chamberlain was out in front with the scouts and skirmishers.

Chamberlain was what might be called a "scientific worrier." While seeking or awaiting contact with the enemy he had a habit of studying all the features of the terrain, meanwhile continually posing himself a series of problems. What would he do, if suddenly attacked by a dash of cavalry from that screen of woods ahead? Or take that defile on the right, where infantry might well be hidden; what would be the proper course of action if Confederate riflemen fired from there? And so on. At Little Round Top, this sort of worrying had paid off when he had sent Morrill's company out to guard his flank. Now it was about to come in handy again. There was a whizzing noise in the air as a shot passed over him—and a commotion behind in the Corn Exchange Regiment, where a man was struck and killed by the projectile. From a wooded hill ahead, white smoke was drifting up. A Confederate battery on the hill had opened on Chamberlain's column. But the Colonel had been worrying about that hill, and he had a plan ready-made. With the objective of capturing the battery, he sent part of the brigade to attack the hill frontally; the rest flanking wide and—he hoped—unobserved through the fields. Orders: never mind the cannoneers at first; shoot the horses.

The 20th Maine and the Corn Exchange Regiment were together in the flanking party. Nearly up to the woods where the exposed flank of the battery lay, a small but apparently deep and muddy stream stopped them. Chamberlain, eager to get at the battery, saw a plank fence on the near side of the stream. He shouted, "Take the fence along with you . . . throw it in, and yourselves after it!" They pulled up the fence, threw it across the stream, and rushed over on the planks. But the fuss had attracted the Confederate artillerymen; they whirled part of the battery around, dusted Chamberlain's force with canister, hitched up and took off.

Memorable, too, in this advance was a curious and somehow pathetic incident. They came in sight of a Confederate major, sitting on a gray horse, with his hand cupped to his ear, listening intently. Apparently his faculties were in some way impaired for he seemed neither to see nor hear the Union troops. While an officer circled around to get between the Major and his avenue of escape, Chamberlain halted the skirmish line and raised his hands in a gesture of silence. The officer came up behind the Confederate major and informed him that he was a prisoner.

"Not so, sir," said the Major. "You are *my* prisoner." He was reaching for a weapon when he saw the jig was up. As the Major was led back through the lines, it could be seen that his face was ashy white. When asked to hand over his sword, he angrily drove it into the ground and broke it off at the hilt.

As the two armies moved with intermittent contact there would be dozens of skirmishes like this—unexplainable and forgotten fights completely mystifying to troops following the advance guards. No historians for fights like these. No markers, except upturned soles on the boots of dead soldiers lying on their backs beside the road, pathetic little monuments striving to the last to preserve the identity of a man. No record. No finding out what ever happened—unless, by chance, years later some old veteran might write an account of the affair on such-and-such a day at such-and-such a creek or crossroads.

When the armies massed at major points of resistance, the action would be like that of two great wheels grinding together —Grant moving troops from his right wing around to his left in continual flanking efforts—Lee moving troops to his right to meet them. The Confederates could march within the curve; but the Union men had to march outside the arc, and the demands on the troops were brutal and unceasing. And there were also the rivers, which often forced an additional move to the left to find a suitable crossing. On May 23, the 20th Maine crossed the North Anna, wading the river at Jericho Ford. There was a noisy fight on the other side where the Confederates threatened their bridge-head for a time; a great deal of ammunition shot off, the Confederates retiring, Major Spear slightly wounded. On the night of the twenty-sixth they recrossed the North Anna on another flank movement to the left. It was, as one of the soldiers of the 20th described it, "fight all day and march all night."

On May 28 they crossed the Pamunkey and there was more resistance, more throwing up of earthworks. By now, no one had to urge the Maine men to dig; it was automatic and they used bayonets, knives, sticks, tin plates, cups, or any tool that was handy, in order to get under ground. But the digging, coming on top of the fighting and the marching in the heat, was adding to the total of exhaustion. Since crossing the Rapidan on May 4 they had had little to eat except hardtack and coffee—no vegetables and only a little stringy meat from equally exhausted cattle being driven along with the army. There had been almost continual marching, fighting, labor or watchfulness. Against Grant's grinding wheel Lee's army was wearing down, but so was the 20th Maine.

Private Gerrish told how it would be at the end of a long day's march through stifling heat. About the time the stars were coming out, the welcome order to halt and break into companies would be heard up at the front of the regiment. Then the commands, "Halt . . . halt . . . halt . . . halt . . ." coming back through the companies. Subsequent orders would follow rapidly: "Front face . . . order arms . . . fix bayonets . . . stack arms . . . break ranks." If a company was lucky, it would have fifteen men at the end of a march. Five of these would probably be detailed for picket duty and would have to report to the adjutant within ten minutes; they would be out on the picket line all night without hope of rest or sleep. Of the remaining ten men, half would be so exhausted that they would stretch out on the ground and go to sleep without eating. The others would search out wood and water and prepare an evening meal. The night's rest would not be too satisfactory. Gerrish believed that the ground of Virginia was inherently hostile; there would always be a hummock where a man wanted a hollow for his hip, and a hollow where he wanted a hummock for his head. Often there would be an outbreak of firing in the course of the night, and the whole company would have to turn out. Faithful stragglers, trying to rejoin their commands, were moving through the bivouac area all night; often a man would be nudged or kicked awake by one of these wanderers asking where his outfit was. Private Dick Quinlon of the 20th, when roused out of a sound sleep and asked, "What regiment is this?" would roar, "The 9th Ireland!" Long before sunup they would be awakened, and from the heaviness and tiredness of their bodies, it would not seem as though they had been asleep at all.

By early June they were close to Richmond, with Lee across the roadways at Cold Harbor—a road junction a few miles north of the Chickahominy. There was a big and costly attack by the Union forces there on June 3, the Army of the Potomac losing nearly six thousand men in one hour. The 20th Maine fought at Bethesda Church two or three miles north of the road junction, with twenty-six casualties which it could ill afford. This was followed by more moving around and digging, and they seemed to be settling down for another spell of trench warfare.

It was a bad place to settle down. They were now in the lowlands of the Chickahominy, a sluggish stream running in places through a kind of Dismal Swamp. The sun was hot. The mosquitoes were thick. The stench of hundreds of unburied men and horses at Cold Harbor blew over the country with every breeze. Water for the troops had to come almost entirely from surface drainage. Malarial ills, known as Chickahominy fever, began to be prevalent.

With Lee's entrenchments so strong, this was a poor place for an army—made worse by the memories of the ill-fated campaign McClellan had fought near here—and Grant did not intend to stay. He had one more "jug handle" up his sleeve. Moving at night, the Army of the Potomac slipped out of its trenches in front of Cold Harbor, crossed the Chickahominy, made a feint toward Richmond, then slid away to the left again on a long march to the James. Grant's plan was to go below Richmond and capture Petersburg, through which main lines of communication led to the south. If the plan succeeded, and if at the same time supplies from the Shenandoah Valley could also be destroyed or cut off, Richmond would die on the vine. More important, Lee would be starved out of the strong fortifications surrounding Richmond, and the Army of Northern Virginia might then be defeated by the numerically superior Union force.

And so it was—after more hard marching—that the 20th Maine on the morning of June 16 found itself on a small steam transport, the *General Hooker*. They were crossing a river they had never expected to see—the James, a sunlit expanse of open water with refreshing breezes coming in from the sea. It was like coming out into the light after a long period spent in a tunnel or mine, and everything looked different.

Toward the last of this campaign from the Rapidan to the James, morning reports had not been called for because, as officers confidentially explained, the country would not stand for it if they knew the casualty figures. There was no such tender regard for the feelings of the infantrymen. They were not only standing it, but they'd have to stand it some more. This in spite of the fact that the 20th Maine was down to the strength of a couple of companies. The regiment had suffered around 175 battle casualties besides numerous losses caused by disease and exhaustion. Uniforms were ragged and dirty. The soldiers were thin and haggard; their eyes seemed to have gone far back into their heads, and they looked, one man thought, twenty years older than they had looked before the Wilderness.

Gazing back over the wake of the steamer, back across the James, the experiences of the past six weeks seemed, as one of them recalled, "more like a fearful nightmare to us than a reality." It was past all remembering. There had been too many rivers, too many roads, too many days, too many deaths, too many stupid night marches. Many of the rifle pits and graves they had dug would soon be overgrown with bushes and weeds; those who returned would not be able to find them. Somewhere there was a plan, a reality, even a destiny perhaps, but a big part of the regiment had vanished in a dream.

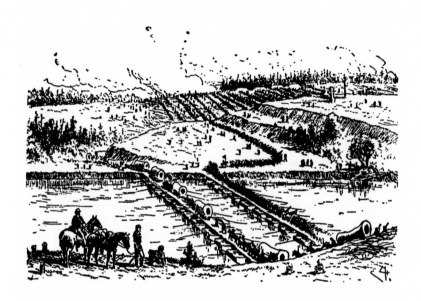

CHAPTER TWELVE

Woodchuck Warfare

LTHOUGH they were near enough for weeks to hear its church bells ringing on Sunday mornings, the men of the 20th Maine never saw the streets of Petersburg while the war lasted. The letters they wrote—and there was time for writing many— were always headed "In Front of Petersburg." And the reason they never got into town was that the Army of the Potomac, after making a brilliantly deceptive and rapid move across the James, moved too slowly in the final stages of the attack on Petersburg. Advance elements of the Union forces cracked the outer defenses, then sat down to await reinforcements; but in the reinforcing columns there were mix-ups and delays. By the time the Fifth Corps arrived and got into the fight, almost three days had gone by; General Lee had moved many of his veteran brigades south and into the defenses of Petersburg; and the Confederates had withdrawn to stronger, shorter, more easily defended lines, where the earthworks of red Virginia soil were rising higher by the hour.

On the hot afternoon of June 18 there was a big Union attack against these defenses, across ground that was rough and intricate, chopped up by ravines and a railroad cut. The 20th Maine was lucky. It advanced through woods offering good concealment, then halted on the edge of a field facing the enemy works with orders to dig in and remain in reserve. But coming in across open ground on their left, the division's 1st Brigade, now commanded by Colonel Joshua Chamberlain, was badly cut up.

As he led his brigade in for the attack, the Colonel could see ample evidence of approaching destruction ahead. There was little cover for his troops; they would have to advance for a long distance over ground that would be lashed with fire from enemy entrenchments on a height of land, and from a fort on their left. If men went out there they would have to be led. Chamberlain formed his line, got out in front with his brigade staff and colors, and ordered the advance. As they came within range of the enemy guns a blast of canister and shot ripped into them, and everything seemed to go down at once, the colors falling, staff officers pitching off their horses, Chamberlain's own horse—just as unfortunate as all the horses he ever rode—floundering down bloodily, shot through with a twelve-pound projectile. The Colonel arose, caught up the colors and continued on foot, keeping the infantry going. After what seemed an eternity they reached the Confederates and drove them from their entrenchments in a brief and frantic action.

But this, it appeared, was only an advance line. The main Confederate entrenchments were just beyond, and from this line a storm of fire was sweeping Chamberlain's captured crest. He ordered the men to keep low, had emplacements dug in the rear slope, and sent for artillery. When the guns came up he placed them on the sunken platforms so that the muzzles were resting on the grass on the crest and the gun crews could work under complete cover.

An order to continue the advance arrived, and this seemed so unreasonable and even suspicious to Chamberlain that he wrote this message to his superiors:

> I have just received a verbal order not through the usual channels, but by a staff officer unknown to me, purporting to come from the General commanding the army, directing me to assault the main works of the enemy in my front. Circumstances lead me to believe the General cannot be aware of my situation, which has greatly changed within the last hour.
>
> I have just carried an advanced position held by the enemy's infantry and artillery. I am advanced a mile beyond our own lines, and in an isolated position. On my right is a deep railroad cut; my left flank is in the air, with no support whatever. In front of me at close range is a strongly entrenched line of

infantry and artillery, with projecting salients right and left, such that my advance would be swept by a cross-fire, while a large fort on my left enfilades my entire advance, as I experienced in carrying this position. Along my front close up to the enemy's works appears to be bad ground, swampy and boggy, where my men would be held at a great disadvantage under a severe fire.

I have got up three batteries, and am placing them on the reverse slope of this crest, to enable me to hold against an unexpected attack. To leave these guns behind me unsupported, their retreat cut off by the railroad cut—would expose them to loss in case of our being repulsed.

Fully aware of the responsibility I take, I beg to be assured that the order to attack with my single Brigade is with the General's full understanding. I have here a veteran Brigade of six regiments, and my responsibility for the welfare of these men seems to warrant me in wishing assurance that no mistake in communicating orders compels me to sacrifice them.

From what I can see of the enemy's lines, it is my opinion that if an assault is to be made, it should be by nothing less than the whole army.

In spite of this clear and carefully worded description of the situation, word came back that the order was intended. Chamberlain was to go ahead and attack.

Picking out what seemed to be the weakest point in the enemy line, Chamberlain launched a second attack, leading his men on foot. He was just turning his side to the enemy to give a command when a bullet crashed through his body from hip to hip. The shock destroyed him as a human mechanism, but the spirit of the man would not go down. Nor did the instinct of command fail. Balancing himself on the point of his sword, with blood gushing hotly down his legs, Chamberlain kept waving the infantrymen on. Then, when the light was fading, and the graying forms had rushed past him into the smoke, he let himself down.

In the backwash of the attack, which secured an advanced position but failed to carry the enemy works, Chamberlain was picked up and carried to a field hospital in the rear, a bloody ruin of a man. The regular surgeon on duty examined him and at once declared there was no hope; this was a wound that Chamberlain would die of. In this prognosis he was correct; Chamberlain did die of it finally, but not for another fifty years. Also, there were surgeons in the old 3rd Brigade who, hearing of his imminent demise, would not be content with this opinion until after they had seen for themselves. Dr. A. O. Shaw of the 20th Maine searched through the woods half the evening until he found the hospital where Chamberlain was lying. Dr. M. W. Townsend of the 44th New York and others joined him, and through much of the night they worked desperately on the shattered colonel. In addition to penetrating both hips, the bullet had passed through the pelvis, and the wound involved the bladder. The surgeons had a job on their hands. At one point they almost decided to give up, feeling that they were only making Chamberlain's last hours miserably painful. But another try was made and, as recorded, "This time good fortune rewarded intelligent persistence, severed parts were artificially connected, and to the great joy of patient and surgeon, there was a possibility of recovery."

In army headquarters, Chamberlain's exploits of the day had not gone unnoticed. Without waiting for authority from Washington, U. S. Grant issued a special order promoting him to brigadier general, with date of rank of June 18—the day of his wounding—subject to the approval of the President. Chamberlain had already been recommended for promotion several times. The approval was now, of course, forthcoming, and this is said to have been the only instance of a battlefield promotion to brigadier general during the war.

So they shipped Chamberlain off to the hospital at Annapolis, a brigadier general. But it seemed to many in the 3rd Brigade that the promotion had come a little too late, as it had for poor Strong Vincent after Gettysburg. Many of their recorded comments have the tone of an obituary, as in this one from a man of the Corn Exchange Regiment, concerning Chamberlain: "A man of high scholarly attainments, a soldier of great ability, infinite resources and distinguished courage, he had endeared himself to the officers and men of the 118th Pennsylvania from their earliest knowledge of him."

Following the unsuccessful attacks of June 18, the army dug in and the 20th Maine entered upon a new experience—siege warfare. Under cover of darkness, the Union lines were pushed up close to the Confederate works; then, perspiring in the hot June night, the men dug quietly and desperately. By daylight, they would all have sunk into the ground. Their works began as simple trenches, with the soil thrown up to form a parapet against the enemy. Then the wall toward the enemy was shored up with logs, sandbags, sods or other sustaining material. At this time, the 20th Maine was in a sector where the lines were fairly close. For a while, until the enlisted men of both sides came to their inevitable agreement, there was destructive sniping back and forth. It was hard to get used to. A man would wake up in the morning, stand up half asleep, inadvertently stick his head above the parapet, and be dead before he really woke up. Captain Samuel T. Keene of the 20th Maine was shot through the heart by a sniper, fell into the arms of Major Ellis Spear, asked Spear to write to his wife, said everything was all right with him, and died quickly and apparently painlessly. This sort of thing held a new and subtle terror; a man could die unexpectedly and for no purpose whatever.

To gain added protection, the troops dug works of increasing complexity. There were, at first, lines of trenches, then along these, at intervals, redoubts and forts (completely enclosed earthworks) were constructed. Running to the rear, and connecting certain works, were deep, canal-like excavations, some of them large enough to drive through with a team of horses and an ammunition or supply wagon. Where trenches ran toward enemy lines, they were zigzagged to keep them from being fired into lengthwise—or they were, in some cases, roofed over with dirt-covered logs. Out beyond the main lines, toward the enemy, the pickets stood in deep holes in the ground; these were connected with the main entrenchments by zigzag trenches or little tunnels. In all, it looked as though millions of martial woodchucks were at work. The two armies stood confronting one another, with pickets out, as they had on many fields previously, but here they stood for the most part below the surface of the ground.

On or about June 19, the coughing rumble of a new engine of war—or at least new to the 20th Maine—was heard. The mortar, that necessary adjunct of trench warfare, had arrived. An ugly, short-range weapon with a tremendous caliber, the mortar tossed its huge projectiles upward at an extreme angle of elevation— and because a trajectory is much nearer to a vertical line coming down than it is going up, the shells fell almost straight down, thus being ideal for dropping explosives into trenches.

At night the path of the shell could be followed by the light of the burning fuse. The little spark rose slowly, almost lazily into the summer sky; it lingered among the stars for a second; and then, if it seemed to be hanging directly overhead and getting brighter and brighter, it was time to duck, for there would shortly be lightning, thunder and an earthquake. The Maine men began a diligent study of mortar trajectories and they learned quickly. If the ascending spark veered to the right or left on its upward course, all was well. It would fall a safe distance to the right or left. If it began to descend before it was directly overhead, it would drop safely short. But if it went up straight and then stopped and did not move and kept getting brighter, a big parcel of hell was about to be delivered. A sharp-eyed sentinel could spot mortar shells in daytime, too; a little black dot in the sky could be judged much in the same way as the spark at night. The shells also made a characteristic noise, a peculiar creaking whistle caused by the fuse as the projectile revolved. "We always told short stories when we heard them coming," was a comment by one of the Maine soldiers.

The flight of shells from field artillery pieces was harder to predict. On one occasion six men from the 20th Maine were preparing to eat a feast of potatoes, soft bread (as distinguished from hard bread, or hardtack), onions, pickles and other delicacies provided by the Sanitary Commission. The banquet was set up under a "dining pavilion"—shelter tents spread across rough posts to shade them from the blazing sun. The soldiers had just sat down to the feast when the air began to quiver with the shriek of an incoming shell. The men leaped for a bombproof shelter, upsetting the table, knocking down the pavilion, and scattering the goodies through the dust. One of the aggrieved participants wrote that "the dinner was almost a failure, and what rendered the circumstances more aggravating . . . was the fact that the shell did not strike within several rods."

The bombproof shelter referred to was a special type of excavation made necessary by the mortar shelling. The usual procedure in constructing a bombproof was to dig a large, square hole—often big enough for a dozen men—roof it over with logs, and then cover the logs with two or three feet of soil. The mortar shell, dropping into the soft earthen cover, did little damage. A couple of men in the brigade tried to improve on bombproof architecture by raising the layer of logs slightly above the level of the ground, so that the air could get in and ventilation would be helped. They forgot about the flatter trajectories of enemy artillery. One day a twelve-pound shell skittered through the opening, rolled under a bunk where two men were sleeping, and exploded. A mournful and somewhat squeamish corpse-recovery party gathered around, waiting for the smoke to clear. To their amazement, the two men emerged, blackened and shaken, but still alive. However, after that all bombproofs were tightly covered.

Life was not pleasant in the trenches. For weeks there was no rain; the earth, torn up as it was, yielded itself easily to the wind; great clouds of fine, red dust swept up and down the earthworks. Flies were thick. Water was hard to get, disappearing from surface sources entirely, so that wells had to be dug, in addition to the day and night digging that was required in the entrenchments. And the sun beat down relentlessly. The dust, the flies and the heat were likely to keep a man from sleeping by day; and a digging detail was likely to keep him awake at night. The men of the 20th baked thin and brown, their eyes withdrawing into their skulls, faces becoming lean and lined.

While the terror of the mortars contributed to an ever-present tenseness, the sniping and picket firing gradually died away in front of the 20th Maine. Wherever the two armies stood facing each other inactively for any length of time, the enlisted men usually came to this agreement, the implied fact being that personal shooting of this nature would not greatly influence the war one way or another. Actually, whether they knew it or not, they had some legal precedent for their forbearance. General orders for the volunteer forces had a section that was a sort of precursor of the modern *Rules of Land Warfare.* Among other refinements of modern war, it prescribed that "outposts, sentinels, or pickets are not to be fired upon, except to drive them in, or when a positive order, special or general, has been issued to that effect." More than likely the enlisted men knew nothing about this rule; and orders, either special or general, had no bearing either. All they knew was that private shooting of a man here and a man there was not going to have anything to do with deciding the war, so why not have peace when peace was to be had?

This amiable state of affairs prevailing, a group of men from the 20th Maine, 1st Michigan, 18th and 22nd Massachusetts were in the habit of playing cards under a shade tree that stood between the Union and Confederate lines. One day a grass fire broke out near by; a Union man ran to stamp it out; an excitable Confederate fired, smashing the fire fighter's forearm. The card players ran for the trenches, and there was great indignation in the 3rd Brigade—an anger which was reflected on the Confederate side. Next morning the criminal who fired the shot was seen parading on the enemy parapet with a log tied across his shoulders, while his Confederate companions loudly extended an invitation to the 3rd Brigade to shoot him. The Unionists refrained. As one wrote, "Vengeance slumbered in the satisfaction of the execration visited on the creature by his own associates."

Over in front of Burnside's Ninth Corps on their immediate right, relations were not so friendly. In the Ninth Corps there were colored troops, and the Confederates were not kindly disposed toward them. The Southerners were further aggravated when the Ninth Corps blew them up with a mine—an extraordinary venture attended by Burnsidean misfortune.

For some time remarkable rumors had been running along the line. A regiment of Pennsylvania miners in Burnside's Corps, so the stories went, was digging a five-hundred-foot shaft to a point under the Confederate works. This sounded impossible, so there was joking back and forth, and since the Confederates seemed to be aware of the rumor too, there were jovial warnings—pickets shouting, "Johnny, you're going to Heaven!" and the like.

Meanwhile the Pennsylvanians had been accomplishing the impossible. They had completed their shaft, placed eight thousand pounds of powder under a section of the Confederate line and laid a long fuse back through the tunnel to the Union side. Official information and orders came to the 20th Maine on the evening of July 29th. The mine was under a fort within full view to their right. It would be exploded at three-thirty o'clock next morning. At the same time Union artillery would open, and an assaulting column from the Ninth Corps, including a division of colored troops, would rush into the breach. The 20th Maine and other regiments of the 1st Division, Fifth Corps, were supposed to open a severe musketry fire and then advance when it seemed that the breakthrough was well on its way.

Long before three-thirty the Maine men were up, staring over the parapets into the darkness, waiting for the blast. But the appointed time came and went, with no explosion. (The fuse had gone out somewhere in the tunnel, and two men had crawled in to re-light it.) More than an hour went by, with tension mounting steadily, and dawn was lightening the eastern sky.

Then it happened—the Hiroshima of the Civil War. The ground under the fort swelled, then mushroomed upward in a mass of earth, flame and smoke. Theodore Gerrish recorded his impression of the blast. "The first intimation we had that the time had arrived was a dull, heavy roar, and the jarring of the ground upon which we stood. It seemed like the shock of a powerful earthquake; we looked, and saw that the air above where the fort had been was filled with smoke, dirt, men, guns, and pieces of fortifications, all falling in one mass of terrible confusion."

The explosion opened a crater 170 feet long, 80 wide and 30 deep. It overwhelmed a battery, killed nearly three hundred Confederate troops and spread such consternation that the Confederate trenches were abandoned for some distance on each side. Simultaneously, the crash of Union artillery fire echoed all along the line, wherever a gun could be brought to bear on the shattered portion of the enemy lines. The gate to Petersburg was wide open. But as the Maine men watched from their

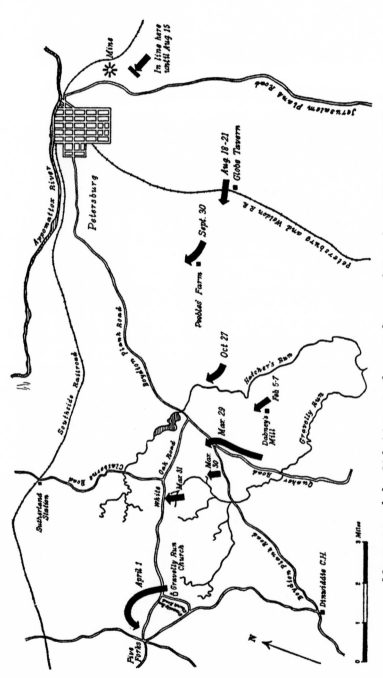

Movements of the 20th Maine in the encirclement of Petersburg, 1864 and 1865

trenches, it seemed that the Union troops were almost equally stunned. Some of them had rushed backward under the impression that the whole mass of debris was falling on their heads. A smoky haze settled down, and nothing seemed to be happening. The attacking column from the Ninth Corps, when it finally got started, appeared to be wandering forward and jamming itself down into the crater. It was hard to see what was taking place, but the mounting roar of Confederate artillery being brought in to face the gap, and the steadily increasing clamor of Confederate musketry told the Maine men what was happening. Rallying under the leadership of a redoubtable Southern general named Mahone, the Confederates were pouring fire into the Union masses crowded into the crater. The dismal affair ended around noon with some four thousand Union troops lost, against a loss of possibly fifteen hundred for the Confederates.

A few days more of the midsummer heat, and an intolerable stench came from the crater when the wind blew from that direction. Hundreds of Union corpses were lying there unburied, along with Confederates blown up in the explosion. There was another unpleasant aftermath in the increased hostility of the pickets, who considered the springing of the mine a work of iniquity, and the employment of colored troops even more dastardly. The colored soldiers had been paid off just before the attack and the Confederates had taken a great deal of money from the dead, wounded and prisoners. There were taunts from the enemy earthworks, soldiers waving fistfuls of greenbacks and yelling, "Send them in on another charge when they get their money."

On the night of August 14, the Fifth Corps began pulling out of the trenches, with the Ninth Corps extending its lines to cover the vacated sector. The 20th Maine was relieved on the morning of the fifteenth, and no one was sorry to go. The Maine men had been living in holes in the ground for so long that any move on the surface of the earth and in the open air would have been welcome. The regiment marched to the rear and went into camp in the woods. The afternoon was memorable to one of the men. "On that day letters came from home, and we lay down upon the ground, in the midst of vines and flowers, under the shade of the pine trees, and read the messages from our loved ones who were so anxious for our safety." Lying there in the heat, under the pitchy-smelling southern pines, a man could remember the coolness of a Maine lake, or the salt breeze coming in from Monhegan, and Maine had never seemed so far away. Victory seemed equally distant. They were strategists enough to know that the Petersburg fight had only begun and that the failure to capture Petersburg in June and July had radically changed the nature of the campaign. Petersburg was the key point on the transportation system linking Richmond with the rest of the South. All but one railroad—the Richmond and Danville Railroad—bringing supplies to the Confederate capital ran through Petersburg. It was the center of a big system of radiating railroads and highways. Had the initial attack of the Army of the Potomac succeeded, all of these roads would have been cut at their nexus, Richmond would have begun to wither away, and Lee would have been forced out into the open. But the attack had failed. So the campaign was no longer the siege of a small city. It would have to be a far-spreading effort, reaching out through fields and forests and swamps to sever these lines of communications one by one, at points far removed from Petersburg itself. And before it could end, the campaign would cover the largest single battle area of the Civil War.

This would involve a continuation, on a smaller scale geographically, of the leftward-flanking maneuver that Grant had begun at the Wilderness three and a half months before. To encircle Petersburg, there would have to be another "jug handle," and right now less than a quarter of the jug handle had been completed. The Maine men knew they would have to drive westward and cut the Petersburg and Weldon Railroad (commonly called the Weldon Railroad). Then, beyond that, the Boydton Plank Road. And finally, as the jug handle curved up and around to the west of Petersburg, they would snap the one remaining link between Petersburg and the rest of the South— the Southside Railroad—and that should just about do the trick.

On the map, it looked easy. But the map didn't show the skill and determination of Confederate soldiers who would be fighting deep in their own territory for survival. Nor did existing maps give any clear idea of the difficulties of the terrain. Around Petersburg, where the initial fighting had taken place, the country was hilly and piny, somehow reminiscent of southern Maine. But south of the city the ground flattened out and sank away into swamps in many places. Here the pine forests were extremely thick; as trees were cut back away from camps and entrenchments, the landscape began to look as though it had been drawn in a child's picture book. In the foreground would be smears of orange-red earth thrown up from the trenches—on the horizon a mass of closely placed, dark, vertical lines—these the trunks of the tall pines—surmounted by the heavy, ragged crayoning of the green tops. Across this flat ground, offering few natural observation points, and through the dense, dark-shadowed pine forests, it was hard for the army to see where it was going. Much of the country was crisscrossed by trails and cart roads which presumably the Confederates knew and the Union commanders did not know. Much of the ground was low; there were streams which would become rivers after a few hours of rain; and rain would also turn the clayey, sandy soil into a bottomless morass. This character of the ground accounted for the many "plank roads"—dirt roads on which logs or planks had been laid to bear the wheels of wagons.

It was raining, in fact, when the push started early on the morning of August 18—a warm, steaming drizzle that soon had the artillery lurching and skidding over the miry roads. The 20th Maine moved out at six o'clock and everyone knew that the Weldon Railroad was the goal. They marched for an hour westward through wooded country. Confederate cavalrymen appeared; and the 20th Maine and the rest of the brigade swung out into line of battle; but Union cavalry drove in, there was a spiteful cracking of carbines, and the gray horsemen scattered away into the rain-misted pines. The advance continued. Soon they were out into open country, and suddenly and surprisingly—there was the railroad. The Fifth Corps was across the Weldon Railroad by noon, in the vicinity of Globe Tavern.

Orders came to dig in and await an attack. Sweating in the muggy heat, the Maine men felled trees and piled up breastworks. In this labor they needed no urging; the veterans realized that painful twinges from the cutting of the railroad were being felt all the way back to Petersburg, and the Confederates would not leave them long unmolested.

Next day a great clamor arose in that direction. North of the 20th Maine's pcsition, two divisions of the Fifth Corps faced Petersburg, and judging by the sound, they were being violently set upon. During a plunging rainstorm in the afternoon, the roar of gunfire swelled to new heights, with echoes rolling in weirdly. There were rumors of catastrophe. Once the 20th Maine double-quicked northward to help, only to halt and march back again. Word came that the line was holding. The Maine men waited tensely behind their breastworks. Soon, they expected, the counterattack would be enveloping their own portion of the line.

When the Confederate blow against this portion of the line came, on Sunday morning, August 21, it was delivered with a lack of skill quite uncharacteristic of their estranged brethren of the South. For once in their lives the Maine men saw troops of the C. S. A. being led straight into a deathtrap that could, it seemed, have been avoided with a determined reconnaissance. The trap was relatively simple and may not, in fact, have been intended as a trap. After swinging across the railroad about three miles below Petersburg, the Fifth Corps line ran south, parallel with the railroad and about 450 yards west of it. Then the main line ended abruptly. But a couple of hundred yards or so nearer the railroad another line continued southward. This was the line of breastworks occupied by the 1st Division of the corps, which included the 20th Maine.

Apparently the Confederates (Johnson Hagood's Brigade) believed that the end of the main line represented the flank of the Union position—and were unaware of the second line nearer the railroad. They came in from the left front in line of battle, with the evident intention of striking what they thought to be the Union flank and rolling it up. In doing so, they ran into a surprise cross fire from the 1st Division, which resulted in wholesale murder.

It was something to see. The Confederate force was advancing from a dense woods. A racket of musketry arose from the forest, and the 1st Division pickets came running in, badly shaken up.

Then out of the woods came the gray line of battle. The Confederates advanced through a cornfield, their heads just visible, the red battle flags waving above the green. For a few moments the men of the 20th Maine watched in wonder and disbelief. This was a situation they had dreamed about but never expected to

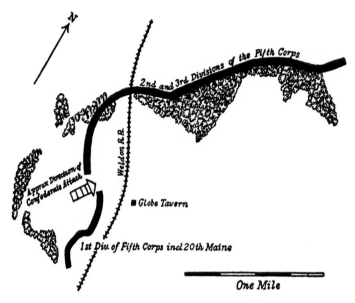

Weldon Railroad, August 21, 1864

see. Here they were, safe behind breastworks, looking over their rifles and watching a Confederate line of battle walk its flank into their sights. It would be like firing lengthwise down a sidewalk crowded with people.

An officer shouted, "Fire!" The breastworks crashed and flamed, and the volley went out with a hiss, the cornstalks toppling as though lashed with an invisible knife, the red flags shivering under the impact. As the ramrods rattled in for another round, there was a sentiment in the 20th Maine that was singularly inappropriate for a Sabbath morning. As described by one of the shooters, ". . . our men enjoyed it very much, for they remembered how often we had been obliged to charge upon their lines, and

223

be shot down by thousands, while they were screened from our fire, and we now rejoiced that for once the tables were turned, and that to our advantage."

But the feeling of elation soon changed to a more sporting instinct. Out across the cornfield, Confederate soldiers were dropping in a continuous fall, like hay before a scythe. Then gray-clad infantrymen were running toward the breastworks with hands held high, calling upon the Union troops to cease fire. Others were running back toward the woods; still others rushed blindly into the space between the two Union lines, where they were pocketed.

A man in the brigade remembered that "we then had them between two fires and could have slaughtered them like sheep in the shambles, but our men instinctively forbore to again fire upon them after they had given this indication of a surrender." Ten minutes later there was a brief flare-up when a chivalrous Confederate general on a horse led a dash for freedom out of the pocket. The General got away, but most of the men following him were shot down or captured. This battle, ending in disaster for the Confederate force, was the last serious attempt to recapture the Weldon Railroad. For General Warren it had been another brilliant achievement in a career that had its high points. For the Union, it had been a signal victory—of an importance which has been largely overlooked by historians. For the 20th Maine it had been a bloodless battle—none killed, none wounded, a rare entry in the records of that regiment.

But a little more than a month later they were back in their accustomed role of charging enemy earthworks. On the morning of September 30, the westward push of the Fifth Corps continued. Rumor had it that the objective was a strong point covering an important road junction. There was a promise of action, because the division commander, General Griffin, was personally leading the advance. Griffin could always smell a fight, and now he was up front with eyes alert and heavy moustache bristling. The troops moved cautiously through dense, scrubby pine for more than two miles, brushed away a screen of skirmishers, and emerged into a large open field.

The cleared space—to be remembered as Peebles' Farm—was

a large area, fringed with woods on all four sides. The ground immediately ahead of them sloped downward to a set of buildings, and then ascended to the far side of the farm. There, at the crest of the green slopes, the Maine men saw an old familiar sight. It was a horizontal slash of brownish orange across the green—Confederate earthworks that appeared to extend on either side of a square earthen fort. Something moved in the air, and caught the light occasionally above the fort—a flag, flapping idly. There were dark little holes in the side of the fort; from these came flashes and puffs of smoke. A couple of seconds or so later heavy thumps of cannon shook the air. To the veterans it looked and sounded as though the guns were half a mile or more away—a long stretch for a man to march or run in the face of artillery fire. The air around them was now agitated by plaintive howls and swishings, and by explosions of distressing violence. There was an order to lie down and take cover from the shelling.

The prospect ahead had the old look of imminent death, but the Maine men regarded it with a certain professional competence. They would pay for this ground. But they would have it by night, and they would bury their own dead. Captain Weston H. Keene, for the first time in a major engagement, had brought his money along. A prudent Maine Yankee, Keene had always thought previously that there was no use in a man's losing his life and his cash too; he had always left his purse behind with some non-combatant. If he were killed today, Keene apparently felt confident that his fellow officers could recover the money; it was to be used, he instructed them, to have his body embalmed and sent home to Maine, where he could have a proper funeral.

So there was this, and there were other provisions for an uncertain future, and around noon the 3rd Brigade charged out across the long, open field with what was described as "a devil of a yelling . . . troops running toward the enemy works whooping like so many demons." The long lines of blue, with the colors fluttering over them like low-flying birds, swept on, growing more and more irregular as Confederate shot broke up the ranks. Going down into a ravine they had momentary cover, but as they emerged on the other side and ascended the final slope toward the fort, the Confederate gunners changed to canister, converting their cannon into giant shotguns, and the Union lines thinned and scattered. Confederate rifle fire, too, was beginning to take effect, and blue figures were falling queerly, awkwardly, some lying still where they fell, others rolling and clawing at the grass. Stretcher-bearers were busy, and one of those they picked up was Sergeant Will Owen, only recently returned to duty from the hospital. "It was a sharpshooter that hit me, I think," he reported later, when he was able to think about it at all. A bullet had gone through him just above his left breast, coming out below the shoulder blade; and the stretcher-bearers lugged him away toward another stay in the hospital. It was the end of the war for Owen, and he was lucky that it was not the end of his life.

But most of the regiment kept moving, up the slope, across a ditch, and through the sharp-pointed teeth of an abatis directly in front of the fort. One officer, Lieutenant Albert E. Fernald, was well ahead in the race. When matters came to the pass they were in now, Fernald always seemed to have an unquenchable desire to close with the enemy—a desire that would eventually lead him to the Congressional Medal of Honor—and he was now a considerable distance in the lead. Inside the fort, Confederate artillerymen were hitching up their horses, trying to get the guns away. They had three safely out of the works and were hauling the fourth away when Fernald came bounding through an opening in the wall of the fort. The Maine officer's revolver, pointed at the driver's head, had a suddenly persuasive effect. The horses were halted. The retreating Confederate infantrymen, seeing Fernald holding up the cannoneers, paused to load and snipe at him, but their fire only succeeded in killing one or two of the horses, making it impossible to remove the gun.

The 20th Maine had been in the forefront of the attack, capturing the gun and seventy prisoners. And of course it had paid. The regiment had left a trail of wounded all the way up the slope to where, within the works themselves, Sergeant James A. Horton was lying with his face getting whiter and whiter, his blood draining out through a canister-shot wound in his thigh. Horton was one of the old hands and a top-notch soldier who hadn't missed a day of duty in two years. There was silent grief among the Maine men as they watched him being carried away; by now they were experienced prognosticators of battle wounds and they knew they would never see Horton again.

But the day was not over. In the afternoon, troops of the Ninth Corps moved through the captured line and continued the advance, disappearing to the northwest. A tumult of firing arose in that direction. To the Maine men, it seemed that the noise grew louder and ominously nearer. Then they, too, were being marched in that direction, meeting Ninth Corps troops who were running as though all the Confederates in the world were after them. Their probing toward the vital Boydton Plank Road had apparently touched off a massive Confederate counterattack, which was now rolling down from the northwest. And someone else would have to halt it; the Ninth Corps boys were going home for supper.

"General Griffin," as one of the Maine men recalled, "entered into the spirit of the occasion, and soon formed us into line on a low crest of land covered with a scattering growth of wood. The enemy must advance in our front, and climb up the ascent. . . ." The crest was right across the path of the Confederate advance. If the 1st Division could stay there, it could stop the counterattack. But it was strung out into not much more than a heavy skirmish line, and they were taking a wicked plastering from Confederate artillery. In the 20th Maine there was a burst of flame and smoke, a spattering of blood, and a dozen men were knocked out by one shell. In the fading light ahead, musketry was spitting redly, its rattle growing to a steady roar. General Griffin, the old artilleryman, decided that it was time to get a line of fieldpieces up on the crest, exposed though it was. And it was here that he made his famous pronouncement on the Griffin doctrine of artillery employment. A battery commander, pointing to the thin line, had cried to General Griffin, "My God, General, do you mean for me to put my guns out on that skirmish line?"

Whereat Griffin, with much vehemence, it is said, replied, "Yes, rush them in there; artillery is no better than infantry, put them in the line, and let them fight together." And the guns came up, loaded to the muzzle with canister. Meanwhile there had been a certain amount of confusion. Officers were seeing men in front dressed partly in blue and were under the impression that some of the Ninth Corps troops were still on the ground and were trying to get back through them. "Cease fire, cease fire!" the officers called, but the enlisted men had better sense. These blue-clad men were shooting at *them*, and whether they were Ninth Corps soldiers or Confederates, they had damn well better be shot back at. Disregarding the orders, the men poured a destructive volley into what was, in fact, a Confederate assault—just in time to avert a possible disaster. Rifles flamed in the gathering dusk; Griffin's requisitioned artillery sent blasts of canister sweeping down the slope, and the enemy went scattering back into the darkness, beaten off and defeated.

As the 20th Maine men picked up their wounded and counted the soldiers present for duty in the darkness of that September evening, they could reckon that they had just been through one of the fiercest days of the war. Seven definitely dead, fifty wounded, was the score. Major Ellis Spear was the only field officer left in the entire 3rd Brigade, so he was now in command of the brigade. Command of the regiment had passed from Spear to Captain Atherton W. Clark. Lieutenant Alden Miller was wounded, also Captain Henry F. Sidelinger. And Captain Weston H. Keene—he who had brought his cash along—was on the way to the embalmer's; the money would be used as he had directed.

Next day, loud cheering. Generals Grant and Meade were riding along to inspect the newly won lines. Better dig in here, Meade told Griffin. But Griffin's blood was still up. He retorted, "I don't need any breastworks; I can whip the whole rebel army with my little division." But, as a man in the 20th put it, "Entrenchments were made, notwithstanding this remarkable fact."

For the 20th Maine, the month of October was peaceful—the countryside around their entrenchments calm in the beauty of Virginia autumn. The sunshine was bright and mellow, but a coolness was coming into the air now, and intermingled with the green of the pines were the yellows and crimsons of oak, dogwood and maples, while persimmons and wild grapes were ripening in the forests. Yet the red scars of the earthworks were being steadily extended westward, and on October 27, the army made another stab in that direction, across Hatcher's Run. This was a confused action; as usual when the army was attacking, it rained, and the dense forests obscured the action and caused entire regiments to get lost. There were heavy Confederate counterattacks and the expedition was a complete failure. The 20th Maine participated, losing one man killed and two wounded.

After that, for the remainder of the year, there was little fighting for the 20th Maine to do, but on November 8 they were coming up to what might be their greatest victory, or most dismal defeat. This was Election Day, offering a choice between Lincoln and McClellan, and for the Army of the Potomac it presented both an emotional and a political crisis. As Private Theodore Gerrish wrote, "McClellan was our first commander, and, as such, he was almost worshipped by his soldiers. The political friends of General McClellan well understood that fact, and it was a very crafty thing for them to nominate him as their candidate for the Presidency. . . ."

Along with McClellan, however, the Democratic Party had asked the country to accept a platform which had declared that the war was a failure and ought to be stopped while negotiations aimed at the restoration of the Union by peaceful means were carried on. For these views there had been some justification in August, when the Democratic Convention had met. In his series of actions from the Wilderness to the Chickahominy, Grant's casualties had reached the enormous total of sixty thousand—more men than Lee had in his entire army at the beginning of the campaign. Meanwhile Lee's Army of Northern Virginia had lost only a third of that number, had successfully defended Richmond and, conscious of the terrible losses inflicted on the attackers, was in high spirits. This had been the situation in midsummer, when the morale of the North was at a record low.

But the victories of Sherman at Atlanta and Sheridan in the Shenandoah Valley in late summer and early fall had restored Northern confidence. And the political tide had also changed. The Democratic Party included a certain number of plotters, extremists, and Southern sympathizers whose activities were actually disloyal to the Union government. There were many others whose attempts to discuss matters freely could be taken to be disloyal, and on this basis the whole Democratic Party was vigorously smeared with the tar of treason charges. So the picture of the party and its aims, as it reached the soldiers in the field, was not likely to be favorable.

In his letter accepting the nomination McClellan had virtually repudiated the Democratic platform, out of deference, as he implied, to his old comrades in arms. But the old comrades could not forget. McClellan had accepted nomination by a party which had asked them to step up and vote, as Gerrish put it, "that our campaigns had all been failures, and that our comrades had all died in vain." The thought of voting thus was abhorrent to most of the men in the 20th Maine. It touched their pride—always a powerful force—and also went against all their ideas of a frugal and businesslike transaction. If a man paid for something, he ought to get it, and looking back over the long and bloody road they had traveled, it did not seem that all the hardships and deaths could properly lead to any result less conclusive than victory.

Yet the election imposed a test of resolution unique in the history of armies. To some extent, the soldiers were voting on whether they would fight or go home. A vote for Lincoln was unquestionably a vote for fight. A vote for McClellan was a vote for the side that—whatever its nominee now declared—had said, "Let's stop the fighting and try to negotiate the southern states back into the Union." A very appealing, if unlikely prospect, for the soldier who wanted to go home.

So there were dangers in this election, any way you looked at it. And even the process of voting was hazardous. On November 6 the army chief of staff had issued this warning: "In view of the fact that a general election is to be held on Tuesday next, the 8th instant, it is considered probable that the enemy may attack with the hope of finding us unprepared and of breaking up the election." In the Fifth Corps, officers were instructed to have their men vote as promptly as possible, so that the polls could be closed early and the troops held ready to meet the expected attack.

But the Confederates had no wish, apparently, to interfere with the election. Election Day was not only quiet along the front, but unusually quiet. When the ballots were counted, the 20th Maine had cast 13 votes for McClellan and 138 for Lincoln. In the Fifth Corps the Lincoln majority was better than two to one—quite remarkable since this had always been considered a "McClellan corps." In the Army of the Potomac as a whole the vote was decisively for Lincoln.

And Private Gerrish concluded, "That grand old army performed many heroic acts . . . but never in its history did it do a more devoted service. . . ." It was an army that voted to send its own lines charging again at parapets where thousands of the voters would meet certain death.

When news of Lincoln's re-election reached the Army of the Potomac, the men went wild with excitement. All the way from the Weldon Railroad, along the lines up past Petersburg, men cheered until they were hoarse. Hearing the cheering, and supposing that some great victory had been won elsewhere, the Confederates made anxious inquiry. At a point where the enemy breastworks were within shouting distance, this exchange was reported:

"Say, Yank."

"Hilloa, Johnny."

"Don't fire, Yank."

"All right, Johnny."

"What are you'uns all cheering for?"

"Big victory on our side."

"What is it, Yank?"

"Old Abe has cleaned all your fellers out up North."

There was a pause and then Johnny answered, "Well, Yank, we cheered when we heard that your little Mac was nominated, but we don't feel much like cheering now." The Maine men believed that Lincoln's re-election cast a deep gloom over the Confederate soldiers and was an important factor in their final defeat.

Concerning all this Joshua Chamberlain was forming certain opinions. Now a brigadier general, although a badly used-up one, Chamberlain was back with the army as autumn ended. He was scarcely able to stand, let alone mount a horse. But he was back, and perhaps the results of the election inspired him. Of them he wrote, "Our volunteer soldiers felt that they were part

231

of the very people whose honor and life they were to maintain; they recognized that they were entitled to participate so far as they were able in the thought and conscience and will of that supreme 'people' whose agents and instruments they were in the field of arms. . . . The result of this vote showed how much stronger was their allegiance to principle than even their attachment to McClellan, whose personal popularity in the army was something marvelous. . . . The fact that this war was in its reach of meaning and consequent effect so much more than what are commonly called 'civil wars'—this being a war to test and finally determine the character of the interior constitution and real organic life of this great people—brought into the field an amount of thoughtfulness and moral reflection not usual in armies."

Thoughtful or not, the Maine men were still capable of behaving as soldiers have often behaved, once relieved from the mud of the trenches. Early in December they went on a most enjoyable raid with the Fifth Corps, about forty miles down the Weldon Railroad and nearly to the North Carolina border. The Confederates had been using the railroad up as far as Stony Creek Station, then hauling the supplies in wagons on a long detour around to the west and up to Petersburg. The purpose of the Union raid was to tear up the railroad so far south that this route of supply would no longer be practicable.

After a hard two-day march in the inevitable rain, they struck the railroad on December 8 a few miles below Stony Creek Station. The weather had cleared. The troops immediately went to work that night destroying the tracks. The procedure was simple. The whole corps was stretched out along the railroad, by divisions. The soldiers stacked arms, dug up the ties, and with groups of men all lifting together, overturned ties, tracks and all. The ties were then wrenched off, placed in large piles and set afire. The rails were laid over the burning ties so that they heated and bent out of shape. In addition, many of the heated rails were wrapped around trees. As soon as a division destroyed the track in its front, it leapfrogged on to another section and repeated the process. Soon the Weldon Railroad was burning for miles—a long line of bonfires glowing in the blue December moonlight. At Jarratt's Station the 20th Maine ceased work for the night and went into bivouac, but there appears to have been little sleeping.

It had by now been discovered that this was excellent country for foraging—with pigs, hens and cattle in abundance. There were also quantities of applejack which could be presumed to be giving aid and comfort to the rebellion. It might, in fact, have been the source of the rebellion, judged by its effects on the regiment for the next two days. All during that moonlit night at Jarratt's Station, foragers were returning to camp in varying degrees of exhilaration. One little fellow came flapping in wearing a white linen shirt that was several sizes too large for him, the collar reaching far above his ears, the cuffs extending inches beyond his hands, the whole ensemble surmounted by a stovepipe hat. Under the influence of applejack, groups of men formed lines and fought sham battles along the burning railroad. And there were other evidences of the sweetly deceptive power of this liquor which should have forewarned the troop commanders.

Next day, with the weather getting colder, the 20th Maine with the 1st Division of the corps moved along down the railroad and encamped near the plantation of one Ben Bailes. So far, no interference from enemy troops. There didn't seem to be a male Southerner left in the territory. But Ben Bailes had unintentionally left an explosive booby trap for the bluecoats, and the 3rd Brigade walked into it. The explosive, concealed under haystacks, was twenty-five barrels of applejack. The men of the regiment that discovered the applejack undertook to keep it to themselves. But there was too much of it, and the effects were too evident. Attracted by the noisy singing and shouting, the whole 3rd Brigade gathered and men began filling canteens and coffee pails. "Alas!" one wrote. "Dew of the Orchard captured the men in turn." The disorder reached such an extent that a regiment of cavalry was sent to suppress it, but the cavalrymen, too, were overcome and only added to the uproar. The Provost Guard rushed in and poured the little applejack that was left in the barrels onto the ground. General Joshua Chamberlain, who was in command of a widely extended infantry guard designed to keep the enemy at bay, had to use half his force to keep drunken soldiers from running off into the countryside.

A sleet storm began in the night, and it completed the devastation that Ben Bailes had inaugurated with his applejack. By morning the bushes, trees, and many recumbent soldiers were beautifully coated with sparkling ice. Besides this, the enemy seemed to be appearing in some force, and the crackle of picket firing was breaking out around them. Orders came to get out, in a hurry. But many of the men were so badly hung over that it took an hour to get them started. And many had disappeared completely. The 20th Maine, it is recorded, marched northward "very rapidly" and made twenty miles by nightfall.

Next day they were back with the main body of the army, and started building winter quarters on the Jerusalem Plank Road. During the whole expedition, the 1st Division had not been engaged. But there were losses, and General Griffin, adding up the figures, must have noted the effects of the applejack. No casualties in the 1st Brigade, only fifteen stragglers in the 2nd Brigade, but in the 3rd Brigade, forty-three missing.

Perhaps the worst loss of all would be that of Joshua Chamberlain. The hard march and the sleet storm had been too much for the wounded and still-suffering Chamberlain. In January, by order of General Warren and the corps surgeons, Chamberlain was bundled up and sent north again. And this time he seemed to be in such bad condition that it was probably good-bye.

CHAPTER THIRTEEN

The Winds of March

GRANT'S campaign in Virginia had a classic, almost a symphonic form. His leftward-flanking theme had its exposition following the battle of the Wilderness, then was developed with variations in the massive drive south to the James, and recapitulated in the cutting off of Petersburg. But as 1864 ended and 1865 began there were accompaniments in a descending scale that saddened many listeners. The sensitive ear of Joshua Chamberlain had caught the sound of muted trumpets, the notes of bass strings going down in ever-deepening, tragic tones. He wrote: "The men of the rank and file in our army of volunteers before Petersburg besides being seasoned soldiers were endowed and susceptible according to their spiritual measures. Their life was not merely in their own experiences but in larger sympathies. Their environment . . . consisted for them not only in material things but also much in memories and shadowings. Things were remnants and reminders. Lines stood thinner; circles ever narrowing. Corps fought down to divisions; divisions to brigades; these again broken and the shattered regiments consolidated under the token and auspices of their States as if reverting to their birthright, and being 'gathered to their fathers.' Old flags—yes, but crowded together not by on-rush to battle, but by thinning ranks bringing the dear more near. . . . And even the coming in of new, fresh faces was not without its cast of shadow. The officers, too, who had gone down were of the best known, trusted, and beloved. . . . All the changes touched the border of sorrows.

"The strength of great memories, pride of historic continuity, unfailing loyalty of purpose and resolve held these men together in unity of form and spirit. But there seemed some slackening of the old nerve and verve; and service was sustained more from the habit of obedience and instinct of duty, than with that sympathetic intuition which inspires men to exceed the literal of orders or of obligations."

Attrition in the ranks of the 20th Maine and replacement by recruits during the last four months of 1864 had greatly changed the character of the regiment. September through December, the regiment received over two hundred recruits. Its strength at the end of the year was 425 enlisted men, with 315 present for duty. Thus, around half of the men were new. One of the veterans who had been wounded in the Wilderness and who returned about this time was sobered by the change. "Alas," he wrote, "how many forms had vanished! How many voices had been hushed!"

The recruits received by the 20th Maine were of about the same class as the original members of the regiment—Maine boys, most of them draftees, all of them untrained, and of varying character. It has been noted throughout the war (by Captain Judson of the 83rd Pennsylvania and other students of military psychology) that the best soldier corresponded to the ordinary reliable citizen, having a sense of responsibility and good principles. A few of the 20th Maine recruits were completely lacking in any sense of duty. Detailed for guard, one of them said, "I won't go on guard, I'll be damned if I'll go on guard, I'll go under guard first." Go under guard he did—to a court-martial.

But most of the men were more responsible. Private Ezekiel Benn, for example, had exceptionally strong principles, some of these being directed, by parental training, against the use of alcohol and tobacco. Private Benn also had a sense of humor; writing home on January 28, he teased the folks back in Maine. "It has been so cold for the last few days that we draw two rations of whiskey each day now. I suppose you would think it looked kind of strange for me to walk up and take the pipe out of my mouth and take a drink of whiskey but you know the army is a great place for drinking, smoking and chewing and you know that it would look odd for one not to join them, but enough nonsense. I of course do no such thing." (Private Benn swapped his whiskey ration for coffee, and later his folks called his attention to the impropriety of this—he should have destroyed the whiskey, they pointed out.)

Physically, Private Benn was far from being a well man and had no business even being in the army. Yet on the long marches leading to Appomattox Benn managed, with the help of his companions, to keep up—and it was, perhaps, old-fashioned Maine moral hardihood like his that could be counted among the main assets of the reinforced as well as the original 20th Maine.

The 20th Maine was no longer the volunteer regiment that had fought at Little Round Top. Yet it was still thought of as a veteran regiment and was one of the bulwarks of the 3rd Brigade, now increased to eight regiments by the consolidation mentioned by Chamberlain. Three of the regiments which had made up the brigade at Gettysburg—the 20th Maine, 16th Michigan and 83rd Pennsylvania—still remained. The new regiments were also "veteran" units—old regiments built up by recruits and by the addition of men from the same state whose terms of service had not expired with the term of their regiments. The 32nd Massachusetts, for example, had "leftovers" from three other Massachusetts regiments that had gone home.

So all in all there had been marked transformation. It could be said that the old 20th Maine had had its last great day at Peebles' Farm. The new 20th Maine would have to carry on, and its work would not be easy. The capture of the entrenchments around Peebles' Farm had brought the Union line to within about four miles of the Southside Railroad, the capture of which would mean the doom of Petersburg. The space between Peebles' Farm and the railroad, however, was so strongly fortified in depth that further direct assaults in that direction were thought to be inadvisable. Grant's tactical theme dictated the next move: try another run around left end.

This would mean driving westward into a gloomy region of forests, swamps and streams. At least two of the streams, Gravelly Run and Hatcher's Run, could be natural obstacles after a heavy rain. Then there were roads where the enemy could be expected to have formidable dispositions—the Quaker Road,

Boydton Plank Road and White Oak Road. And all through the forested region, the Confederates had constructed a maze of earthworks. Capturing one line, the Union troops might find themselves facing still another, even stronger; advancing to the second line, they would be likely to find it swept by fire from a third, or enfiladed from works to the flank. There were infinite possibilities for ambush, surprise and confusion.

These possibilities were well developed by the partly green 3rd Brigade when the Fifth Corps went crashing into the labyrinth of the Hatcher's Run forests on February 6. Late in the afternoon of that cold winter day, the brigade struck a Confederate line near Dabney's Mill, drove the gray troops back half a mile, and then ran into another line of entrenchments where the Confederate general Mahone was waiting to smite the Yankees hip and thigh. The results of Mahone's counterattack were reluctantly chronicled by Private Gerrish of the 20th Maine. "I think that I will not attempt to describe that affair; the boys will all remember it, and there are some facts connected with that battle which we would not want everyone to know. We all remember the thick pine bushes, the tangled brush, the running vines, the thorn bushes, the streams of water, the deep holes filled with mud and mire, how the rebels fired on us, and how we fired in return, and how we got frightened, and 'skedaddled' back through the woods like a flock of sheep."

An officer in the 83rd Pennsylvania also described the affair as "the greatest skedaddle that has taken place yet." He thought, however, that bad handling of the troops had had something to do with it. "The generals got excited and did not keep their reserves well in hand: and when Mahone charged with his division, he drove the front line before him and they, in turn, carried everything back with them."

The 155 Pennsylvania, one of the regiments just added to the 3rd Brigade, had the further misfortune of being fired into by raw Union troops in its rear. Understandably angered, the Pennsylvanians charged into their misguided brethren, and the confusion was further confounded. The whole disorganized mob poured back over a ridge where, fortunately, a line of fieldpieces was waiting, gunners standing with their hands on the lanyards, waiting for the refugees to pass. A blast of canister discouraged the pursuing Confederates, and the fall of darkness brought the miserable action to a close.

The day was particularly unhappy for Colonel Charles D. Gilmore. Although nominally colonel of the 20th Maine from June 18, 1864, onward, Gilmore had been absent on detached service in Washington from December of 1863 to October of 1864. Thus he had had no opportunity to command the regiment in a major action. At Hatcher's Run, Gilmore fell into the hands of the enemy and was a prisoner for a short while, but in the magnificent confusion he made a desperate dash for freedom and got back to the Union lines. Two weeks later he was ordered back to Washington to serve on a military commission.

The cost of the battle for the 20th Maine was twenty-four men and a grievous wounding of the regimental pride. For the army as a whole, the only result of the affair was the extension of the Union lines westward to Hatcher's Run. Here the 20th Maine went into camp for a few weeks of relative peace. The weather was fine; bands played on the sparkling winter afternoons, and there were brigade and division reviews. There was also time for instructing the recruits in military matters. The drill and discipline of the regiment improved.

This was the farthest south the Maine men had ever wintered, and they noticed striking differences. Spring was coming on weeks ahead of anything they had ever experienced. In early March there was a softness in the air on fine days, and the frogs were singing in the swamps around Hatcher's Run. The frogs, too, sang differently, with a certain easygoing calmness in their voices, whereas the frogs of Maine had sung with a continuous high-pitched note not unlike that of the rebel yell. (The frogs of the two states, they might have observed, should have swapped places.) Around March 20 it is recorded that the winds blew furiously, sighing through the pines around Hatcher's Run, flattening the rusty brown grass with roaring waves of air and casting a haze over the landscape with clouds of fine dust. The wind yanked up tent pegs, whipcracked loose canvas loudly, harried small birds across the sky like specks of chaff. And this spring the winds of March evoked, more than usually, their strangely moving mood of sadness and gusty optimism, for they were blowing the Confederacy away, blowing toward peace and —for many of the young men who would bring all this about— toward death.

There were rumors that another big push was about to begin and a general feeling that this would be the last campaign. Although the regiment was now so big and so altered with new blood that it seemed altogether different, elements of the old 20th Maine still provided a strong backbone of determination. Typical of this spirit was the desire expressed by Private Edmund Morrison, one of the original members of the regiment. Twice wounded, suffering from injuries from which he could never fully recover, Morrison was told by the surgeon that he was in no condition to withstand the hard marches of the campaign coming up, and that he had better go back to the hospital and get his discharge. His old friends in the regiment also tried to persuade him to go home, but to no avail. Morrison had been on a long road with the 20th Maine, and he wanted to see the end of it. If the 20th Maine was marching, he was marching with it.

And it may have been this same spirit of the old 20th Maine that brought about the miraculous reappearance of Brigadier General Joshua Chamberlain. Having been sent north in January, he had escaped from the doctors and returned to participate in the spring campaign. Although somewhat shattered he was considered to be serviceable, so the appreciative Griffin gave him the command of the 1st Brigade.

As the spring campaign opened, Walter G. Morrill, now a lieutenant colonel, was commanding the 20th Maine. Ellis Spear, who had risen to the rank of colonel, was on staff duty at division headquarters. These officers had a good conception of Grant's plan for the campaign. Orders were clearer, more complete than they ever had been before. The enemy situation and capabilities were well understood. The Confederate lines were now getting extended to a high degree of vulnerability. Besides covering Petersburg, Lee was attempting to protect the remaining supply routes leading into the city, and this would eventually prove to be an impossible assignment against superior Federal manpower. Extending from Petersburg the Confederate lines of entrenchments ran westward at distances varying from two to four miles below the Southside Railroad, also covering the Boydton Plank Road as far as Hatcher's Run. From this point the main Confederate line ran along the White Oak Road as far as the Claiborne Road, where it bent back in a "return" toward the north. Four miles to the west—on the White Oak Road but detached from the main line—there was another line of Confederate works covering an important road junction known as Five Forks.

Grant's plan was to make a flanking thrust around the extreme right of Lee's line with a force consisting of three divisions of cavalry, headed by Sheridan, and the Fifth Corps of infantry, followed if necessary by the Second Corps. The plan would present General Lee with a set of uncomfortable choices. If he remained in his line of entrenchments, Sheridan's cavalry could sweep on past his right, cut the Southside Railroad, and then go on to sever the Richmond and Danville Railroad farther to the north—thus isolating Richmond. If, on the other hand, Lee moved out of his entrenchments, he would have to meet a powerful force in the open; and if he moved troops from the immediate front of Petersburg, extending the lines westward for the purpose of blocking Sheridan and the flanking Union infantry, the defenses of the city would be so weakened that the rest of Grant's numerically superior army could launch an attack that would probably succeed.

With all these possibilities, something was bound to happen. And whatever happened, Grant hoped to be ready. Perhaps for that reason he was placing much of the tactical responsibility for the performance of the cavalry-infantry task force on the shoulders of Sheridan. Unlike some of the generals in the Army of the Potomac, Sheridan was a hurry-hurry leader who could get his troops moving fast when the time came—and it would be necessary to move fast if Lee was to be cornered even now.

There was something about Sheridan, apparently, that moved men to action—a dynamic quality that photographs have never quite conveyed. Theodore Gerrish wrote, "I have carefully examined many pictures of Sheridan, which I suppose are lifelike, but somehow I have always been disappointed. . . . This is how he appeared on the field: A short, thick-set man, with very short legs, his broad shoulders a little stooping as he sat upon his horse, having a very large head, with hair clipped close, a short, thick mustache; his uniform being usually the worse for wear and spotted with mud; wearing a soft felt hat, at least two sizes too small, and for safekeeping usually pressed down upon a portion of the back of his head. He rode a splendid horse, usually went at a round gallop, and rolled and bounced upon the back of his steed much as an old salt does when walking up the aisle of a church after a four years' cruise at sea."

Sheridan's entourage was equally colorful. Beside him, usually, rode a dozen or so scouts clad in Confederate uniforms—useful if somewhat hazardous for making dashes inside the rebel lines. At least twenty captured battle flags ranging all the way from battery guidons to brigade headquarters standards were borne unfurled behind Sheridan as he galloped along. Not to be outdone in showmanship, one of his division commanders, General George A. Custer, was clad in a blue uniform decorated with gold lace, sported a red necktie and wore his hair in flowing locks.

To the plodding infantrymen of the 20th Maine, the cavalrymen were a bunch of showoffs as this campaign opened, and later they would have more cause for resentment directed at Sheridan. They could take comfort, however, in the fact that one of their own, General Joshua L. Chamberlain, would rise to heights that would rival even the bright eminence of the great Sheridan. Physically, the ex-theologian was in striking contrast to the bull-headed cavalry leader, but he entered the final conflict with equal zest. And with something more. Chamberlain was still ailing from his fearful wound, and his exploits in the spring campaign seem to have been sheer triumphs of the spirit rather than of animal energy. In many of his writings and recorded utterances, he gave evidence of this spiritual quality all through his life. (One day, for example, when he was a very old man, someone asked him if there was any truth to the report that George Washington had been seen riding around on a white horse on that morning in 1863 when they were approaching the field of Gettysburg. The old warrior did not reply for a long while, then said, "Yes, that report was circulated through our lines and I have no doubt that it had a tremendous psychological effect in inspiring the men. Doubtless it was a superstition, but yet who among us can say that such a thing was impossible? We have not yet sounded or explored the immortal life that lies out beyond the Bar. We know not what mystic power may be possessed by those who are now bivouacking with the dead. I only know the effect, but I dare not explain or deny the cause. I do believe that we were enveloped by the powers of the other world that day and who shall say that Washington was not among the number of those who aided the country that he founded?")

In his actions along the Quaker and White Oak roads, Chamberlain may not have been George Washington riding on a white horse, but his examples appear to have been happily inspirational and impressive. On March 29, a warm spring day with a moist wind blowing in from the south, birds singing, buds breaking into green tufts and troops throwing off excess clothing along the line of march, Chamberlain and his brigade led the advance of the 1st Division up the Quaker Road, northward toward that vital portion of the Confederate line that stretched along the White Oak Road. Since the Quaker Road—sometimes called the Military Road—was one of the important avenues of approach, the Confederates had strong advance forces on it. These had destroyed the bridge across Gravelly Run and were waiting on the north bank. "We soon found," Chamberlain recalled, "this road better entitled to its military than its Quaker appellation." There was a preliminary bickering of musketry back and forth across the stream, then Chamberlain led his brigade in an impetuous dash across it, men wading through water up to their waists and scrambling up the north bank to break the Confederate line and sweep it into a mile-long retreat up the Quaker Road. But just beyond a set of farm buildings, the gray line reformed again behind strong breastworks in the edge of a wood, and the advance quivered to a halt with the smoke and noise of battle extending to the flanks as supporting troops came up.

Chamberlain thought that it looked like a job for foot-cavalry—

243

a straight run at the enemy works with little halting to fire, then over the entrenchments with the bayonet. Putting part of his brigade on the right of the Quaker Road and part on the left, Chamberlain himself took six companies of infantry and dashed straight up the road, his objective a heap of sawdust where a portable sawmill had once stood—now the center of the Confederate line.

As they neared the sawdust pile, Chamberlain's horse was going wild with excitement and getting a little too far ahead of the troops. Chamberlain gave him a quick check. The horse reared up, and a bullet apparently aimed at Chamberlain's breast went through the big muscles of the horse's uplifted neck, thence up the General's arm, ripping the sleeve to tatters and bruising the flesh. Striking a brass-mounted hand-mirror in Chamberlain's breast pocket and dealing him a staggering blow just beneath the heart, the bullet then followed two of his ribs around and came out the back seam of his coat. Knocked unconscious, Chamberlain fell forward and instinctively clasped the neck of his horse, which had stopped and was bleeding profusely. The two, man and horse, bled together for a moment, making such an exceedingly gory sight that a dispatch went back and reached the New York morning newspapers as a notice of the Maine general's death.

Just as Chamberlain was coming to, General Griffin rode up to him, put an arm around his waist and murmured, "My dear General, you are gone."

"Yes, General, I am," Chamberlain responded, but he had completely misunderstood Griffin's remark. A dazed glance had shown him that the entire right of his attacking line had broken and was scattering toward the rear. He was "gone" indeed, in a military sense, unless something were done—and done quickly. Straightening back in his saddle, Chamberlain spurred his wounded horse away from the astonished Griffin and rode into the midst of the fleeing troops. There he evidently appeared as an apparition, his cap gone, bare head smeared with gore, clothing bullet-torn and soaked with blood. Properly impressed, the troops rallied and swarmed back to get a foothold inside the enemy works.

Waves of cheering followed Chamberlain as he rode back toward the sawdust pile and the center of the line. Some of it was coming from the Confederates. "I hardly knew what world I was in," Chamberlain recalled. His unfortunate horse, however, was sinking lower and lower from loss of blood, until its nose finally touched the ground and the General dismounted. At this point he remembered that Colonel Ellis Spear came up and "with a mysterious and impressive look, as if about to present a brevet commission," drew from his pocket a Jamaica-ginger bottle full of wine. Chamberlain tipped it up and drank long and deeply, the level in the bottle lowering so drastically that Spear began to wear a "melancholy, martyr-like look." Chamberlain was a long way, now, from the Bangor Theological Seminary.

But he needed the drink. In the edge of the woods where the enemy breastworks ran, the fight was still roaring and the outcome was not at all certain. General Griffin came up again, looking pale—an unusual complexion for Griffin. Whenever there was serious trouble, Griffin's first thought was artillery. He shouted, "If you can hold on there ten minutes, I will give you a battery."

Someone produced a strange-looking, mud-spattered white horse; warmed by his draught of wine, Chamberlain climbed into the saddle and returned to the fray, shouting, "Once more! Try the steel! Hell for ten minutes and we are out of it!" The soldiers regarded him with appreciation. A general's place was normally behind the line of battle, but here was a general right out in front and with blood on him, at that. The troops held on in front of the breastworks, and soon Griffin's promised artillery fire swished overhead, thundering in the trees around the Confederates, showering them with sharp metal and falling branches. Union infantry launched another attack following the artillery closely, and this time the defenders gave way, heading for their main entrenchments farther north. The way to assault the line on the White Oak Road had now been opened, and Chamberlain had been about as sensational as it is possible for one officer to be in one afternoon. Not long afterward he received a brevet commission of major general, "for conspicuous gallantry in action on the Quaker Road, March 29, 1865."

That evening the rain began to fall heavily, drenching the wounded, turning roads and fields into mire. During the day Sheridan's cavalry had moved to a position around Dinwiddie Court House, off to the left and rear of the Fifth Corps. But the developments on the Quaker Road had caused Grant to modify his plans somewhat for the cavalry. He sent word to Sheridan to forget, for the time being, the plan to dash northward and capture the enemy railroads. Instead, Sheridan was to work with the infantry, pushing around the Confederates and getting on their right rear. There was a chance now, Grant felt, to deliver the knockout blow. Later in the night, Sheridan was ordered to seize Five Forks early the next morning. In the Fifth Corps, Chamberlain and other infantry officers were wondering why Sheridan hadn't seized Five Forks already. What had he been doing all day? Experience had shown that it didn't take Robert E. Lee very long to size up a situation of this kind. Within a few hours Lee would probably know all about Grant's plans, and would have a strong force waiting at Five Forks to knock the cavalry back on its haunches.

The 20th Maine, with the 3rd Brigade, now again under the command of General Joseph Bartlett, had supported Chamberlain's advance on the Quaker Road during the twenty-ninth. During the night, the Maine soldiers worked on entrenchments to secure the advanced line, blundering around in the rainy darkness, one man falling into a twenty-foot well and causing some bewilderment with his cries for help, coming from deep underground, before he was finally found and fished out. They had a few hours' sleep in rain-soaked blankets, then awoke to find new work waiting for them in the foggy dawn. Around four hundred yards ahead, the Confederates had established a lightly held line covering their main works a little farther north. There was a Union attack in the afternoon—rain still coming down in torrents —and the first enemy line was carried. During this attack, and in standing off a counterattack that soon followed, the 20th Maine lost several men wounded. It also got muddied up. By nightfall, except for its colors, the regiment was completely unrecognizable. Men had been lying and crawling all day; the reddish mud covered uniforms from head to foot.

During the night they were relieved by troops of the Second Corps and moved to the left, where the Fifth Corps was now within close striking distance of the White Oak Road. Their division, Griffin's, went into a reserve position. The other two divisions of the corps were moving toward the enemy. Rumor had it that one of these divisions was going to make an exploratory thrust at the Confederate line very shortly; but back here where the 20th Maine was resting, everything seemed peaceful. The storm had ceased, and bright spring sunshine was pouring down through the breaking clouds. The men lighted fires and spread soaked blankets out on the ground to dry, while coffee pails bubbled over the coals. Up front, the expected roar of battle swelled up, and men stopped munching hardtack momentarily to cock an attentive ear in that direction. The sound kept getting louder and seemed to be coming closer. Soon musketry could be distinguished from cannon fire, and cheering could be heard which sounded suspiciously like the rebel yell. It appeared that the attack was proceeding in the wrong direction. It was, in fact, coming straight at them—so with a screaming of bugles and frantic orders to "Fall in! Fall in!" the Maine men grabbed their muskets from the stacks, formed, and went double-timing with Bartlett's Brigade to a crest overlooking a branch of Gravelly Run. By now, troops of the other two Fifth Corps divisions were in sight, retreating in such numbers that the high-pitched voice of General Griffin could be heard yelling, "For God's sake, let them through or they will break our line!"

Coming down the slope on the other side of Gravelly Run was a line of wolf-gray forms, yipping, shooting, running through the smoke of their own firing and seemingly about to drive the Fifth Corps into one of the real panics of its career. But the volleys from Bartlett's Brigade, slashing across the stream, struck the oncoming Confederates like an evil wind; Union artillery opened fire; bands began to play to hearten the defenders, and in the face of music and musketry, the enemy advance staggered to a halt.

The Confederates had run into another instance of good generalship by the hero of Little Round Top. Expecting a counterblow by Lee, General Warren had not placed his divisions in line.

Instead, he had arranged them in echelon, so that the Confederate counterattack had met the increasing resistance of a defense
in depth. But even though he had stood off the blow successfully,
Warren was badly shaken. The honor of the Fifth Corps, if not
completely blackened, had been badly dimmed. Warren approached Chamberlain with a request that he lead an attack to
regain the lost positions.

Chamberlain was lying on a heap of straw, suffering from his
old pelvic wound, plus the new ones he had received on the
Quaker Road. It might have seemed to the Maine general that
he was being put upon—that he had done enough during the past
two days; in fact, he pointed out to Warren that Bartlett had a
much bigger brigade than his own, and Bartlett might be just the
person for the job. "We have come to you; you know what that
means," was Warren's grim reply. So the incredible Chamberlain
got up and led the counter-counterattack—which not only recovered the lost ground, but roared right across the White Oak
Road, securing a lodgement on this important Confederate artery.
It now seemed to Chamberlain that they were ready for the final
stroke that might bring the war to a rapid conclusion. The Fifth
Corps was on the White Oak Road; if Sheridan could now come
up from the left rear with even one of his cavalry divisions and
strike in on their left, the enemy line would be turned and they
could start rolling it back toward Petersburg.

But instead of the cavalry coming to their aid, the Fifth Corps
was destined to go to the rescue of Sheridan. In late afternoon
they heard heavy firing in the direction of Dinwiddie, and it
seemed to be receding. The meaning was clear to officers of the
Fifth Corps. Sheridan was being driven backward, and their own
left flank was being rapidly exposed to whatever Confederate
force was driving him. Chamberlain and Warren had a talk about
it, wondering whether or not help ought to be sent to Sheridan.
Chamberlain expressed the opinion that if they believed the enemy had the advantage of Sheridan, they would be criticized for
not going to his support, even though they had no specific orders
to do so.

"Well, will you go?" Warren asked.

"Certainly, General, if you think it best; but surely you do not want me to abandon this position," Chamberlain replied. Upon further reflection, Warren decided to detach the 3rd Brigade, Bartlett's. So at about five o'clock Bartlett pulled out of line and started directly across country, following a narrow, muddy woods-trail off toward the sound of the firing in the southwest. For a detached unit, this was a dangerous mission and a man in the 20th Maine remembered a feeling of great uneasiness when the sun went down and the shadows of the forest enveloped them. As darkness fell, there was skirmishing ahead. They halted, and Bartlett threw out a long line of pickets. South of them enemy campfires blossomed in the night, seeming to stretch for miles. They could hear the Confederates talking, chopping wood and moving wagons. They had come up behind the left flank of the force that was threatening Sheridan at Dinwiddie.

Meanwhile, back on the White Oak Road, nightmarish confusion was setting in. Word had arrived that Sheridan had been driven back to Dinwiddie Court House by Fitzhugh Lee's cavalry, plus Pickett's infantry division. The reaction to this was exposing one of the weaknesses in this campaign, which was too many generals giving orders. Involved in the operation were: General Grant, commanding all the Union armies but making his headquarters with the Army of the Potomac; General Meade, commanding the Army of the Potomac; General Sheridan—as the cavalry commander, independent of Meade—but using Meade's Fifth Corps as a supporting force; and finally the unfortunate General Warren of the Fifth Corps, who was receiving instructions and orders from all directions. All of these generals wanted to get help for the cavalry, but each had a somewhat different idea of what troops ought to be sent where. Over the miry fields and roads, across the rain-swollen streams and through the darkness, all communications were slow and erratic, so that conflicting orders became even more confusing when their arrival sequence was mixed up.

The net of all these orders was that the Fifth Corps was to disengage itself from its grapple with the enemy and move five or six miles backward through mud and intense darkness to the support of Sheridan. But the immediate effect was that the corps was picked apart, into divisions and brigades, and as orders

changed there was much shuttling of troops back and forth, with
enormous difficulties in the inky darkness. One division found a
roaring torrent across its designated route and the bridge out.
The men tore down a house and built a forty-foot bridge in the
blackness of the night. Along the White Oak Road, the troops
were in such close proximity to the enemy that they could not
be summoned by bugles. Officers and non-coms had to creep
along from one unit to another and give the commands verbally.
All this took time. Further, the actions of the enemy were suspicious; the Confederates had been carefully putting out their
fires, and it seemed that they might be getting ready to launch
an attack into the rear of the withdrawing Fifth Corps—which
would be, of course, disastrous. Chamberlain finally got his 1st
Brigade out of line as dawn was beginning to gray the east, not-
ing as he did so that Warren was remaining behind to supervise
the ticklish business of disengaging the rest of the corps. Chamberlain started down the woods-road that Bartlett had followed
in going to Sheridan's support. He met Bartlett's Brigade coming
back. In the confusion of orders, the 3rd Brigade had been recalled. The 20th Maine men and others in the brigade now had
to turn and follow Chamberlain, wallowing along this road for
the third time. They had had little rest and no rations, and
Chamberlain recalled that they were using "expressions that
could be conjectured only by a veteran of the Old Testament
dispensation."

When he got back down to the position that Bartlett had occupied during the night, Chamberlain, at the head of the column,
saw a mile in front an array of advancing cavalry and supposed
that it was the Confederate force Bartlett had run into. But as
the distance shortened, he made out the distinctive blue of Union
cavalry, and presently Sheridan himself came galloping up with
his swallow-tailed battle flag flashing in the morning sunlight.
Chamberlain was apprehensive as he rode out to meet the cavalry commander, for Sheridan's eyes were dark with anger, and
there was a feeling of doom in the air. Chamberlain saluted: "I
report to you, General, with the head of Griffin's Division."

Sheridan returned the salute, barking, "Where is Warren?"

"He is at the rear of the column, sir."

"That is where I expected to find him. What is he doing there?"

"General, we are withdrawing from the White Oak Road, where we fought all day. General Warren is bringing off his last division, expecting an attack."

At this point Griffin rode up, and Chamberlain thankfully withdrew. The great Sheridan was evidently in an ugly mood, and he obviously had it in for someone, believing that the Fifth Corps had been criminally slow in coming to his assistance. Later in the morning Griffin told Chamberlain of his own talk with Sheridan. The cavalry general, Griffin said, was greatly put out about the performance of the Fifth Corps. Worse yet, the Fifth Corps was now acting under Sheridan's orders and Grant had given Sheridan permission to relieve Warren from command if he thought it necessary. Chamberlain felt that personal animosities were involved. Both generals agreed that trouble was building up, and something unpleasant would happen before the day was over.

But the cool bright morning had brought at least one favorable disclosure. The enemy troops had completely disappeared from Sheridan's front. They had been alarmed by Bartlett's presence in their rear during the night, imagining in the darkness that his picket line represented the advance of the whole Fifth Corps. So the 20th Maine and the other foot-weary, mud-spattered regiments of Bartlett's Brigade had accomplished a great tactical stroke with the expenditure of very little gunpowder. Later in the day Sheridan's cavalry reconnaissance brought back word that the enemy had retired to Five Forks. At this important point, the reports said, there were strong breastworks running along the White Oak Road, bending back at the east end to make an angle and "return." Behind the breastworks was a sizable body of troops, it was said, including Pickett's Division.

Sheridan got his infantry-cavalry force in hand and went marching up toward Five Forks. Dismounting at Gravelly Run Church, where officers of the Fifth Corps had assembled, Sheridan explained to Warren his plan of attack, scratching a diagram in the dirt with the point of his sabre. According to the plan the Fifth Corps was to go in on an oblique approach and hit the angle and "return" of the Confederate line, while Sheridan's cavalry charged their front and right. Warren made his own diagrams and sent them to his division commanders.

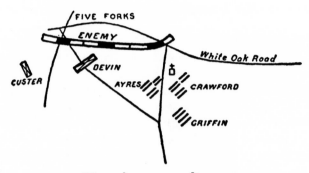

Warren's erroneous diagram
for the attack at Five Forks

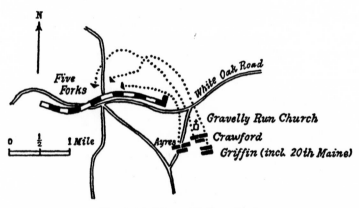

True situation, and the attack
as it actually took place

The Fifth Corps formed in the fields and light woods around Gravelly Run Church and at four o'clock in the afternoon the whole corps moved forward in splendid array—Ayres' and Crawford's divisions in the front line of battle, Griffin's following Crawford as a support. But they were heading for a surprise quite appropriate to the day, April Fool's. The diagram, as drawn by Warren from Sheridan's reconnaissance information, was wrong in one important respect. It showed the Confederate breastworks extending to the intersection of the White Oak Road with the Gravelly Run Church Road. Instead, the end of the works was around eight hundred yards to the west. This meant that the Fifth Corps, or most of it, would miss the breastworks entirely and go barging off into the woods and ravines to the north.

Even when the advance of the Fifth Corps crossed the White Oak Road the misapprehension apparently continued in Crawford's division, for there the infantrymen found Confederates who disputed with them in a most hostile manner. There were also light breastworks of rails, which might be the expected "return" of the Confederate line—or, if not here, the main line should be somewhere just beyond, for there was enough shooting going on and they certainly were in a battle. Actually, the troops in front were dismounted Confederate cavalrymen who had been thrown out on the White Oak Road as a covering force; but they were apparently strong enough to give Crawford a fight and mislead him, and Crawford's Division went on, pushing these gray people off to the north, and leaving a bloody trail of wounded behind it.

Griffin's Division was following Crawford. But as the woods got thicker and thicker and the expected kind of resistance did not develop, General Joshua Chamberlain began to be troubled. Something, he now knew, was definitely wrong. A sudden burst of musketry off to his left drew the General's attention. Spurring his horse to an elevated piece of cleared ground, Chamberlain looked to his left—which was now southerly—and saw a confused whirl of smoke and fighting that seemed to be involving Ayres' Division. Instantly Chamberlain realized what had happened. Crawford and Griffin had gone completely past the earthworks and were now to the north of and somewhat behind the Confederate line. But Ayres had come close enough to the enemy "return" so that he had drawn fire upon his left and was now wheeling to attack down the rear of the breastworks.

Besides being in command of the 1st Brigade of Griffin's Division, Chamberlain now had the 2nd Brigade acting under his orders. Chamberlain yanked these two brigades out of the advance by the left flank and then led his troops up a gulley and into the rear of the Confederate breastworks. Coming out of the gulley, they found themselves practically on top of the Confederates; there were smashing volleys at close range, and the two lines came together, as Chamberlain remembered, "like shutting jaws."

Sheridan, who seemed to be everywhere at once in this fight, saw Chamberlain putting his troops in. "By God, that's what I want to see!" the cavalry commander roared. "General officers at the front!" He thereupon dashed up and told Chamberlain to take command of all the infantry he could see. By now there were scattered groups of Union men around who didn't know where they were or what they were supposed to do. Chamberlain began gathering them up and throwing impromptu lines of battle at the rear of the Confederate works. He found one man behind a stump and yelled at him, "Don't you know you'll be killed here in less than two minutes? This is no place for you. Go forward!"

"But what can I do?" the man cried. "I can't stand up against all this alone!"

"No, that's just it," Chamberlain shouted. "We're forming here. I want you for a guide center. Up, and forward!"

The man came out from behind the stump, stood as a guide while Chamberlain formed about two hundred of the scattered bluecoats on him, and then this strange battalion of odds and ends went swarming into the gathering smoke clouds to add its weight to the Union attack. Next Chamberlain found one of Ayres' brigades, which had become undecided where to go, and threw it, too, into the fray.

Meanwhile General Bartlett—with his brigade plowing on through the wooded country north of the White Oak Road—had been making a discovery similar to that previously made by Chamberlain. He noticed that there was no firing at all in his front, but that the rattle of musketry was swelling up to an alarming volume off to the left. He, as Chamberlain had done, rode to an open field and saw the enemy works, now far off to the left. General Griffin had made the discovery at about the same time. Together the two officers dashed back through the woods to where the big 3rd Brigade was moving northwestward in three lines of battle. The 20th Maine was in the third or rearmost line. It was therefore one of the first of the regiments to be recovered and turned around by the strenuous efforts of Griffin and Bartlett. Along with the 1st Michigan and the 155th Pennsylvania, the Maine regiment wheeled sharply to the left and headed toward the Confederates.

It was the last big fight of the war for the 20th Maine. In the uproar of the battle the regiment, with the 1st Michigan beside it, went over a hill and down through a wooded descent so quietly that it was not observed by the Confederates until the Maine and Michigan men came charging into their rear with a yell. The Confederates at this point immediately threw down their arms, and the attackers found themselves with an embarrassment of prisoners who outnumbered them, one man estimated, about ten to one. Still the two regiments might have carried it off, with many lives saved, had it not been for the actions of a couple of incendiaries. One of these was a Confederate officer who came dashing down the lines calling on his men to rally. The other was an enlisted man who picked up a discarded but loaded rifle, yelled, "We can whip you yet!" and shot a captain of the 1st Michigan. A private of the 20th Maine immediately bayoneted the impulsive Confederate, and the fight was on—soldiers firing muskets in each other's faces, yelling, stabbing, knocking each other back and forth across the breastworks. Because of the premature surrender, the troops had moved in to close quarters and were already more or less mixed with the enemy. The vicious fight that resulted was of the Little Round Top-Laurel Hill variety, and many of the old-timers of the 20th Maine demonstrated that they hadn't lost stomach for this peculiarly horrible brand of conflict. Private Edmund Morrison—the man who'd been wounded so badly that he had been supposed to go home—was seen completely surrounded by the gray infantrymen, busily crashing his rifle butt down on the heads of his assailants. For a few moments the regiment arose, nearly, to its old heights of combat greatness, but it had too many Confederates to deal with alone. Morrill sent to Bartlett to hurry up with support, and just as the right flank of the 20th Maine was about to give way, one of Bartlett's other regiments arrived to take the pressure off, followed by more Union infantry pouring in to overwhelm the defenders of the works from the rear.

At this critical moment also, the Maine men heard bugles and the U. S. Cavalry came dashing to their rescue in traditional style. There was a final rush at the enemy. Lieutenant Albert Fernald, the human bombshell who had bounded into the works in advance of his troops at Peebles' Farm, this time chose the flag of the 9th Virginia as his target. There was a wild scuffle, and out of it came the fearless Fernald with his flag-earning, for this exploit, the fourth Medal of Honor to be awarded to members of the 20th Maine. Now, all along the line, Confederate troops were casting away their arms and running. Sheridan rode past like a madman, swinging his clenched fist and shouting, "Smash 'em! Smash 'em!"

In the pursuit by Union forces, over thirty-two hundred prisoners were taken, and so many muskets were thrown away that they were gathered up and used for corduroying roads on the following day. But even as Five Forks has been a mixed-up event of history (Union infantry attacking from the rear, Custer riding Indianlike with the encircling forces, Pickett making a Last Stand, and other oddities), it was followed by mixed emotions.

In the 20th Maine that night there was a feeling of exhilaration such as the men had never known. The victory at Five Forks clearly heralded the imminent end of the war.

There was a feeling of pride at hearing the stories of Chamberlain's exploits during the battle. Here was a 20th Maine boy who had made good in a spectacular way. Among the veterans it was recognized that Chamberlain had been lucky in being in the right places at the right time, but even so he had demonstrated that he could make the most of his opportunities and had been, without a question, the outstanding infantry commander from March 29 onward.

There also was deep resentment in the 20th Maine following the report of a momentous incident on another part of the field. The report had it that Crawford's Division of the corps, unlike Ayres' and Griffin's, had not changed direction immediately after passing the Confederate earthworks. Instead, it had continued to go blundering off to the north, pursuing the dismounted cavalry. In an agony of effort, General Warren had finally overtaken the division and turned it around, leading the troops in a charge into the rear of the Confederate works. Then, the story went, Warren had sent his chief of staff to Sheridan, telling him that he was in rear of the enemy, cutting off his retreat and taking many prisoners. Sheridan's reply to the messenger had been, "By God, sir, tell General Warren he wasn't in the fight!" And shortly afterward Warren had been relieved—an action which the men of the 20th Maine never forgot or forgave.

And there were other sorrows of a more personal kind. Some time after dark, the regiment having returned from the pursuit, Private Theodore Gerrish and a companion took candles and went looking around the area where the 20th Maine had fought. In time they found what they were looking for: Private Morrison, shot through the body, dead; and another old friend, Private William Gilmore, shot through the heart. The men put down their candles and began to dig two shallow graves under an oak tree. The tree was a big one. And perhaps, if they ever came back, they could find it—along with the two makeshift headboards they still had to find and carve. Ahead of the 20th Maine now, the glow of victory was clearly discernible. But dead men's eyes in the candlelight do not seem to see anything at all.

CHAPTER FOURTEEN

Hungry Victory

N April 2, the Fifth Corps—now under the command of General Griffin—cut across the Southside Railroad, Chamberlain's Brigade capturing the last Confederate train that tried to make the run out of Petersburg. Meanwhile guns had been thundering in the east, and the next day a staff officer dashed past the 20th Maine shouting that Petersburg had fallen, the government in Richmond was breaking up and Lee was in full retreat. Although this had been understood to be almost inevitable following the battle of Five Forks, the Maine men found the report hard to believe. For too long now, Petersburg had been the Forbidden City—a citadel seemingly invulnerable against all attacks; and too many times, during the course of the war, the veterans had heard news of victories that had been merely hopeful fictions. Now they hurled at the messenger all available expressions of complete derision and disbelief known to masters of repartee in the ranks.

But Lieutenant Colonel Walter G. Morrill rode back along the column to assure the men that the report was true. In an instant caps were flying in the air, men were shaking each other's hands, and the Maine soldiers were cheering themselves hoarse. It was, however, a little early for cheering. Robert E. Lee was pulling his troops out of the entrenchments and heading west and south, with the idea of circling around the Union army and reaching North Carolina, where he could join forces with General Joseph E. Johnson, commanding a large body of Confederate troops in that area. With this accomplished, the war could still go on for no one knew how long. The enlisted strategists in the ranks of the 20th Maine understood this as well as Grant himself, and the regiment prepared for some of the hardest and fastest marching of the war.

They had had races with the Army of Northern Virginia before: up and down the Blue Ridge Mountain range, up and down the Orange and Alexandria Railroad. But there had never been anything like the race that now started westward along the course of the Appomattox River. On April 4, the Fifth Corps made a march of more than thirty miles with Sheridan's cavalry; by midnight it was at Jetersville in line of battle squarely across the Richmond and Danville Railroad, which was Richmond's last supply line and Lee's best route of escape. Here, for a day, they waited apprehensively, expecting an attack by Lee's whole army. The attack never came. Finding the railway blocked, Lee was circling farther to the west before attempting his break for the south—and Jetersville, which might have marked a famous battle, relaxed into being just another name on the map.

Late on April 5, the Second Corps and the Sixth Corps arrived to join the Fifth at Jetersville. The Army of the Potomac was together again at last. But it would not remain together very long and would never, in fact, seem like an army again to those who marched in it. Ill part of the time, and overshadowed by Grant and Sheridan, Meade was watching his army scattered as the three corps were directed along various courses in the Appomattox race. The Second and Sixth Corps pursued generally the line of march of the retreating Confederate army. In the latter stages of the pursuit, the Fifth Corps, acting as "foot cavalry," followed Sheridan's horsemen, keeping to the south of Lee and trying desperately to get ahead of him so that his retreat could be cut off.

So the 20th Maine marched where the hard marching would have to be done. The men were pushing ahead with everything they had because what they were pushing for now was the end of the war. When the "accordion action" of a column opened a gap, men double-timed to fill it up again. Going across streams, they waded water almost shoulder-deep, holding haversacks and cartridge boxes on bayonets high over their heads. Ordinarily soldiers did not like to march on wet feet; but now, coming out of a stream they scrambled up the banks and pushed on without stopping to pour the water out of their boots.

Meanwhile Union cavalry was slashing at the Confederate columns, and infantry rear-guard actions were flaring up, distant guns thumping, columns of black smoke soiling the horizon. Sheridan's cavalry, they heard, was creating havoc—flying columns cutting off trains, blowing up ammunition wagons, destroying, burning.

And the Second and Sixth Corps were smashing into the rear of Lee's tortured army, capturing thousands of prisoners. Surrendering Confederates reported that the Army of Northern Virginia was literally dying of hunger. Men were constantly dropping muskets because they were too weak to carry them any farther—or falling, themselves, from exhaustion. A few were living on parched corn, but there was very little corn to parch, no time to stop and parch it anyway, and things otherwise were about as bad as they could get.

All of this was very encouraging to the men of the 20th Maine, but there was a gnawing in their own stomachs, and a suspicion that they would soon be starving themselves, for they seemed to be outmarching their ration supply. On April 6 they trudged thirty-two miles and food was getting scarce. During halts, and even on the march, foragers darted away from the column to see if anything edible could be found. In one foraging expedition, a small private in the 20th Maine fell head-first into a cask of syrup and went gooily on his way, wiping syrup off his face and licking his hands.

On April 8 rations gave out entirely, and there was an enormously difficult march of twenty-nine miles. The difficulty started about noon, when they were halted to allow troops of the Army of the James, under General Edward O. C. Ord, to pass them. These troops had come all the way from Petersburg to assist Sheridan and the Army of the Potomac; they'd had a long march and were tired; but Ord was senior to Griffin in rank and availed himself of the privilege of passing Griffin's corps. The halt meant a good rest for the Fifth Corps infantrymen, but as they sat by the roadsides and in the fields waiting for Ord's weary troops to struggle past, they began to grumble. Unless

Ord's people moved faster than they were going now, the whole column was going to be held up and Lee would probably get away after all. This thought sent the men into an almost insane rage. Their anger was intensified when they moved out to follow Ord's column and found the tail end dragging ever farther from the front. Chamberlain recalled that "it fretted our men almost to mutiny. . . . The head of our column seemed more like a mob than our patient well-disciplined soldiers. The headquarters wagons and pack mules which made the bulk of that real rabble ahead got unceremoniously helped along. Whoever blocked the way was served with a writ of ejectment in quite primitive fashion."

The 20th Maine that day had the further misfortune of being at the rear of its division, a position where, because of the peculiarities of a marching column, stops and starts are magnified into endless delays followed by sudden jerks. For men under arms nothing is more tiresome than standing in ranks and waiting and nothing more annoying than dashing to catch up with a regiment ahead that has suddenly moved off at the double. As darkness was falling the 20th Maine entered a forest, through which the route led on a narrow, crooked road. Here the regiment got into one of the ill-tempered brawls that General Ord's passage had left boiling up along the route of the Fifth Corps column all afternoon. The 20th Maine's trouble was with artillery. In the darkness, the artillerymen started throwing their weight around on the narrow woods-road—and the weight of six horses, followed by a rumbling gun could be fatal to an infantryman who failed to jump out of the way fast enough. The foot soldiers were already half mad with weariness, hunger and frustration. This new annoyance moved them to homicidal anger. Soon men in the rear ranks were turning to bat artillery horses over the heads with their musket butts. The enraged drivers struck back with whips, and so with a great deal of whacking, whipping, cursing and whinnying of frightened horses, the mixed-up column floundered on through the darkness. Around midnight, the dispute rose to a climax. A heavy gun came thundering down a hill into the rear of the regiment, a soldier turned and struck a horse; the horse fell, piling up the following animals and bringing the gun section to a tangled halt. An artillery sergeant rode up to have someone arrested. A 20th Maine lieutenant, who happened to be carrying a musket for one of his men, used it to knock both horse and sergeant to the ground. By the time this fracas was over, the 20th Maine was far behind, completely separated from the rest of its division. As the regiment pushed on in an effort to catch up, men were falling out continually, turning out of the column and falling as they turned, knocked out by sheer exhaustion.

At two o'clock in the morning the 20th Maine overtook the rest of the division, which had halted for two hours and was just now arising to form column and move on. For many of the 20th Maine marchers—on their feet for nearly twenty-four hours—this had been a point of probable rest toward which they had been focusing all their thoughts and energies. And now when the point got up and moved on, there was nothing to do but collapse. After a brief rest, part of the regiment kept on. At daylight there were, however, less than seventy-five men still marching. Rations had been promised at a place about six miles ahead. The name of the place—Appomattox—wasn't important; what was important as the men stumbled on in a half stupor with hunger overcoming their fatigue, was that there would be food at this place and if they could keep on putting one foot ahead of the other they would eventually get there and be able to eat again.

In another part of the column, Joshua Chamberlain as a general officer had a more elevated view of what was taking place. By the light of a match he read a message sent by Sheridan to the infantry commanders. "I have cut across the enemy at Appomattox Station, and captured three of his trains. If you can possibly push your infantry up here tonight, we will have great results in the morning." So Sheridan had done it! He was in front of the Confederate army, barring Lee's way. But no cavalry line that Chamberlain had ever heard of could withstand a determined rush of infantry. If Sheridan didn't have Union infantry in his line by morning, he would be swept away with heavy losses and the race would go on. Chamberlain had his brigade bugler sound the "Forward" and was amazed to see the men moving— stiff-jointed, staggering, numb with weariness—but still ready to plod on.

By sunrise they had reached Appomattox Station, where staff officers were waiting to turn them square to the right on a course that would bring them in behind Sheridan's cavalry and across the path of the Confederates. It was one of those soft gray-and-green April mornings with clouds over the rising sun, but with foliage seeming to reflect a luminous warmth of spring. Through these gentle airs from somewhere on the right was coming the ringing reports of Sheridan's horse artillery and the sputtering of his carbines, answered by the booming of heavier Confederate fieldpieces and the deeper roll of enemy infantry muskets. A cavalry officer came galloping out of the woods to Chamberlain, who was marching with his command at about the middle of the Fifth Corps column—the 2nd Division and the 3rd Brigade of the 1st Division being ahead of him.

"General, you command this column?"

Chamberlain replied, "Two brigades of it, sir; about half the 1st Division, Fifth Corps."

"Sir, General Sheridan wishes you to break off from the column and come to his support. The rebel infantry is pressing him hard. Our men are falling back. Don't wait for orders through the regular channels, but act on this at once."

Taking his two brigades, Chamberlain hurried them through the woods directly toward the sound of the firing. As he emerged from the woods into the fields that were now smoking and echoing with the roar of Sheridan's battle, he could begin to sense the pattern of the corral into which the Army of Northern Virginia had moved. The all-important western barrier had initially been Sheridan's battered cavalry, but Ord's infantry had now come up to take over this vital portion of the line across Lee's escape route, the Lynchburg Road. As the Union infantry came up behind him, Sheridan was moving cavalry rapidly across to form the south and southeast sides of the enclosure. To the Confederates, advancing westward, the effect of this cavalry movement was like the drawing away of a curtain, disclosing the solid blue wall of infantry barring their way. Their natural tendency might then have been to turn south and drive through the re-forming cavalry. But this fence also was being strengthened—by the Fifth Corps coming in from the southwest and south. (It had been Sheridan's need for infantry support here that had caused him to detach Chamberlain's troops from the Fifth Corps column and bring them in on a short-cut.)

From the northeast, close behind Lee's army and driving it into Sheridan's corral, came the Second and Sixth corps of the Army of the Potomac.

All routes of escape were now effectively closed.

True, there was a gap in Sheridan's fence to the north; but north was not promising; it was not, by any stretch of the imagination, a way that offered hope for the Confederate army any longer.

Coming into line from the southwest, the 20th Maine found itself in the front ranks of the Fifth Corps. As the color-bearers uncased their flags and shook them out, the sun was breaking through the clouds and illuminating a scene so memorable that a member of the 20th Maine could later describe it in detail. "Before the concave line of infantry, visible from flank to flank, sprang out the skirmishers, dotting the greensward. Behind, the artillery was moving up. The lines of infantry in order of battle, a long array of bright muskets spaced with colors, on an open field, more than twenty thousand men in sight, formed an unusual and inspiring spectacle even to veterans. But in front of this, and between it and the enemy, appeared a moving panorama still more picturesque. A body of cavalry, apparently relieved by the infantry on the left, came galloping across the field toward the right. In front, apart from the rest, conspicuous, clear against the sky as if in silhouette, on a black horse, in swift gallop, rode Sheridan. . . . Next behind him spurred on his color bearer, with the broad and swallow-tailed flag marked with crossed swords, and standing out and quivering in the rapid motion. . . .

"Behind this, in quick succession, followed staff and orderlies and a hurrying body of horsemen. Over all this and over the infantry lines shrieked the shells of the enemy, bursting in the air, with white puffs, that one after another drifted and disappeared; or, plowing the ground, rebounded in the air. Sheridan, with his staff and escort and their flutter of flags, passed the front, and the infantry moved on, silent and steady, for what they thought the final grapple with the enemy."

There was a ridge in front of the 20th Maine, and on the crest of the ridge a house, barn and outbuildings. The regiment moved toward this crest in line of battle, the infantrymen plodding doggedly forward, squinting in the brightening sunlight. The main body of the enemy was not visible, but Confederate artillery was thumping somewhere on the other side of the crest and shells were swishing over.

As the regiment approached the building, one of the enemy shells struck the barn. Boards and splinters flew from the walls, fire burst up through the roof, and out came a cloud of frantic hens and chickens. It was too much for the hungry 20th Maine. The men forgot shell fire, the enemy, military discipline, glory of victory, and everything else. Ranks broke apart as the soldiers went chasing after the hens. And so as the drama of Appomattox approached its climax, there were a few minutes of incongruous comic relief with officers shouting and swearing, trying to get the men back in formation, hens squawking, soldiers, almost as hysterical as the hens, running, screaming, laughing. On the crest the regiment was finally re-formed. Looking down the slope, across a plain and toward another ridge in front, the men saw a sight that quickly sobered them. There, familiar as death, was the line of enemy skirmishers in hastily dug rifle pits; and in rear of these, higher on the hillside, the gray line of battle with its reddish colors, waving. And beyond this, artillery flashing and puffing. The infantrymen pulled the visors of their forage caps down over their eyes, gritted their teeth and moved forward, thinking it would be a pity to be killed here, with the war so nearly over.

The Maine men were not worried too much about the artillery, but they dreaded the moment when the little tongues of flame would go dancing along the Confederate infantry line and aimed rifle fire would come whistling out to meet them. In an orchard behind the enemy line of battle they saw a white object flutter; this was taken by many to be the signal for the infantry to open fire. But no fire came, and the white object seemed to be changing its position. It was advancing down through the Confederate

line and coming out to meet them. It was a white flag, borne by
a galloping horseman. A hundred yards away from the Union
line, the rider suddenly turned to his left and dashed away in
the direction Sheridan had taken. Shortly afterward a mounted
Union staff officer came dashing along their lines swinging his
hat like a lunatic and shouting, "Lee has surrendered! Lee has
surrendered!"

Over to the right of the 20th Maine, where Chamberlain was
advancing with his command toward Appomattox Court House,
he, too, came to a ridge where the view was even better. It was
a sight that Chamberlain would remember for the rest of his
days. "For there burst upon our vision a mighty scene, fit cadence
of the story of tumultuous years. Encompassed by the cordon of
steel that crowned the heights about the Court House, on the
slopes of the valley formed by the sources of the Appomattox,
lay the remnants of that far-famed counterpart and companion
of our own in momentous history—the Army of Northern Virginia—Lee's army!

"It was hilly, broken ground, in effect a vast amphitheater,
stretching a mile perhaps from crest to crest. On the several confronting slopes before us dusky masses of infantry suddenly resting in place; blocks of artillery, standing fast in column or
mechanically swung into park; clouds of cavalry small and great,
slowly moving, in simple restlessness. . . ."

Chamberlain pushed his battle line toward the village, and
there was a lot of wild scuffling that looked like fighting but
wasn't—at least not to the Maine general's experienced eye. "Not
much killing, not even hurting," he remembered. And he noted,
with amusement, how youngsters who hadn't been in the army
long were dashing around making heroes of themselves—collect-
ing tolerant prisoners and armfuls of swords. But there wasn't
much time left for making military reputations. Chamberlain's
advance had reached the village when white flags began coming
in. They came to several points on the Union front, and two
came to Chamberlain. The first was a towel, and Chamberlain
wondered where, in either of the two mud-spattered armies, it
would have been possible to find a white towel. The second flag-
bearer was accompanied by a Union cavalryman, who was es-

corting a Confederate staff officer. The cavalryman shouted, "I am just from Gordon and Longstreet. Gordon says, 'For God's sake, stop this infantry, or hell will be to pay.' " One of the last cannon shots from the Confederacy tore through the chest of a young lieutenant in Chamberlain's front line. And about this time also, over in front of the 20th Maine, a shell burst on a private of the 155th Pennsylvania out in the skirmish line, and he seemed to fly into dozens of pieces, his rifle, canteen and other equipment tossed in the air by the explosion. Both of these individuals, and others, were claimed as the last man killed at Appomattox. It was not, Chamberlain reflected, a proper subject for dispute.

All along the lines now, the firing had ceased, leaving a strange and unaccustomed silence, for never before in the experience of the Maine men had a battle ended just like this. Men began climbing haystacks, fences, trees, even houses to get a better view. Then, when they realized what was going on, Private Charles E. Dunn recalled that in the 20th Maine "muskets, knapsacks, haversacks, canteens, dippers, everything that a man could get his hands on went into the air" and that men were laughing, shouting, shaking hands, hugging each other and even crying.

But still the surrender was not final. A truce was declared until one o'clock, and the armies settled down for a period of tense waiting. Sheridan didn't like it, and according to Chamberlain "his natural disposition was not sweetened by the circumstance that he was fired on by some of the Confederates as he was coming up to the meeting under the truce." The cavalry commander was all for unconditional surrender and wanted to charge in and settle things once and for all. But still the armies waited. One o'clock came. No word. Griffin had just said to Chamberlain, "Prepare to make, or receive, an attack in ten minutes!" when General Lee rode through Chamberlain's lines on the way to his meeting with Grant. Not long afterward Grant rode past.

The two figures had even now passed into the realm of history. Each with his own trademarks of individual greatness, they were quickly recognizable yet somehow unreal, as though they were already waxworks or statues. Chamberlain was about equally awed by both generals: Lee noble, imposing, beautifully uniformed and mounted, all grayness and grandeur, wearing an unconquerable, unapproachable dignity even in the sadness of defeat; Grant small, shabby-looking, yet with a presence all his own. Grant as described by Chamberlain: "Slouched hat without cord; common soldier's blouse, unbuttoned . . . high boots, mud-splashed to the top; trousers tucked inside; no sword, but the sword-hand deep in the pocket; sitting his saddle with the ease of a born master, taking no notice of anything, all his faculties gathered into intense thought and mighty calm. He seemed greater than I had ever seen him—a look as of another world about him. No wonder I forgot altogether to salute him."

With details of the surrender settled, there was much visiting back and forth between the lines. There had always been a strange kinship between these armies—the Army of Northern Virginia and the Army of the Potomac. It was an understanding that had allowed them to swap coffee and tobacco and converse in friendly fashion across the picket lines, or drink from the same spring after a battle—and yet with battle joined, they had fought each other as fiercely as men had ever fought anywhere on earth. Now there was a brief time remaining in which to talk and swap again, and to study closely the men they had seen over distant parapets or briefly through the smoke of infantry clashes in the open field.

Thomas Chamberlain, who was now division Provost Marshal, was greatly impressed by the Confederate officers. In a letter to his brother John he wrote, "I saw Lee—Bushrod Johnson —Gordon—Longstreet—Pickett & all of their great Generals. . . . They are as well dressed as our Generals and certainly better looking. Gen'l Gordon is the best-looking soldier I ever saw in my life."

The appearance of the Confederate foot soldiers was in striking contrast to that of their generals. Theodore Gerrish described them as tall, thin, spare men with long hair and beards, clad in ragged, dirty gray uniforms and broad-brimmed, slouched hats. Another man in the 20th, seeing how thin they were, said, "No wonder we didn't kill more of them; either one of them would split a minie-ball if it should strike him." Private Dunn thought he had been having a hard time, but when he saw the Confederate foot soldiers, he decided he'd been having a picnic. The 20th Maine had three days' rations in its baggage wagons; when the wagons arrived the rations were shared with the Confederates, who were on the point of starvation. Soon the blue and gray camps began to get so intermingled that it was necessary to forbid further visiting in order to expedite the paroling and other businesses of the surrender.

Late on the night of April 9, Chamberlain was summoned to corps headquarters and Griffin gave him a summary of the day's negotiations. The Confederates, Griffin said, had requested that they be allowed to stack their arms on the ground where the troops were resting, and where they could be picked up by the Federal authorities after the troops had gone home. But Grant did not think that this procedure would be sufficiently respectful to the United States. He wanted the Southern army to march out in military order and formally lay down its arms and colors thereby acknowledging that all organized hostility to the Union was ending. Grant wanted the ceremony kept simple—there would be no large body of troops to receive the Confederates— and nothing was to be done that would seem to humiliate the Southern soldiers. But Grant did want the Confederate arms surrendered in the immediate presence of some representative portion of the Union army. And now came the surprise. The officer to command the parade at this ceremony, Griffin announced, was General Joshua L. Chamberlain.

Chamberlain's first thought appears to have been for his companions of the 20th Maine and other veteran regiments. He immediately asked to be transferred back to the old 3rd Brigade. This was a brigade that had taken its name from many famous commanders; it had been Butterfield's Brigade, Vincent's Brigade, Chamberlain's Brigade, Rice's Brigade, Bartlett's Brigade, besides being commanded at various odd times by several other well-known officers. It now reperesented much of the original 1st Division of the corps, for as the regiments of the division had been beaten down into remnants by the remorseless flailing of battle and disease, some meanwhile going home upon expiration of their terms, the old 1st Division had been gradually consolidated into this one brigade. The surrender ceremony, Chamberlain felt, would be an incident of some importance in history, and he wanted the veteran regiments to be present with him in recognition of their long service. His request was granted and the old 3rd was, again, Chamberlain's Brigade.

And so April 9, Palm Sunday, approached its end. But around midnight there was another arrangement in recognition of peace which the generals did not anticipate. It was described by Private Dunn of the 20th Maine, who was out on picket duty. "The two picket lines were within speaking distance, and we were on speaking terms with the 'Johnnies' at once. There was nothing that resembled guard duty that night. It resembled a picnic rather than a picket line. They like ourselves were glad the war was over. We exchanged knicknacks with them, and were reminded of the days when at school we swapped jewsharps for old wooden toothed combs. The articles we exchanged that night were about the same value . . . It came on to rain about midnight, and the camp fires of the Fifth Corps on the hillside half a mile away looked mighty attractive. To our Johnnie friends (not our enemies now) the camp fires of their army in the valley below had the same attraction. After a short conference both sides voted unanimously to desert the picket line and go to camp."

When Dunn got back to camp he found only a few soldiers awake. For the first time the two armies rested side by side without fear or tension, the soft April rain falling on their shelter tents, fires dimming, men breathing heavily in the sleep of total exhaustion.

The night wore on, and at three o'clock, a man in Bangor, Maine, was awakened by the sound of bells ringing, and of cannon firing. Getting up in the middle of the night didn't seem the sensible thing to do, but he had been sleeping soundly and felt refreshed—also, it was obvious that something important had happened in the war. He got up, dressed and went out. The sky was clear, but a south wind was blowing up the river, and there was a dampness in the air that seemed to be magnifying the clangor of the bells and the booming of the cannon. People were acting in a manner quite uncharacteristic of Bangor, Maine. As he walked downtown, he saw houses illuminated, and excited people running around without much idea, apparently, of where they were going. There was a big crowd in front of the *Whig & Courier* office. The man pushed through, bought a paper and learned what had happened.

He left an account of several subsequent impressions: . . . of Willard B. Heath, with a tenor drum, and Z. L. Bragdon, with a bass drum, marching across the lower Kenduskeag Bridge, shouting, "Fall in" . . . of an impromptu parade of citizens . . . of bonfires, music in the night . . . and of an incident which struck him as being movingly symbolic of the gladness that prevailed. "A bird—having been aroused by the cannon probably—sang a beautiful shrill and clear song—this being long before daylight—she sitting on a tall fir tree. . . ."

That morning someone in Brewer—Chamberlain's home town —made a huge kite, twelve feet long, and on the kite string, some twenty feet below it, fastened an American flag. The kite is reported to have gone two thousand feet into the air, and an observer wrote, "Looking at it from the side, the cord did not show, owing to the distance, and it appeared as though the beautiful flag, doubly dear and precious now, was supported by unseen hands in the Heavens."

While celebrations of this sort were going on all over Maine, ceremonial affairs reached their climax on April 12, at Appomattox Court House. At sunrise Chamberlain had his lines formed for the parade. Some of the Confederate troops, mostly cavalry and artillery, had already turned in their arms, but this would be the main event, the surrender of weapons by the once-great Confederate infantry corps.

Chamberlain's formation was on the main street of the town, extending from the Appomattox River—here just a stream—on the right, almost to the Court House on the left. The 3rd Brigade as it stood that day consisted of the 20th Maine, a company of the 1st Maine Sharpshooters, the 32nd Massachusetts, the 1st and 16th Michigan, and four Pennsylvania regiments—the 83rd, 91st, 118th (Corn Exchange) and 155th.

But intermingled with these veteran regiments were remnants of many others famous in the Army of the Potomac, including the 2nd Maine, 9th, 18th and 22nd Massachusetts, the 4th Michigan and the 62nd Pennsylvania. The group, as Chamberlain noted, "held in it the soul of the famous 'Light Brigade,' and of the stern old First Division, Porter's, which was the nucleus of the Fifth Corps, men among them who had fired the first shot at Yorktown, and others that had fired the last at Appomattox, and who thus bore upon their banners all the battles of that army."

Besides the 3rd Brigade, Chamberlain had also arranged to have the other two brigades of the 1st Division present—the 1st Brigade in line a little to the rear of the 3rd, and the 2nd Brigade on the opposite side of the street. Thus for the ceremony he was in command of the whole 1st Division, and this was a little awkward, for it left the actual division commander—now General Bartlett—with no troops to command. Chamberlain felt that this situation bothered Bartlett, but the senior general made no comment; instead he rode around the surrender area most of the day with his division staff and flag, talking with Confederate officers.

Across the stream they could see the Confederate troops breaking their last camp, taking down shelter tents, forming slowly in ranks. Then the vanguard of the gray column crossed the stream and approached. Some of the Confederate color-bearers were keeping their flags tightly bound to the staffs, but most of the colors were flying, although crowded so thickly together by the depletion of the ranks that it seemed to Chamberlain that the column was crowned with red. On they came, at the swinging route step that had taken this great infantry for so many miles. As the head of the column drew nearer, Chamberlain was certain that these men deserved a salute of arms. He was well aware of the howl of criticism that would follow, from politically embittered people of the North. He resolved to order the salute anyway, because, as he explained it, "My main reason . . . was one for which I sought no authority nor asked forgiveness. Before us in proud humiliation stood the embodiment of manhood: men whom neither toils and sufferings, nor the fact of death, nor disaster, nor hopelessness could bend from their resolve; standing before us now, thin, worn, and famished, but erect, and with

eyes looking level into ours, waking memories that bound us together as no other bond;—was not such manhood to be welcomed
back into a Union so tested and assured?"

Instructions had already been given to regimental commanders. And when the head of the gray column came opposite the
right of the 3rd Brigade, a bugle sounded; there was the soft,
ordered slapping of hands on wood and metal, and along the
whole line, regiment by regiment in succession, muskets rose with
a simultaneous gleaming to the position of the old "carry"—the
marching salute.

At the head of the Confederate column, General John B. Gordon, riding disconsolately with bowed head, caught the sound
of shifting arms. The meaning suddenly dawned on him, and in
an instant the spirit of the occasion changed. Gordon wheeled
toward the 3rd Brigade. Rider and horse made one superb uplifted figure, the Confederate general dropping his sword point
to the toe of his boot as he returned Chamberlain's compliment.
Then, facing his own command, Gordon ordered his troops to
pass with the same position of the manual, the two armies honor-
ing one another in a final salute.

The classic description of the moment is Chamberlain's. "On
our part not a sound of trumpet more, nor roll of drum; not a
cheer, nor word nor whisper of vain-glorying, nor motion of man
standing again at the order, but an awed stillness rather, and
breath-holding, as if it were the passing of the dead!"

The Confederate column marched on until its front came
abreast of the 3rd Brigade's left. Then with the commands, "Halt!
Close up! Front face! Stack arms!" the troops faced Chamberlain's brigade, stacked their muskets, and hung their cartridge
boxes on the stacks. The color-bearers laid the colors on the
stacks. Many of them were weeping, and it was noted throughout
the day that men tore bits of cloth from the flags, hastily tucking
them away inside their uniforms. Some of the colors were thus
torn up completely, leaving only bare staffs to lay upon the
stacks.

As the first brigade of disarmed troops moved away, a detail
of Union men took the stacks and moved them up closer to the
line of the 3rd Brigade. Another portion of the Confederate col-

umn then moved up and front-faced as before. Their stacks were then moved and piled around the first line of stacks—a single line of muskets, colors and unslung equipment that kept growing as successive Confederate brigades moved up and surrendered their arms. At intervals, Union wagons came to remove the equipment, the wagon-crews emptying cartridge boxes in the street when the ammunition was discovered to be unserviceable.

For the most part, the Union troops were silent and respectful. There was no cheering. Officers conversed in the background and at intervals during the day. The general tenor of these conversations was one of hope for reconciliation and for the future of the nation. As one Confederate officer put it, years later, "They were proud of their success, and we were not ashamed of our defeat; and not a man of that grand army of one hundred and fifty thousand men but could, and I believe would, testify, that, in purely personal grounds, the few worn-out half-starved men that gathered around General Lee and his falling flag had the prouder position of the two. Had the politicians left things alone, such feelings would have resulted in a very different condition of things."

There was, however, one notable exception to this general civility. This was an encounter between General Henry A. Wise of Virginia, and Chamberlain. General Wise had been hungry and ill for several days. Chamberlain was sore from his wounds. Chamberlain approached Wise with a polite expression of hope for future good will between North and South. Wise snapped at him, "You may forgive us, but we won't be forgiven. There is a rancor in our hearts which you little dream of. We hate you, sir." Later, as though trying to mitigate his harshness, he spoke of the holes in Chamberlain's coat and asked him where he got them.

The question could hardly have been more unfortunate. It had probably been one of Wise's men who had fired the bullet, for Chamberlain had driven Wise's Brigade up the Quaker Road in his notable fight on March 29. So Chamberlain answered that he had got the holes in his coat on a field from which General Wise had departed. There was another flare-up from Wise. "I suppose you think you did great things there! But I stopped you until I saw I was fighting three divisions!"

Chamberlain told him he had three regiments.

"I know better!" Wise shouted. "You go home and take those fellows home, and that will end the war."

"We are going, General," said Chamberlain. "But first let us escort you."

But for the most part this day at Appomattox was a procession of memories, a consciousness of a national kinship which the enmities of war had not entirely sundered, and of another, more remarkable bond which had been forged in the flames of many battles. A soldier in one of the passing regiments shouted to the 20th Maine, "Well, old fellows, we have met you again." Facing the Maine men at close range were Confederate organizations that had, indeed, met before . . . the corps until recently commanded by A. P. Hill, which, in the long ago, had chased them across the Potomac at Shepherdstown Ford . . . Longstreet's men, and the Maine soldiers noted that Longstreet's was the best-marching corps present . . . and also many divisions that the 20th Maine recognized . . . the remnants of Hood's old division, which they had first seen through the smoking woods at Little Round Top . . . Pickett's, lately encountered at Five Forks, now a pitifully small group, decimated in the April Fool's Day engagement . . . and many other famous and familiar units whose passing brought, along with the exultation of victory, an inexplicable trace of sadness.

After the last of the gray troops had passed, and the April dusk was settling over the little Virginia village, the long lines of dumped cartridges in the street were set afire. The little cylinders of gunpowder burned with a flaring brilliance, then sputtered out in the darkness. The Army of Northern Virginia had passed on into song and story, where it has since continued to do very well.

CHAPTER FIFTEEN

The Last Review

The pageant has passed. The day is over. But
we linger, loath to think we shall see them
no more together—these men, these horses,
these colors afield.
——JOSHUA L. CHAMBERLAIN

HE fact that they had been one of the regiments chosen to receive the surrender of Lee's troops at Appomattox appears to have been an honor that was, at the time, largely unappreciated by the men of the 20th Maine. For one thing, there was a lot of work to do, gathering up the discarded equipment. In the woods where the Confederate army had encamped, thousands of rifles were found. Whole regiments had simply stacked arms and departed without taking any part in the surrender. These arms all had to be gathered up and carried to places where they could be destroyed or shipped to Washington.

And for another thing, the Maine men were uncomfortable—cold, ragged, and desperately hungry. They had raced to Appomattox in the lightest possible marching order, discarding overcoats and blankets. Railroad bridges had been destroyed, so that trains could not reach them, and the roads were in such bad condition that supply wagons had not been able to keep up with the needs of the troops. The men had shared what food they had with their Confederate "guests." Now rations were exhausted. Foraging expeditions went out and came back reporting slim pickings. Poor country. No food to be found. The 20th Maine got hold of a little beef, but it was so stringy and tough and so

tainted with garlic that few could eat it. The men searched out
places where corn had been fed to the horses and trampled into
the ground. The kernels were dug out of the mud, washed,
parched and eaten greedily.

On the day they left Appomattox, April 15, it was raining in
torrents. Mud was ankle-deep in the roads. Hungry and ill-
tempered, the men made no attempt to keep in ranks but straggled along picking their way as best they could. Officers kept
them going with the rumor that they would draw rations that
night, but darkness brought only a rain-soaked bivouac in a bog
—nothing to eat. Wood too wet for fires. Not much sleep in wet
blankets. Next morning—cold and raw as November. Thick, black
clouds. Driving rain.

Muttering and snarling, they pressed on. But at noon the
clouds cleared away, the sun came out warmly, and the wagons
were waiting at Farmville with rations and mail. Basking in the
sun on that pleasant Sunday afternoon, lying in the grass and
reading letters from home, they began to realize for the first time
that the war was over.

But late in the afternoon they were again cast into gloom. A
dispatch arrived bringing word that Lincoln had been assassi-
nated. Theodore Gerrish recalled that "at first we did not believe
the report, but when we were compelled to do so, we supposed
that he had been shot by some of the rebels made desperate by
their recent defeats. I never saw men so deeply moved as were
those soldiers. It was a fortunate affair for both sides that the
rebel army had been paroled before that deed of assassination
took place, for with the intense feeling that existed when that
intelligence reached us, there would have been a conflict of the
most deadly character."

A double guard was immediately put on the camp, the officers
fearing an outbreak of violence. There were rumors of chaos in
Washington, fears that a plan was afoot to destroy the government by assassination, and talk of the army moving on to the
capital and making Grant a military dictator until order could
be restored.

On April 19 they halted on the march while Lincoln's funeral
was taking place in Washington. Headquarters tents, colors and

sword hilts were draped in mourning. Minute guns sounded. Bands played dirges. The 1st Division (now commanded by General Joshua Chamberlain) formed in a hollow square and listened to a memorial address by an Irish chaplain who very nearly emulated Mark Antony, carried away by his own grief and eloquence. He finally had to be restrained by General Chamberlain, who feared that the men would be fired to some act of vengeance upon the surrounding populace.

On the twenty-third the 20th Maine went into camp at Sutherland Station, a few miles from Petersburg, with the assignment of guarding the railroad and restoring order in the region—now disrupted economically, overrun with marauders, and troubled (as General Chamberlain noted) with unruly Negroes. Upon their arrival, the 20th Maine got mixed up in an incident that was both disgraceful and significant. It involved a sutler and a regiment of colored cavalry. The sutler of the Civil War was a civilian who operated a sort of private-enterprise PX, with a portable stock of merchandise that included candies, cheese, canned fruit, tobacco, sardines, cookies and other delicacies for sale to the soldiers. Although hundreds of respectable fortunes were made from the war in locations farther removed, there always seemed to be something slightly immoral in taking a profit so close to the front lines, where men were dying and the wounded lay. And there were other conditions working against the sutler. His place in the army was fixed by law and army regulations, so he was the semi-official sort of person not always well regarded by soldiers. His prices, because of the risks and difficulties involved, were likely to be high. He was often the object of suspicion; soldiers thought he might be in cahoots with some officer, defrauding the troops, and splitting up the profits with his "higher-up" accomplice. And he was also allowed a lien on one-sixth of a soldier's monthly pay if the man did not make good on his bill. This was charged on the payroll, deducted, and turned over directly to the sutler—a procedure which could lead to real or imagined grievances. So the sutler had a public relations problem, and he was not a public relations expert, but just a determined little peddler with money on his mind. Frequently there was trouble. The sutler, if he were wise, would see to it that he stayed under the protection of the Provost Guard or some other responsible authority. (One regiment in the brigade, the Corn Exchange, raided a sutler about that time and ate everything he had except two kegs of nails.)

The sutler at Sutherland Station had set up shop with a new regiment of colored cavalry. Although the men of the 20th Maine had fought and bled for almost three years for purposes that included the liberation of their colored brethren, they were apparently far from ready to accept them as equals. The Negro cavalrymen, proud of their new uniforms, were accused of "putting on airs." Ragged soldiers of the 20th Maine, Corn Exchange Regiment and the 1st Michigan crowded around the sutler's stand and began eyeing his stock with hungry eyes. The sutler became nervous. Negro soldiers on guard ordered the white soldiers to fall back, but were disregarded. A corporal of the guard came up and attempted to make an arrest. He was promptly knocked down by a sergeant of the Corn Exchange Regiment, and the fight was on. Officers of the cavalry regiment came charging into the melee; their swords were seized and sent flying; their new gold-tasseled hats were kicked around like footballs. Care was taken, in all this confusion, to upset the sutler's tent. Soldiers began running off in all directions with cookies, cakes, canned peaches, cheese, tobacco, raisins, sardines and other goodies.

This natural dispersion might have ended the fight, but matters took a serious turn. The colonel of the cavalry regiment ordered "Boots and Saddles" sounded and came dashing to the fray with mounted troopers. The 20th Maine and the 1st Michigan grabbed their muskets, which were stacked conveniently near, with fixed bayonets. In an instant the unpleasantness had turned into a minor battle, with sabres swinging, horses rearing, and infantrymen circling and stabbing with extended bayonets, trying to keep the horsemen at a distance. The affair finally ended with half a dozen horses wounded, after which the 3rd Brigade commander advised the cavalry colonel to move his troops away or some of them might get killed.

Most of their experiences with colored people were, however, far more pleasant. One soldier, who took charge of a colony of "contrabands" on a near-by abandoned plantation, reported that he was treated like a king, with everyone obeying his orders and the finest hoe cakes, bacon and good rich milk brought to his table. A bandsman told of how the liberated slaves formed in groups along the road to welcome them with plantation songs. Then the band would respond with spirited music—to the great delight of the colored folk.

On May 3, the Fifth Corps was moving and the 20th Maine joined the march again toward Petersburg. General Chamberlain recorded the impression that "it had a certain majesty of tone—that returning army of august memories. A solemn march it was —past so many fields from which visions arose linking life with the immortal." For several miles before reaching the city, they passed inside the line of fortifications that had so long withstood their attacks. Seen from the enemy side, the abandoned forts and breastworks had a spectral look, like a land much imagined and sought for, now revealed with dreamlike unreality. In the city itself they encountered a more recent remnant of the past, General Warren, who had been relegated to the command of Petersburg after his summary dismissal by Sheridan at Five Forks. Warren was waiting with his wife and members of his staff in front of the Bolingbroke Hotel. Just a month before, he had been within one day, or at the most a few days, of the summit of a distinguished career in the army. Now he had descended a long way into the shadows that even a court of inquiry fourteen years later would never entirely clear away. But as the Fifth Corps passed the Bolingbroke Hotel, Warren did receive one vindication which he might have valued more than any other. Going past the hotel the corps was supposed to be marching at attention, as part of a formal salute to its old commander. Instead, the men raised their caps and gave vent to vociferous cheers.

They passed through Richmond, marred by fire and wearing a melancholy beauty in defeat. The bands played national airs but there was little cheering in response. The men marched quietly, on their good behavior, and it was pleasantly recalled that ladies came from many of the houses in the intense heat to offer them cool water. They passed out of the city and neared the old battlefields, crossing rivers with bloody names—the Chick-ahominy, the Pamunkey, the Mattapony. There were sad remind-ers along the way. One night in bivouac not far from Hanover Court House, Chamberlain's tethered horse pawed up skulls and other bones from the dead leaves and fallen pine cones. The 2nd Maine and other old regiments of the 1st Division had fought a battle here in the long, long ago—under McClellan. Veterans of the division identified the bones—by means of initials on the equipment and other marks—as belonging to comrades who had been reported missing in that battle. The bones were packed in empty cracker boxes and carried north in the supply train.

On the night of May 9 they camped near Fredericksburg. Some of the men of the division visited the old camp site at Stoneman's Switch, and one wrote, "How changed! the tall weeds, rank grass and undergrowth overran everything. Here and there the ruins of a chimney, or one still standing, around which we had listened to the merry jest and cheering words of many a comrade. . . ."

In the twilight a soldier of the 20th Maine walked through Fredericksburg and visited a churchyard where he had been brought with a shattered leg after the battle of the Wilderness. Not so long ago the churchyard had been full of suffering, moan-ing men. Now it was as though they had never been there. A service was going on inside the church; the worshipers were singing, and the hymn was one he had heard many times back in Maine.

> Jesus, lover of my soul
> Let me to Thy bosom fly . . .

The man passed on, up toward the heights where regiment after regiment had dashed itself against the stone wall, and the words of the hymn followed him—

> When the nearer waters roll,
> While the tempests still are high.

On the fields once blue with Union dead and wounded, few traces of that agony remained. Green grass covered the places where the 20th Maine had dug its little earthworks and scooped shallow graves for its dead. The soldier recalled that the air was soft and balmy; and the tinkle of a cowbell came from a distant field. He sat there a while, but the ghosts crowded in around him; the stillness became oppressive and he went back to the bivouac of the 20th Maine.

It seemed that the place was bad luck. On the next morning, just as they were breaking camp, a careless wagoner discharged a carbine. The bullet passed through several tents and struck Lieutenant George H. Wood. A brave officer, Wood had fought with the 20th Maine all through the war; now he had a mortal wound. It was an accident, but General Chamberlain wrote bitterly, "I did not treat it as such."

As he lay dying in the hospital, Lieutenant Wood was troubled with regret. He was a devout young man, and thinking back over the past three years of death and destruction, it occurred to him that he could hardly have been known as one who was doing the work of the Lord. Talking to the Reverend Edward P. Smith he said, "Chaplain, do you suppose we shall be able to forget anything in heaven? I would like to forget those three years."

The last day of the march, May 11, was the worst of all. The road surface was muddy, with men sliding and slipping as though they were on ice, and it was up-and-down-hill marching most of the way. In the afternoon, a violent thunderstorm swept over them. Lightning struck the column, running along the muzzles of the rifles, killing one man and stunning several. Streams rose to the size of rivers; they struggled across the Occoquan on a pontoon bridge, wading through deep mud to the approaches, then crawling up the slippery slopes on the other side. At nightfall, for some incomprehensible reason, the march continued at a rapid rate. In the intense darkness, they floundered over a corduroy road; the bark had worn off logs slippery with rain; there were deep holes in the road where logs had been swept away by the flood, and men fell into these cursing and sputtering. The order to halt was not given until after midnight; then they were forced to bivouac in a marsh, where the men suffered intense discomfort in the rain and freezing cold. Many stated that this was harder than any march they had made during the war; the rumor was that two corps commanders were racing to see who could get into Washington first. It was long afterwards felt that the health of many men had been impaired by this march, and the soldiers never ceased to damn the higher-ups responsible.

Muddy, and haggard with weariness, the 20th Maine reached the crest of Arlington Heights early on the morning of May 12. Looking eagerly toward Washington, they were disappointed to find that the city was completely hidden by a dense bank of fog. But as they watched, the fog began to scatter in the morning sun, buildings emerged in outline, then more distinctly, and finally the capital city stood serene and clear, like the crystallization of a nation's dream. They felt, as one said, like crusaders who had finally caught sight of the Holy City.

Issued new tents and equipment, the 20th Maine made a regulation camp on the Heights, tents in perfect lines, grounds policed up, everything according to the book. Then they began cleaning uniforms and boots, polishing muskets and getting ready for the Grand Review. In many units of the army, men were getting new uniforms with fancy embellishments, while the officers were blossoming out with bright sashes, epaulettes and gaudy trappings for their horses. This was thought, however, to be not quite appropriate to veterans; so the 20th Maine and other regiments of the 1st Division decided to "let their plainness tell its own story." The men simply brought themselves up to regulation field inspection, with uniforms, arms and equipment neat and clean—but not so new that they would be made to look like recruits. The officers restricted themselves to unadorned open saddles with an army blanket folded underneath, service uniforms with plain belts and scabbards—no sashes or epaulettes.

Chamberlain admitted, however, that in all this there might be "a scornful pride more sinful than that of vanity." Over in Sherman's army, which had come up from its march to the sea to an encampment near by, there was even more scornful pride. Mostly troops from the West, they looked upon the Army of the Potomac as parade ground soldiers.

The Army of the Potomac men had, in fact, ever since the days of McClellan always taken a certain pride in their soldierly bearing. This attitude was particularly characteristic of the Fifth

Corps, which had included nearly all of the army's Regular troops, and which had West Pointers commanding in most of the superior grades. Both officers and men took pride in a strict observance of army regulations. For example, when Tom Chamberlain was a private he never dared sit down in the presence of Joshua, his brother, even when the two were alone together in a tent. Things like that just weren't done in the Fifth Corps. This tradition, plus the early influence of Adelbert Ames, had made the 20th Maine, if not professional, at least a recognizable imitation of a Regular Army regiment.

The Maine men were therefore, somewhat shocked and disgusted at the appearance of Sherman's men, who were apparently trying hard to live up to their reputation as a rough, tough and ready group of combat soldiers. Private Gerrish of the 20th Maine put down some of his impressions. "Their uniforms were a cross between the regulation blue and the Southern gray. The men were sunburned, while their hair and beards were uncut and uncombed; they were clad in blue, gray, black and brown; huge slouched hats, black and gray, adorned their heads; their boots were covered with the mud they had brought up from Georgia; their guns were of all designs, from the Springfield rifle to a cavalry carbine. . . ."

There was visiting back and forth between the two camps, and the Westerners cast aspersions. The effete Army of the Potomac, they asserted, had done its work in trenches and fortifications, while Sherman's army had done all the fighting and marching. And if they hadn't marched two thousand miles to drive Lee into a trap, the Easterners would never have caught him.

The Maine men retorted that if Sherman had come up against Robert E. Lee instead of a bunch of backwoods bushwhackers, they never would have reached the sea and probably would have been exterminated anyway if Lee had not been defeated at Petersburg and Appomattox. From throwing words, it was not far to throwing punches. Fist fights broke out involving individuals, and then entire brigades. The affair between the North and South had been settled, but now it appeared that there was almost as much feeling between East and West. Division com-

manders eventually had to take strong measures; double guards
were placed on the camps; special reserve details were kept
ready to suppress disorders; Chamberlain found himself sleeping
some nights in his boots, with sword and pistol by his side. He
might as well, he figured, have been back on duty in the Petersburg lines.

But in the memory of those spring days at Arlington this was
really only a minor unpleasantness, eclipsed by the splendor of
the Grand Review of the Army of the Potomac. On the morning
of May 23, the Fifth Corps moved into Washington starting at
four A.M. and halted near the Capitol.

It was a fine, sunny spring morning, the air clear, Washington
bright with banners and thronged with spectators. When their
turn came in the order of march, a bugle sounded, and General Griffin and his staff swung into their saddles to lead the Fifth
Corps up Pennsylvania Avenue. Next, Joshua Chamberlain,
mounting painfully—his staff, which included Ellis Spear and
Tom Chamberlain, lining up behind him—the white 1st Division
flag with its red Maltese cross swaying aloft above them. More
bugle calls, an echoing of commands down the column, and the
division was moving. At the head of the troops marched the old
3rd Brigade in column of companies closed in mass, making a
wide front across the street. There were more marchers than
there had ever been fighters; the division was about ten thousand strong—twice the number it had mustered at Appomattox,
and some regiments had as many as fifteen companies. The 20th
Maine was augmented by the 1st Sharpshooters, so it was a big
regiment. And this was a big day.

They marched at the route step and right shoulder arms until
approaching the turn of the avenue near the Treasury Department building; then the bugle sounded "Prepare for Review";
the bands struck up the cadenced march; the troops took up
the step, lines dressing guide left, muskets coming to the "carry."
Over their heads, a sensation of colors hovering and moving like
bright, proud wings; and on either side they felt, rather than
saw, banks and tiers of people, clouds of banners and red-white-
and-blue bunting. They moved through great waves of sound:
cheering that rose and fell; bands playing; and the rolling thun-

der of salutes fired by the artillery stationed around Washington.

When they passed the President's reviewing stand opposite the White House, drums ruffled, colors dipped, and mounted officers saluted. After riding past, Chamberlain and other high-ranking general officers turned out of the column, dismounted and ascended the reviewing stand at the President's invitation to watch the passing of the troops.

It was an honor for which the Maine general had been an extremely unlikely candidate three years before as a theologian and a college professor. But there is no telling what sort of man will do well in battle. The war had been Chamberlain's dish; he had swallowed it whole and savored it to the full. He had been in battles, reconnaissances and skirmishes without number; had been seriously wounded; and had narrowly escaped with his life. He was even now in need of surgical attention, and his injury would cause him untold pain and misery for the rest of his life.

And yet Chamberlain would have disagreed with Sherman's "War is Hell." In fact he wrote, later on, "In the privations and sufferings endured as well as in the strenuous action of battle, some of the highest qualities of manhood are called forth—courage, self-command, sacrifice of self for the sake of something held higher . . . and on another side fortitude, patience, warmth of comradeship, and in the darkest hours tenderness of caring for the wounded and stricken. . . . Such things belong to something far different from the place or sphere assigned in the remark of the eminent exemplar of the aphorism."

As he stood here on the presidential reviewing stand, Chamberlain could not know that his whole life had been transformed by his war record—that the Congressional Medal of Honor, the governorship of Maine, and the presidency of Bowdoin College awaited him. But he did know that something was passing that would never be regained. As the 20th Maine came past, he could not take his eyes off the men and the battle-worn colors. Of those who had fought with him at Little Round Top, not many were left; but some were left, and there were others, unseen, who marched with a procession of grim names that moved under the cheering like a roll of muffled drums:

THE LAST REVIEW

Antietam
Shepherdstown Ford
Fredericksburg
Middleburg
Gettysburg
Rappahannock Station
Mine Run
The Wilderness
Laurel Hill
North Anna
Bethesda Church
Petersburg
Weldon Railroad
Peebles' Farm
Hatcher's Run
Quaker Road
White Oak Road
Five Forks
Appomattox

Chamberlain watched the 20th Maine until its colors mingled with the flags that had gone before and the many that came after—the Fifth Corps marching for the last time together. For the regiment it was a march that had come full circle. On that September day seemingly so long ago when they had first marched through Washington behind their erratic drum corps, war had been a great unknown. Now, along with the music of victory, they could feel a weight of memories: the vast night-moaning on the field at Fredericksburg; blood running down the rocks and making puddles on Little Round Top; the shot deserter sitting upright but stone dead on his coffin; wounded screaming in the Wilderness as the brush fires engulfed them; the death-smell on the summer winds that blew over Cold Harbor; men dying in the mud at Petersburg; the skulls going home in the cracker boxes; all this and more; a piled-up, pressing-down, suffocating mass of bones, decayed blue fabric, tarnished buttons, the gold and the glory long ago gone.

And yet they had come through the war with a spirit that seemed at times curiously innocent and unsophisticated when compared with present-day standards of soldierly behavior. On the evening of May 25, there took place an incident which cannot possibly be imagined as happening in a modern army. An issue of candles had been made. As darkness settled, it was noticed that the camps of the Second Corps had been illuminated. Not to be outdone, Fifth Corps soldiers placed lighted candles in rifle muzzles and in the sockets of their bayonets.

Individual soldiers began attempting the manual of arms and other antics with the flame-tipped weapons. Then groups formed and moved—one in the shape of a giant revolving Catherine wheel. Soon, perhaps from habit, the candle-bearers assembled in military formations—companies, then regiments, brigades and divisions—a vast, sparkling parade growing spontaneously and forming under the command of enlisted men who had promoted themselves to temporary officers. The air was still. The little flames burned steadily, casting a beautiful, far-spreading glow, and here in this group of battle-hardened veterans was something that very much resembled a candlelight ceremony at a Boy Scout Jamboree. To Sergeant William T. Livermore of the 20th Maine it looked like "an ocean of stars."

Bands and drum corps struck up a cadence. The troops marched to salute their generals. A headquarters clerk described the approach of Chamberlain's division as "an immense column . . . a line of living fire; it was almost inconceivable that the slight ray of a candle, although so many times multiplied, should give so strong a light." And when the division had formed around the headquarters tents ". . . the place was so illuminated that the smallest print could have been easily read."

There were cries of "Speech! Speech!" and Chamberlain, with his background of Oratory and Rhetoric at Bowdoin College, was able to mount a cracker box and produce an appropriate flight of eloquence. The band played and there were patriotic songs and cheers for the generals and the Army. The demonstration went on until, as one soldier-historian put it, "The oratory and exercises . . . were cut short by the ration of candles burning out, leaving all in the dark."

Symbolically, it was good-night and good-bye to the Army of the Potomac. A regiment called the 20th Maine remained at Arlington for a few more weeks, but it was only a name and a number, being made up of recruits and the consolidated fragments of other units. Men whose enlistments expired in the fall were allowed to go home, so the real 20th, the old 20th, was departing. On Sunday, June 4, the veterans were mustered out of the United States service. Next day, under the command of Lieutenant Colonel Walter G. Morrill, they marched into Washington to take the train north.

Here in the lowlands of the Potomac, a muggy hot-weather haze was already dimming the horizon, but beyond, they knew, the Maine sky would be a clear and luminous blue; trout would be biting; and in the cool, shadowed woods it would be so quiet a man could hear a chipmunk scolding a mile away.

THE END

ACKNOWLEDGMENTS

THE foremost acknowledgment is to Jean A. Pullen, who has patiently endured the trials that beset the wife of an author during the researching and writing of a book and whose unfailing understanding and support have made this work possible.

Eleanor Wyllys Allen and Rosamond Allen, granddaughters of General Joshua L. Chamberlain, have been graciously helpful. Important information has been obtained from Helen K. Atchison; the *Bangor Daily News*; the Bangor Public Library and L. Felix Ranlett, Librarian; the Library of the College of Physicians in Philadelphia; Grace N. Darling; the Erie Public Library and Helen E. Rilling, Librarian.

A very special note of thanks goes to Alice M. Fairweather for her interest in this project as well as for her assistance in preparing the manuscript. Alice M. Farrington, niece of General Chamberlain, provided letters and also information from her own memories of the General. Line drawings are from the work of Edwin Forbes (1839-95), who traveled with the Army of the Potomac as an artist-reporter for *Frank Leslie's Illustrated Newspaper*.

Oscar L. Hamlin and the heirs of William T. Livermore made available several important letters, as well as a diary by Sergeant Livermore covering the war years. The author has appreciated the privilege of working in the library of the Historical Society of Pennsylvania and is particularly grateful to Raymond L. Sutcliffe, Librarian, for his friendly and patient assistance. The Free Library of Philadelphia was also an important source of information.

Certain portions of the manuscript having to do with the raising of the 20th Maine and the draft were reviewed by Merton G. Henry, co-author with Colonel Marvin A. Kreidberg of *History of Military Mobilization in the United States Army, 1775-1945* (see Bibliography), a comprehensive and comparatively recent work which is recommended to students of the Civil and other wars. It should be understood, however, that Mr. Henry is in no sense responsible for any errors which may be found in this story of the 20th Maine.

Mr. and Mrs. Charles L. Holden and the heirs of Ezekiel Benn searched out letters and assisted generously in other ways. Emma L. Jones contributed a photograph. Sidney F. Jones answered many inquiries. The staffs of the Library of Congress Manuscripts Division and Prints and Photographs Division assisted the author in making use of their extensive collections.

Tommy S. Lee made the maps for this book. Lippincott's Lynn Carrick and Tay Hohoff have provided tactful professional guidance and steady encouragement. The Maine Historical Society and Marian B. Rowe, Librarian, allowed the author to consult manuscript collections owned by the Society. Jessie Ames Marshall and heirs of Adelbert Ames made available records and correspondence. John E. Maass kindly helped with the selection and planning of illustrations. Peter Mills, U. S. Attorney for the District of Maine, made valuable suggestions.

A great deal of material and good advice was obtained from the National Archives and Records Service and Josephine Cobb, Archivist in charge of the Still Picture Branch; and from the National Park Service and its extremely competent and co-operative historians at three National Military Parks: Ralph Happel at Fredericksburg; Frederick Tilberg at Gettysburg; and Lee A. Wallace, Jr., at Petersburg.

At the New York Public Library, Robert W. Hill, Keeper of Manuscripts, permitted the author to read collections of Civil War Letters; this library's fine collection of regimental histories was also consulted.

The largest group of letters came from Harold M. Owen and the heirs of William H. Owen. Over seventy-five letters written by Sergeant Owen while serving in the 20th Maine were painstakingly transcribed and sent to the author along with a photograph of the sergeant.

Mr. and Mrs. Francis Palmer helped with books and research. The author's parents, Mr. and Mrs. O. W. Pullen, contributed much pertinent information. Ruth Pullen, a sister, has also helped in many generous and important ways.

Thanks also goes to Henry Rothman for his assistance in preparing the photographs; Caroline Dunn Smith for an article written by Private Charles Dunn of the 20th Maine; C. Robert Tittle, Jr., M.D., for advice on certain medical references; and to Louis E. Tuckerman for information concerning the battle of Antietam.

In much of the research, the author has been privileged to use one of the finest Civil War libraries anywhere—the War Library and Museum of the Military Order of the Loyal Legion of the United

States at 1805 Pine Street, Philadelphia—and he was assisted on many occasions by Stephanie Benko and by George A. Landell, former President of the War Library and Museum. James H. Whitcomb helped in the research. The Wyeth Laboratories and Philip H. Van Itallie, Editor of *Pulse of Pharmacy*, provided information that was helpful in writing the account of the 20th Maine's experience with smallpox.

Many other people, for example the Postmasters in several Maine towns, have provided "leads" of great value in the research. To all who in any way assisted in the preparation of this work, the author is sincerely grateful.

As a last-minute note, the author also wishes to record one notable contribution that took place just before the book went to press. A picture of Company G was located by, and appeared in *Down East Magazine*, Camden, Maine. Through the prompt co-operation of Duane Doolittle, the editor, and Mrs. Nelson S. Rundlett of Clinton, Connecticut, the photograph was quickly made available. The author also received from James C. Rundlett copies of more than fifty letters written by his grandfather, James C. Rundlett, who appears third from left in the picture of Company G. These came too late for use in preparing the text but did serve to corroborate several details.

BIBLIOGRAPHY

ACTS OF CONGRESS affecting the armed forces: May 8, 1792; February 28, 1795; July 22, 1861; August 6, 1861; March 19, 1862; July 17, 1862; March 3, 1863.

AMES, ADELBERT, Brevet Major General, U.S.A. LETTERS. Manuscript Division, New York Public Library; and private possession, Jessie Ames Marshall, Jamaica Plain, Mass.

ANNUAL REPORTS of the Adjutant General, State of Maine, for the years 1861 through 1866. Augusta, Maine.

Atlas to Accompany the Official Records of the Union and Confederate Armies. Washington: War Department, 1891-95.

Bangor Daily News, issue of July 1, 1913.

Bangor Daily Whig & Courier, issues of August 22, 1862, and September 14, 1863.

Battles and Leaders of the Civil War. Edited by Robert Underwood Johnson and Clarence Clough Buel. Four volumes. New York, 1887-88.

BENN, EZEKIEL, Private, 20th Maine. LETTERS. Private possession, Charles L. Holden, Millinocket, Maine.

BILLINGS, JOHN D. *Hardtack and Coffee.* Boston, 1888.

Biographical Review (Volume XXIX) *Containing Life Sketches of leading citizens of Somerset, Piscataquis, Hancock, Washington and Aroostook Counties, Maine.* Boston, 1898.

BOYKIN, EDWARD M., Lieutenant Colonel, C.S.A. *The Falling Flag.* New York, 1874.

BROWN, J. WILLARD. *The Signal Corps, U.S.A., in the War of Rebellion.* Boston, 1896.

Camp Fire Sketches and Battle-Field Echoes of 61-65. Compiled by W. C. King and W. P. Derby. Springfield, Mass., 1889.

CARTER, ROBERT GOLDTHWAITE, Captain, U.S.A. "Four Brothers in Blue." Installments appearing in the *Maine Bugle,* issues of October, 1897; January, 1898; July, 1898; and October, 1898. This veterans' magazine was initially published by the First Maine Cavalry Association in 1890 and was called *First Maine Bugle.* Later its scope was widened to include material of interest to other Maine regiments and its name was changed to *Maine Bugle.*

CATTON, BRUCE. *Mr. Lincoln's Army.* Garden City, New York, 1951.
———. *Glory Road,* Garden City, New York, 1952.
———. *A Stillness at Appomattox.* Garden City, New York, 1953.

CHAMBERLAIN, JOHN. LETTERS. Private possession, Alice M. Farrington, Brewer, Maine.

CHAMBERLAIN, JOSHUA, Brevet Major General, U.S.V. *Abraham Lincoln,* an oration delivered at ceremonies in commemoration of the 100th anniversary of the birth of Abraham Lincoln, Philadelphia, February 12, 1909. Papers of the Military Order of the Loyal Legion, Commandery of the State of Pennsylvania.
———. Collections of papers. Manuscripts Division, Library of Congress. Also, Maine Historical Society.
———. "My Story of Fredericksburg." *Cosmopolitan Magazine,* January, 1913.
———. *The Passing of the Armies.* New York, 1915.
———. *The Third Brigade at Appomattox.* Appended to *Army Letters,* by Oliver Willcox Norton. See Norton, following.
———. "Through Blood and Fire at Gettysburg." *Hearst's Magazine,* June, 1913.

CHAMBERLAIN, THOMAS D., Lieutenant Colonel, U.S.V. LETTERS. Private possession, Alice M. Farrington, Brewer, Maine.

BIBLIOGRAPHY

CILLEY, JONATHAN P., Brevet Brigadier General, U.S.V. "Up the Shenandoah Valley and on to Appomattox." Installment appearing in the *First Maine Bugle,* issue of January, 1893.

Civil War in Song and Story. Collected and arranged by Frank Moore. New York, 1889.

CRAIGHILL, WILLIAM P. *The Army Officer's Pocket Companion.* New York, 1862.

Cyclopaedia of Political Science, Political Economy and of the Political History of the United States. Edited by John J. Lalor. Three volumes. New York, 1893.

DANA, CHARLES A. *Recollections of the Civil War.* New York, 1898.

DUNN, CHARLES E., Private, 20th Maine. "The Fiftieth Anniversary of the Surrender of General Lee." *The Aroostook Pioneer,* April 22, 1915.

DWINAL, LESTER, Captain. U.S.V. LETTERS. Private possession, Phyllis Manning, Millinocket, Maine.

EATON, CYRUS. *Annals of the Town of Warren.* Second Edition. Hallowell, Maine, 1877.
——. *History of Thomaston, Rockland and South Thomaston.* Two volumes. Hallowell, Maine, 1865.

FORBES, EDWIN. *Thirty Years After, An Artist's Story of the Great War.* Two volumes. New York, 1890.

FOX, WILLIAM F., Lieutenant Colonel, U.S.V. *Regimental Losses in the American Civil War.* Albany, 1889.

General Orders Affecting the Volunteer Force (1861-62-63). Washington: War Department, Adjutant General's Office, 1862-63-64.

General Orders, Headquarters Army of the Potomac (1861-65).

GERRISH, REV. THEODORE, Private, 20th Maine. *Army Life, a Private's Reminiscences of the Civil War.* Portland, Maine, 1882. (Gerrish, *Army Life.*)

GERRISH, REV. THEODORE and HUTCHINSON, REV. JOHN. *The Blue and the Gray*. Portland, Maine, 1883.

HAPPEL, RALPH. *Appomattox Court House National Historical Park*. National Park Service booklet. Washington, 1955.

HASKELL, FRANK ARETAS, Colonel, U.S.V. *The Battle of Gettysburg*. Published under the auspices of the Commandery of the State of Massachusetts, Military Order of the Loyal Legion of the United States. Boston, 1908.

History of the Corn Exchange Regiment, 118th Pennsylvania Volunteers. By the Survivors' Association. Philadelphia, 1888. (*Corn Exchange Regiment*.)

History of the 122nd Regiment, Pennsylvania Volunteers, from the Diary of George F. Sprenger. Lancaster, Pennsylvania, 1885.

History of the Town of Wayne, Kennebec County, Maine. Written by a group of Wayne citizens. Augusta, Maine, 1898.

Infantry Tactics. Prepared by Brigadier General Silas Casey, U.S.A., and authorized by the War Department, August 11, 1862. Three volumes.

In Memoriam, Joshua Lawrence Chamberlain, late Major General, U.S.V. Circular Number 5, Series of 1914, Military Order of the Loyal Legion of the United States, Commandery of the State of Maine. Portland, Maine, 1914.

Joshua Lawrence Chamberlain, a Sketch. Prepared for the Report of the Chamberlain Association of America. (No date or place of publication.) Copy available at the Bangor Public Library.

JUDSON, A. M., Captain, U.S.V. *History of the 83rd Regiment Pennsylvania Volunteers*. Erie, Pennsylvania. Not dated. Believed published between 1865 and 1870.

KEEN, W. W. "Surgical Reminiscences of the Civil War." In *Transactions of the College of Physicians of Philadelphia*, Third Series, Volume 27. Philadelphia, 1905.

BIBLIOGRAPHY

KREIDBERG, MARVIN A., and HENRY, MERTON G., *History of Military Mobilization in the United States Army, 1775-1945*. Department of the Army Pamphlet No. 20-212. Washington, 1955.

Lincoln County News (Waldoboro, Maine), issue of January 18, 1877.

LIVERMORE, WILLIAM T., Sergeant, 20th Maine. LETTERS. Private possession, Oscar L. Hamlin, Milo, Maine.
———. DIARY, 1862-65. Private possession, Percy L. Hamlin, Milo, Maine.

LONGSTREET, JAMES, Lieutenant General, C.S.A. *From Manassas to Appomattox.* Philadelphia, 1896.

LYKES, RICHARD WAYNE. *Petersburg Battlefields.* National Park Service Historical Handbook. Washington, 1955.

McPHERSON, EDWARD. *The Political History of the United States of America During the Great Rebellion.* Second Edition. Washington, 1865.

Maine at Gettysburg. Report of Maine Commissioners. Portland, Maine, 1898.

MEADE, GEORGE, Brevet Lieutenant Colonel, U.S.A. *The Life and Letters of George Gordon Meade.* Two volumes. New York, 1913.

Medal of Honor of the United States Army, The. Washington: U. S. Government Printing Office, 1948. (*Medal of Honor.*)

Medical and Surgical History of the War of the Rebellion. Two volumes (Volume I, Medical History; Volume II, Surgical History) each in three parts. Washington, 1870-1888.

MELCHER, HOLMAN S., Brevet Major, U.S.V. *An Experience in the Battle of the Wilderness.* War Papers, Volume I, Military Order of the Loyal Legion of the United States, Commandery of the State of Maine. Portland, Maine, 1898.

Military Maps Illustrating the Operation of the Armies of the Potomac

& *James*. Executed under the direction of Brevet Brigadier General N. Michler. Washington: Office of the Chief of Engineers, 1869.

MILLER, SAMUEL L., Lieutenant, U.S.V. Historical address published in *Reunions of the 20th Maine Regiment Association*. Waldoboro, Maine, 1881.

NASH, EUGENE ARUS, Captain, U.S.V. *A History of the Forty-Fourth Regiment, New York Volunteer Infantry*. Chicago, 1911.

NORTH, JAMES W. *The History of Augusta*. Augusta, Maine, 1870.

NORTON, OLIVER WILLCOX. Lieutenant, U.S.V. *Army Letters*. Chicago, 1903.
——. *The Attack and Defense of Little Round Top*. New York, 1913.
    (Norton, *Little Round Top*.)

OATES, WILLIAM CALVIN, Colonel, C.S.A. *The War Between the Union and the Confederacy and Its Lost Opportunities*. New York and Washington, 1905.

OWEN, WILLIAM H., Sergeant, 20th Maine. LETTERS. Private possession, Harold M. Owen, Milo, Maine.

PARKER, FRANCIS J., Colonel, U.S.V. *The Story of the 32nd Regiment Massachusetts Infantry*. Boston, 1880.

Philadelphia Public Ledger, issues of July 4 and 6, 1863.

Photographic History of the Civil War. Edited by Francis Trevelyan Miller. Ten volumes. New York, 1912.

PLUM, WILLIAM R. *The Military Telegraph During the Civil War in the United States*. Two volumes. Chicago, 1882.

POWELL, WILLIAM H., Lieutenant Colonel, U.S.A. *The Fifth Army Corps*. New York, 1896.

PRAY, J. L. "Recollections of Appomattox." In the *First Maine Bugle*, issue of July, 1893.

BIBLIOGRAPHY

Pulse of Pharmacy. Volume IX, Number 1 (1955). Published by Wyeth Laboratories, Philadelphia.

RAUSCHER, FRANK. *Music on the March*. Philadelphia, 1892.

Rebellion Record. Edited by Frank Moore. Eleven volumes and a supplement. New York, 1861-1868.

REGIMENTAL RECORDS of the 20th Maine, including muster and descriptive rolls, letters, orders, reports and returns. From records of the War Department, Office of the Adjutant General, in the National Archives, Washington.

Revised Statutes of the State of Maine passed October 22, 1840 and April 17, 1857.

ROBINSON, REUEL. *History of Camden and Rockport, Maine*. Camden, Maine, 1907.

SCHAFF, MORRIS. *The Battle of the Wilderness*. Boston and New York, 1910.

SCHURZ, CARL. *The Reminiscences of Carl Schurz*. Three volumes. New York, 1908.

SMITH, REV. EDWARD P. *Incidents of the United States Christian Commission*. Philadelphia, 1871.

SPEAR, ELLIS, Brevet Brigadier General, U.S.V. War Papers, Military Order of the Loyal Legion of the United States, Commandery of the District of Columbia.
——. *The Hoe Cake of Appomattox*. Number 93. Read May 7, 1913.
——. *The Story of the Raising and Organization of a Regiment of Volunteers in 1862*. Number 46. Read March 4, 1903.
    (Spear, *A Regiment of Volunteers*)

STANLEY, R. H. and HALL, GEORGE O. *Eastern Maine and the Rebellion*. Bangor, Maine, 1887.

STEELE, MATTHEW FORNEY, Major, 2nd U. S. Cavalry, *American Campaigns*. 1949 edition. Two volumes. Harrisburg, Penna.

SWINTON, WILLIAM. *Campaigns of the Army of the Potomac.* New York, 1866.

TILBERG, FREDERICK. *Gettysburg National Park.* National Park Service Historical Handbook. Washington, 1950.

TILNEY, ROBERT. *My Life in the Army.* Philadelphia, 1912.

TOCQUEVILLE, ALEXIS DE. *Democracy in America.* Translated by Henry Reeve. With a Critical and Biographical Introduction by John Bigelow. Two volumes. New York, 1899.

TREMAIN, HENRY EDWIN. *Two Days of War.* New York, 1905.

Under the Maltese Cross, Campaigns of the 155th Pennsylvania Regiment. Edited by Charles F. McKenna. Pittsburg, 1910.

United States Sanitary Commission, *Sanitary Memoirs of the War of the Rebellion,* including:
———. *Contributions Relating to the Causation and Prevention of Disease, and to Camp Diseases.* Edited by Austin Flint. New York, 1867.
———. *Investigations in the Military and Anthropological Statistics of American Soldiers.* By Benjamin Apthorp Gould. New York, 1869.

UPTON, EMORY, Brevet Major General, U.S.A. *The Military Policy of the United States.* Washington, 1904.

War of the Rebellion: A compilation of the official records of the Union and Confederate armies. 70 volumes in 128 parts. Washington, 1880-1901.

WHITMAN, WILLIAM E. S. and TRUE, CHARLES H. *Maine in the War for the Union.* Lewiston, Maine, 1865.

WOODWARD, JOSEPH J. *Outlines of the Chief Camp Diseases of the United States Armies.* Philadelphia, 1863.

NOTES

THESE abbreviations are used:

OR—*War of the Rebellion*: A compilation of the official records of the Union and Confederate armies. Series I unless otherwise noted.

MeAGR—*Annual Report of the Adjutant General, State of Maine.* This is always preceded by the year of the report.

WDAGO—War Department, Adjutant General's Office.

If an author has only one work listed in the Bibliography, the work is referred to in these notes by the name of the writer, the full title being omitted.

Chapter 1. How D'Ye Do Colonel

THE account of Colonel Ames' arrival in camp, up to and including the drum corps incident: Spear, *A Regiment of Volunteers*, pp. 7-13.

The table of organization of the volunteer regiment varied slightly throughout the war. See the following General Orders, WDAGO: No. 15, May 4, 1861; No. 126, Sept. 26, 1862; and No. 110, April 29, 1863. Also 1862 MeAGR, App. D, pp. 653-677.

Biographical information concerning Adelbert Ames: OR, II, 394; 1864-65 MeAGR, I, 302, 303; and Eaton, *History of Thomaston, Rockland and South Thomaston*, II, 63; *Medal of Honor*, p. 105; and information provided by Jessie Ames Marshall, daughter of General Ames.

Biographical, Joshua L. Chamberlain: *In Memoriam, Joshua Lawrence Chamberlain*, pp. 2, 12; 1864-65 MeAGR, I, 330; *Joshua Lawrence Chamberlain, a Sketch*, pp. 1-10; and information provided by Alice M. Farrington, Chamberlain's niece.

Biographical, Charles D. Gilmore: 1864-65 MeAGR, I, 370, 371; Spear, *A Regiment of Volunteers*, p. 7.

Biographical, Ellis Spear: Eaton, *Annals of the Town of Warren*, p. 404.

Heights of the men: Regimental records, *Descriptive Book*. Also, the U. S. Sanitary Commission's *Sanitary Memoirs, Investigations in the Military and Anthropological Statistics of American Soldiers*, p. 93.

Recruiting: Spear, *A Regiment of Volunteers*, pp. 4, 5.

Commissioning of officers: Upton, pp. 250, 251, 259, 260; Acts of Congress, July 22, 1861 and August 6, 1861.

Politics in volunteer regiments: The letters of Lester Dwinal of the 15th Maine provide a good picture of this activity. The 20th Maine's political meeting mentioned in this chapter was reported in *Bangor Daily Whig & Courier*, Sept. 14, 1863.

Militia in 1840: 1861 MeAGR, pp. 43, 44; *Revised Statutes of the State of Maine* (1840), Chapter 16. There is a good description of the old-time militia muster in *History of the Town of Wayne*, pp. 78, 79.

Militia in 1861: 1861 MeAGR, pp. 5, 47, 51, 52; *Revised Statutes of the State of Maine* (1857), Chapter 10; Kreidberg and Henry, p. 90.

Important legislation affecting militia includes: U. S. Constitution, Article I, Section 8 and Article II, Section 2; Acts of Congress, May 8, 1792, Feb. 28, 1795 and July 17, 1862. See also 1862 MeAGR, pp. 6, 10 and these General Orders, WDAGO: No. 94, August 4, 1862 and No. 99, August 9, 1862; and Kreidberg and Henry, 30, 31, 103, 104.

States' vs. federal rights in raising troops: Upton, pp. 249, 264-266; General Order No. 78, WDAGO, Sept. 16, 1861.

Medical examinations: Spear, *A Regiment of Volunteers*, p. 6.

Bounties and records: 1862 MeAGR, pp. 6, 7, 21-26, 29, 30.

Towns sending extra men: *Bangor Daily Whig & Courier*, Aug. 22, 1862; 1862 MeAGR, p. 25.

Home towns, names and ages: 1862 MeAGR, App. D, pp. 653-677; Miller, p. 11.

Racial origins and occupations: 1864-65 MeAGR, I, 526.

Glazier Estabrook incident: Related by Isaac Simpson.

Dirty ears incident: Gerrish and Hutchinson, *Blue and the Gray*, p. 392.

Uniforms: Spear, *A Regiment of Volunteers*, pp. 9, 10; Gerrish and Hutchinson, *Blue and the Gray*, pp. 50, 52; Miller, p. 12.

Equipment: 1862 MeAGR, App. C, p. 5 and App. G, p. 21; Gerrish and Hutchinson, *Blue and the Gray*, p. 51; Spear, *A Regiment of Volunteers*, pp. 9, 10.

The departure of the 20th Maine: *Lincoln County News*. Issue of Jan. 18, 1877.

The appraisal of the soldier in a democracy: Tocqueville, II, 771, 772.

Chapter 2. Dan, Dan, Dan, Butterfield, Butterfield

The situation in Washington in early September, 1862: Swinton, pp. 193, 197; Steele, I, 260; Livermore diary, entry of Sept. 7, 1862.

The 20th Maine's arrival in Washington and march to Fort Craig: Spear, *A Regiment of Volunteers*, p. 14; Gerrish, *Army Life*, p. 19; Miller, p. 12.

Corps organization: Swinton, p. 64; Upton, p. 257; Gerrish and Hutchinson, *Blue and the Gray*, App. p. 792; Powell, pp. 1-58.

Lack of system for regimental replacements: Upton, p. 258; 1864-65 MeAGR, II, Preface, 7.

Composition and history of the 3rd Brigade: Powell, p. 304; Tilney, p. 11.

Bugle calls: Norton, *Army Letters*, pp. 323-328; *Infantry Tactics* (Casey's), I, 229, 230; Billings, pp. 336, 337.

The march to Antietam: Powell, pp. 261, 262; *Corn Exchange Regiment*, pp. 1-24, 29, 30, 36, 37-39; Gerrish and Hutchinson, *Blue and the Gray*, pp. 53, 54; Miller, p. 12; Norton, *Army Letters*, p. 119; Parker, pp. 86-88; Gerrish, *Army Life*, pp. 27, 28; Carter in *Maine Bugle* for Oct., 1897; Judson, p. 53.

Description of the battle of Antietam: Gerrish, *Army Life*, p. 31; Norton, *Army Letters*, pp. 120, 126; Parker, pp. 91-95, 102; Carter in *Maine Bugle* for Oct., 1897; *Corn Exchange Regiment*, p. 42.

Critical comment, battle of Antietam: Steele, I, 282.

Description of the fight at Shepherdstown Ford: Powell, pp. 295-300; Judson, p. 54; *Corn Exchange Regiment*, pp. 54-71; Gerrish, *Army Life*, pp. 41, 43, 44; Livermore diary, entry of Sept. 20, 1862.

Chamberlain at Shepherdstown Ford: Powell, p. 301.

Lincoln at Antietam: Powell, p. 309; Joshua Chamberlain, *Abraham Lincoln*, and "My Story of Fredericksburg."

Incident of men hanging around officers' tents: Regimental records, Special Order No. 3, Hq. 20th Me. Vols., Sept. 10, 1862.

"Green apple sass" and "juicy hardtack" incidents: Gerrish, *Army Life*, pp. 67, 68.

"Load in nine times": *Infantry Tactics* (Casey's), I, 42-46.

Formation of line of battle: *Infantry Tactics* (Casey's), I, Plate 1, and pp. 9-17; Thomas to Sarah Chamberlain, Oct. 14, 1862.

Marching maneuvers: *Infantry Tactics* (Casey's), I, 83, 127-132, II, 30, 45.

Men's reaction to drilling: Thomas to Sarah Chamberlain, Oct. 14, 1862, and Oct. 26, 1862; and to John Chamberlain, Oct. 30, 1862.

Disciplining young officers: Gerrish and Hutchinson, *Blue and the Gray*, pp. 64, 65.

Joshua Chamberlain's liking for the army life: Thomas to Sarah Chamberlain, Oct. 14, 1862; and information provided by Alice Farrington.

Health conditions: Gerrish, *Army Life*, p. 47; Carter in *Maine Bugle* for Jan., 1898.

Diseases, and susceptibility of rural soldiers: U. S. Sanitary Commission, *Sanitary Memoirs, Contributions Relating to the Causation and Prevention of Disease, and to Camp Diseases*, pp. 100, 103, 181; Thomas to Sarah Chamberlain, Oct. 30, 1862; Woodward, pp. 206, 267, 268; Regimental records, return of deceased soldiers of the 20th Maine, Fourth Quarter, 1862; Miller, p. 14; Gerrish, *Army Life*, pp. 47-49.

Burials: Gerrish, *Army Life*, p. 48.

Mood of the soldiers: William to Abbie Owen, Oct. 19, 1862.

Chapter 3. NEVER AND FOREVER

GENERAL McClellan: Gerrish and Hutchinson, *Blue and the Gray*, p. 248; Swinton, pp. 60-67.

The march into Virginia: Gerrish, *Army Life*, pp. 50, 51; Judson, p. 55.

McClellan's removal, and the reaction of the soldiers: Swinton, p. 227; Powell, pp. 317, 319; Judson, p. 55; *Corn Exchange Regiment*, pp. 107, 108; William to Abbie Owen, Nov. 14, 1862.

The move to Stoneman's Switch: Powell, pp. 360, 361, 363; Parker, p. 117; *Corn Exchange Regiment*, p. 109.

Incident of the two men freezing to death: Powell, p. 366.

General Burnside: Dana, p. 138; Joshua Chamberlain, "My Story of Fredericksburg"; Steele, I, 297; Gerrish, *Army Life*, pp. 331, 332.

Rumors of and preparations for the attack: Nash, p. 112; Swinton, p. 236; Steele, I, 290; *Under the Maltese Cross*, pp. 93-95; *Corn Exchange Regiment*, p. 114.

Morning of December 11, and the march to Fredericksburg: Parker, pp. 121-123; Miller, p. 14; *Rebellion Record*, VI, 247.

Waiting in the field by the Phillips House: Parker, p. 123; Carter in *Maine Bugle* of July, 1898; *Corn Exchange Regiment*, pp. 119, 120.

The bombardment of Fredericksburg and river crossing: OR, XXI, 182, 183; *Rebellion Record*, VI, 247, 248; Swinton, pp. 241, 242.

The bivouac, and impressions of the soldiers on the night of December 11: Carter in *Maine Bugle* of July, 1898; Gerrish, *Army Life*, pp. 73, 74.

Confederate dispositions: Longstreet, pp. 300-305, 311, 313; Swinton, pp. 231, 232.

The second day of waiting, December 12: OR, XXI, 404; Swinton, p. 242.

Watching the attack on December 13: Gerrish, *Army Life*, pp. 75, 76; Longstreet, pp. 307, 309-311, 315; Parker, p. 127; Steele, I, 298, 299; *Battles and Leaders of the Civil War*, III, 111-118; Joshua Chamberlain, "My Story of Fredericksburg."

The river crossing and advance on the field: Joshua Chamberlain, "My Story of Fredericksburg"; *Corn Exchange Regiment*, p. 122; Norton, *Army Letters*, p. 130; OR, XXI, 411; Carter in *Maine Bugle* of July, 1898.

The night of December 13-14: Joshua Chamberlain, "My Story of Fredericksburg"; Chamberlain's account in *Camp Fire Sketches*, pp. 127-130; Gerrish, *Army Life*, p. 78.

Daylight hours, December 14: OR, XXI, 411, 412; Joshua Chamberlain, "My Story of Fredericksburg"; Gerrish, *Army Life*, p. 79.

Retiring from the field, evening of December 14: Joshua Chamberlain, "My Story of Fredericksburg"; Chamberlain's account in *Camp Fire Sketches*, pp. 127-130.

Daylight hours, December 15, resting in Fredericksburg; Joshua Chamberlain, "My Story of Fredericksburg"; Gerrish, *Army Life*, pp. 79, 80; *Corn Exchange Regiment*, p. 137.

Night of December 15-16, covering the retreat: *Corn Exchange Regiment*, p. 137; Joshua Chamberlain, "My Story of Fredericksburg"; Judson, p. 60.

Losses of the 20th Maine: Powell, p. 410.

Conversation between Hooker and Chamberlain: Joshua Chamberlain, "My Story of Fredericksburg."

Chapter 4. STUCK IN THE MUD

DESCRIPTIONS of Virginia mud: Parker, pp. 120, 121, 141; *Rebellion Record*, VI, 399.

Building and furnishing of huts: Gerrish, *Army Life*, p. 63; Billings, pp. 55, 56, 74-76, 95.

Arrangement of camp: Craighill, p. 119.

"The army cough": Parker, pp. 120, 121.

Cutting, carrying and stealing wood: *Corn Exchange Regiment*, p. 142; Billings, p. 180; Gerrish, *Army Life*, p. 63; Gerrish and Hutchinson, *Blue and the Gray*, p. 400; and a reminiscence of Charles L. Holden.

The Sergeant Buck incident: Gerrish, *Army Life*, pp. 69-71.

The reconnaissance to Richards Ford: *Corn Exchange Regiment*, pp. 152-158; Judson, p. 61; OR, XXI, 742-744; Norton, *Army Letters*, p. 132; *History of the 122nd Regiment, Pennsylvania Volunteers*, pp. 170, 171. Compiled from a diary, this book includes frequent descriptions of weather conditions experienced in the Army of the Potomac from August, 1862, through May, 1863.

Letter home: William H. to Abbie Owen, Feb. 24, 1863.

Tossing cartridges down the chimney: Gerrish and Hutchinson, *Blue and the Gray*, pp. 401-403.

Lousiness: Billings, p. 80; Norton, *Army Letters*, p. 137.

Confederate dispositions and Burnside's preparations for crossing the river: *Rebellion Record*, VI, 397, 398.

The Mud March: *Corn Exchange Regiment*, pp. 158-164; Powell, pp. 407, 409, 410, 415; Parker, pp. 139-141; *Rebellion Record*, VI, 397, 399, 400; Whitman and True, p. 492; Carter in *Maine Bugle* of Oct., 1898; Norton, *Army Letters*, p. 137; Billings, p. 72.

Description of General Hooker: Gerrish, *Army Life*, p. 85; Gerrish and Hutchinson, *Blue and the Gray*, p. 252; *Corn Exchange Regiment*, pp. 165, 166.

Hooker's orders for improving camp conditions: OR, XXV, Part 2, 57, 89, 91, 239; *Under the Maltese Cross*, p. 126; Regimental records, General Order No. 7, Hq. 20th Me. Vols., Jan. 26, 1863.

Corps badges: Billings, pp. 254-268; OR, XXV, Part 2, 152.

Review by Lincoln: Norton, *Army Letters*, p. 148; Carter in *Maine Bugle* of Oct., 1898; Livermore diary, entry of April 7, 1863.

Hooker's plan for attacking Lee: Steele, I, 330-334; OR, XXV, Part 2, 199, 200, 213, 214, 220, 221.

The smallpox incident: *Medical and Surgical History of the War of the Rebellion*, I, Part 3, 625-648; *Pulse of Pharmacy*; U. S. Sanitary Commission, *Sanitary Memoirs, Contributions Relating to the Causation and Prevention of Disease, and to Camp Diseases*, pp. 162, 163;

Regimental records, report of Surgeon N. P. Monroe, April 17, 1863; Gerrish, *Army Life,* p. 86; Miller, p. 15; 1864-65 MeAGR, I, 331.

Activities of Ames and Chamberlain following the disclosure of smallpox: 1864-65 MeAGR, I, 331.

Guarding the telegraph line: Brown, pp. 177, 178, 348-350; Plum, I, 364, II, 63; Gerrish, *Army Life,* p. 86; 1864-65 MeAGR, I, 331. See also General Order No. 181, Hq. Army of the Potomac, Oct. 30, 1862.

Reports from Chancellorsville: Swinton, pp. 267-303; Gerrish, *Army Life,* p. 89.

The retreat from Chancellorsville: Gerrish, *Army Life,* p. 93; William H. Owen to his mother, May 7, 1863.

Ames and Chamberlain at Chancellorsville: 1864-65 MeAGR, I, 302, 331.

Manpower status of the 20th Maine: Gerrish, *Army Life,* p. 63; OR (Series 3), III, 803; Regimental records, monthly return for April, 1863.

Transfer of men from the 2nd Maine: 1864-65 MeAGR, I, 331; Joshua Chamberlain, "Through Blood and Fire at Gettysburg"; Miller, p. 15.

History of the 2nd Maine: Whitman and True, pp. 37-42, 44, 55; Stanley and Hall, pp. 55, 56; 1861 MeAGR, pp. 5, 6, 16-19.

Chamberlain's handling of the 2nd Maine soldiers: 1864-65 MeAGR, I, 332; Joshua Chamberlain, "Through Blood and Fire at Gettysburg"; Regimental records, Joshua Chamberlain's letter to AAAG, 3rd Brigade, July 30, 1863.

Chapter 5. SUNSTROKE, SORE FEET AND STUART

PICKETING on the Rappahannock: Norton, *Army Letters,* pp. 155-157; William to Abbie Owen, June 2, 1863; Whitman and True, p. 492.

Brigade flag: Norton, *Little Round Top,* facing p. 262.

Rumors and observations along the Rappahannock: *Corn Exchange Regiment,* pp. 218, 219; Norton, *Army Letters,* p. 158; Swinton, pp. 314-317; Livermore diary, entry of June 12, 1863.

Lee's move northward: Swinton, pp. 309, 310, 317-320; Steele, I, 354.

March from the Rappahannock to Aldie: Nash, p. 136; *Corn Exchange Regiment,* pp. 221, 222; *Under the Maltese Cross,* pp. 147, 150; Parker, pp. 162, 163; Miller, p. 16; Powell, p. 497.

Tactical situation between Blue Ridge and Bull Run mountains: Steele, I, 358, 359; *Corn Exchange Regiment,* p. 222; Judson, pp. 63, 64.

The skirmish on the Ashby's Gap road: Powell, p. 357; Miller, p. 16; *Corn Exchange Regiment,* pp. 223-225; Judson, pp. 64, 65.

The march from Aldie to Frederick: Nash, pp. 137-141; *Corn Exchange Regiment,* p. 230; Miller, p. 16.

Reports and events during the halt at Frederick: *Corn Exchange Regiment,* p. 229; Powell, p. 501; Gerrish, *Army Life,* pp. 96, 97.

Meade's instructions from Washington and method of advance: OR, XXVII, Part 1, 61; Swinton, pp. 324, 325.

Distances marched: Nash, pp. 137-141; Powell, p. 513. Many other regiments in the Army of the Potomac made even longer marches, including those of the Sixth Corps, which moved thirty-four miles in its final approach to Gettysburg. There is a statistical summary of distances, rations, health conditions, and other aspects of the army's march to Gettysburg in the U. S. Sanitary Commission's *Sanitary Memoirs, Investigations in the Military and Anthropological Statistics of American Soldiers,* pp. 603-610.

Procedure when a man left the column: Regimental records, Special Order No. 25, Hq. 20th Me. Vols., Nov. 5, 1862. See also General Order No. 155, Hq. Army of the Potomac, Sept. 9, 1862.

George Estabrook incident: related by William Estabrook.

Gathering wood and water: Parker, p. 164; Tilney, p. 52.

Rations: Billings, pp. 113, 133, 135, 321; Gerrish, *Army Life,* p. 98; Tilney, p. 32 (the mule incident); Spear, *Hoe Cake of Appomattox,* pp. 4-6.

Pitching tents: Tilney, p. 53; Gerrish and Hutchinson, *Blue and the Gray,* p. 56; Billings, p. 52; Livermore diary, entry of July 5, 1863.

The march to Hanover, July 1: Meade, II, 15-18; William to Charles Livermore, July 6, 1863; *Under the Maltese Cross,* pp. 153-156; Judson, p. 66; Gerrish, *Army Life,* p. 99; *Corn Exchange Regiment,* p. 235; Steele, I, 362; Plum, II, 16; *Philadelphia Public Ledger,* July 4, 1863.

News from Gettysburg and the night march: Judson, p. 66; *Bangor Daily News,* July 1, 1913; Gerrish, *Army Life,* p. 101; Joshua Chamberlain, "Through Blood and Fire at Gettysburg"; Powell, p. 510.

Morning of July 2, and approach to Gettysburg: *Corn Exchange Regiment,* pp. 238, 239; Haskell, pp. 16, 17.

Meade's order read to the troops: OR, XXVII, Part 3, 415; *Under the Maltese Cross,* p. 162.

Forenoon of July 2 on the field of Gettysburg; *Corn Exchange Regiment*, p. 239; Haskell, pp. 16-18; *Under the Maltese Cross*, p. 165.

Chapter 6.   UNHOOKED, UNHINGED AND ALMOST UNDONE

DESCRIPTION of General Meade: Gerrish, *Army Life*, pp. 328, 329; Gerrish and Hutchinson, *Blue and the Gray*, pp. 250, 251.

General Meade's mood on the morning of July 2: Meade, II, 66.

Tactical situation on the morning of July 2: Swinton, pp. 335-342.

Description of Sickles: Gerrish, *Army Life*, p. 345; Gerrish and Hutchinson, *Blue and the Gray*, pp. 471, 472.

Captain George Meade's visits to Sickles' position, carrying instructions: Meade, II, 66-68 and Map No. 17.

Sickles' position, disadvantages: Swinton, pp. 343, 344.

Sickles' visit to army headquarters at 11 A.M.: Meade, II, 70, 71.

Hunt's evaluation of Sickles' proposed position: Meade, II, 74, 75; *Battles and Leaders of the Civil War*, III, 301-303.

Removal of Buford's cavalry: Meade, II, 71.

Longstreet's plan, proposed to Lee: *Battles and Leaders of the Civil War*, III, 339-341.

Lee's plan: OR, XXVII, Part 2, 318; *Battles and Leaders of the Civil War*, III, 339-341; Longstreet, p. 358.

Longstreet's march: *Battles and Leaders of the Civil War*, III, 339-341; Longstreet, pp. 365, 366.

Longstreet's mood: Oates, pp. 223, 224.

Absence of Confederate cavalry and Longstreet's order to Hood to send out scouts: Longstreet, pp. 365, 367.

Three o'clock conference at Meade's headquarters: Meade, II, 71, 72.

Times: There is a considerable variance in the times at which the events of this afternoon are reported to have taken place. The times which Longstreet reports, for example, are considerably earlier than those reported by Meade. The times used in this account are mostly from Union reports.

Longstreet's arrival on the Emmitsburg Road, and the position of Sickles' troops confronting him: Tilberg, p. 15; Meade, II, Map No. 18; Oates, pp. 223, 225.

Reports from Hood's scouts, and Hood's recommendation to move farther to the Union left: *Battles and Leaders of the Civil War*, III, 321, 322.

Longstreet's dispositions for attack: Meade, II, 80, 81.

Break-up of the conference at Meade's headquarters: Meade, II, 72.

Description of General Sykes: Powell, portrait opposite p. 500.

Meade follows Sickles to his position: Meade, II, 73.

Exchange between Meade and Sickles, and Meade's removal on a runaway horse: Meade, II, 78, 79; Tremain, pp. 64, 65.

Description of General Warren: Gerrish and Hutchinson, *Blue and the Gray*, p. 240.

Warren's actions on Little Round Top: Norton, *Little Round Top*, pp. 308-311.

Warren's request to Sickles: OR, XXVII, Part 1, 138.

Effects of the attack on Sickles' corps, and on Sickles: Norton, *Little Round Top*, p. 310; Meade, II, 354; Tremain, p. 103.

Sickles' leg bones preserved: Exhibit, Medical Museum of the Armed Forces in Washington.

Arrival of advance elements of the Fifth Corps, including 20th Maine: Norton, *Little Round Top*, pp. 263, 264; OR, XXVII, Part 1, 600, 601; *Maine at Gettysburg*, p. 251.

Chapter 7.   A Hard Day for Mother

Arrival of 20th Maine at the wheatfield and description of the battle as seen from that point: Norton, *Little Round Top*, p. 263; Joshua Chamberlain, "Through Blood and Fire at Gettysburg"; *Maine at Gettysburg*, p. 251.

The move to Little Round Top: Norton, *Little Round Top*, pp. 264, 265; Chamberlain, "Through Blood and Fire at Gettysburg"; Gerrish, *Army Life*, pp. 106, 107.

Placing of the regiments by Vincent: *Maine at Gettysburg*, p. 251; Norton, *Little Round Top*, p. 265; Judson, p. 67.

Occupation of position by the 20th Maine, and deployment of skirmishers under Captain Morrill: Joshua Chamberlain, "Through Blood and Fire at Gettysburg"; *Maine at Gettysburg*, 254; OR, XXVII, Part 1, 623.

The advance to Little Round Top of Law's Brigade: Longstreet, p. 365; Oates, pp. 210-214; OR, XXVII, Part 1, 518, 519; *Maine at Gettysburg*, pp. 349-351; Norton, *Little Round Top*, pp. 258, 259.

First attack, as experienced by the 20th Maine: Joshua Chamberlain, "Through Blood and Fire at Gettysburg"; Livermore diary, entry of July 2, 1863; Judson, p. 67; Norton, *Little Round Top*, pp. 255-258; Gerrish and Hutchinson, *Blue and the Gray*, p. 357.

Discovery of Confederate flanking column and Chamberlain's handling of the regiment to meet the flank attack: *Maine at Gettysburg*, p. 254; Joshua Chamberlain, "Through Blood and Fire at Gettysburg"; OR, XXVII, Part 1, 623; Chamberlain's report to 3rd Brigade Headquarters, July 6, 1863 (copy in Chamberlain Papers, Library of Congress).

Attack by the Alabama flanking column: *Maine at Gettysburg*, p. 256; OR, XXVII, Part 1, 623, 624; Judson, p. 68; Joshua Chamberlain, "Through Blood and Fire at Gettysburg."

Incidents concerning Private Buck and Andrew Tozier: Joshua Chamberlain, "Through Blood and Fire at Gettysburg."

Incident of the prisoners from the 2nd Maine: OR, XXVII, Part 1, 626.

Fighting on the left wing as experienced by Company H: Gerrish and Hutchinson, *Blue and the Gray*, pp. 357, 358.

Intensity of rifle fire, and effects: *Maine at Gettysburg*, pp. 261, 262.

Description of fighting as experienced by Confederates: Oates, pp. 218-220, 227.

Incident of the Confederate soldier, taking aim at Chamberlain: Joshua Chamberlain, "Through Blood and Fire at Gettysburg."

Attack on the right wing of the brigade and the wounding of Vincent: OR, XXVII, Part 1, 624; Judson, p. 67.

Support by the 83rd Pennsylvania: Judson, p. 68.

Status of ammunition and Chamberlain's decision to charge: OR, XXVII, Part 1, 624; Joshua Chamberlain, "Through Blood and Fire at Gettysburg"; *Maine at Gettysburg*, pp. 257, 261.

Lieutenant Melcher incident: *Maine at Gettysburg*, p. 257.

The charge by the 20th Maine: Gerrish and Hutchinson, *Blue and the Gray*, p. 359; Joshua Chamberlain, "Through Blood and Fire at Gettysburg"; *Maine at Gettysburg*, pp. 257, 258; Judson, p. 68; OR, XXVII, Part 1, 624; Gerrish, *Army Life*, p. 111.

Effects of the charge on the Confederates: Oates, pp. 219-221; Norton, *Little Round Top*, p. 112.

Number of men engaged, losses, prisoners: *Maine at Gettysburg*, pp. 270-272; OR, XXVII, Part 1, 625, 626.

Comments on importance of the action: Livermore diary, entry of July 2, 1863; Oates, pp. 219, 225.

Chapter 8. So Nobly Advanced

Colonel James C. Rice and his handling of the 3rd Brigade on Little Round Top: Norton, *Army Letters*, p. 165; Judson, p. 77; OR, XXVII, Part 1, 617, 618.

Arrival and subsequent action of Fisher's Brigade: OR, XXVII, Part 1, 625.

Seizure of Big Round Top by the 20th Maine, actions of supporting troops and capture of men from the 4th Texas: OR, XXVII, Part 1, 625; *Maine at Gettysburg*, pp. 259, 260.

Movement of the 20th Maine to reserve position: *Maine at Gettysburgh*, p. 261; Livermore diary, entry of July 3, 1863.

Visit of General Ames: Livermore diary, entry of July 3, 1863.

Description of artillery firing preceding Pickett's charge: Judson, pp. 70, 71.

Reconnaissances, and descriptions of the dead on the battlefield: *Corn Exchange Regiment*, p. 261; William to Charles Livermore, July 6, 1863.

Conditions in the hospital area following the battle: *Medical and Surgical History of the War of the Rebellion*, I, Part 1, App., 141, 145-147; John Chamberlain to Charles Desmond, July 11, 1863; Smith, p. 162.

Nature of wounds suffered by 20th Maine: *Maine at Gettysburg*, pp. 270-272; *Medical and Surgical History of the War of the Rebellion*, I, Part 1, App., 146.

Piles of amputated arms and legs, witnessed by an army bandsman: Rauscher, p. 95.

Description of the surgeon at work: Schurz, III, 39.

Surgery, and post-operative complications: Keen, pp. 103-109.

Case of Private Byron Hilt: *Medical and Surgical History of the War of the Rebellion*, II, Part 2, 507.

Story of Captain Charles Billings: Smith, pp. 171, 172; *Civil War in Song and Story*, pp. 508, 509.

Burial of the 20th Maine dead: *Maine at Gettysburg*, p. 262; 1864-65 MeAGR, I, 167, 168, 178; Gerrish, *Army Life*, pp. 111, 112.

Chamberlain's visit to Little Round Top in later years: Joshua Chamberlain, "Through Blood and Fire at Gettysburg."

Chapter 9. LIVING IN AWFUL TIMES

MARCH on July 5: OR, XXVII, Part 1, 621; Judson, p. 73; Livermore diary, entry of July 5, 1863.

Congratulatory order read: *Corn Exchange Regiment*, p. 275; OR, XXVII, Part 3, 519.

Condition of the men: Norton, *Army Letters*, pp. 165, 166.

Lee's retreat to the Potomac, and defense dispositions: OR, XXVII, Part 2, 299-301; Swinton, pp. 366-369; *Under the Maltese Cross*, p. 207.

Route of the 20th Maine south from Gettysburg: Powell, p. 564; OR, XXVII, Part 1, 626, 627.

Marches of July 7, 8 and 9: *Corn Exchange Regiment*, pp. 278, 279; William to Charles Livermore, July 9, 1863.

Skirmish at Fair Play and death of 2nd Maine prisoner: Judson, p. 74; Miller, p. 18; OR, XXVII, Part 1, 627; Regimental records, Joshua Chamberlain to AAAG, 3rd Brigade, July 30, 1863.

Listening to the order for Vincent's promotion: Judson, pp. 72, 73.

Union advance to the Potomac and Lee's escape: Powell, p. 567; *Corn Exchange Regiment*, pp. 280, 283; Judson, p. 74; William to Charles Livermore, July 9, 1863; Longstreet, p. 429.

The affair at Manassas Gap: Swinton, pp. 373-375; *Corn Exchange Regiment*, pp. 286-288; Powell, pp. 569, 570; Gerrish, *Army Life*, pp. 121, 122; Judson, p. 76; Will to Etta Owen, Sept. 7, 1863; Miller, p. 18; Norton, *Army Letters*, p. 168; Spear, *Hoe Cake of Appomattox*, pp. 6, 7.

The draft: Act of Congress, March 3, 1863, Sections 11, 13 and 17; *Revised Statutes of the State of Maine* (1857), Chap. 10, Section 4; Norton, *Army Letters*, p. 180; Stanley and Hall, pp. 178-180, 182; 1863 MeAGR, p. 10; 1864-65 MeAGR, I, 35; North, p. 737; OR (Series 3), III, 484, 791; Judson, pp. 76, 77; Robinson, pp. 358, 359; Kreidberg and Henry, pp. 104-109, 111-113.

The execution of deserters: OR, XXIX, Part 2, 102, 103; *Corn Exchange Regiment*, pp. 292-302; Norton, *Army Letters*, p. 179; Gerrish, *Army Life*, pp. 124-126; Parker, pp. 178, 179; Will to Abbie Owen, Aug. 30, 1863; General Order No. 84, Hq. Army of the Potomac, Aug. 23, 1863.

Chamberlain's illness and promotion: Norton, *Army Letters*, pp. 176, 178; 1864-65 MeAGR, I, 332; Gerrish, *Army Life*, p. 122.

The Orange & Alexandria Railroad: Powell, p. 579; Tilney, pp. 50, 51.

Advance to Culpeper and retreat on Oct. 13: Swinton, pp. 375-383; Powell, pp. 574-577; Miller, p. 19.

Action at Bristoe Station and marches of October 14: *Corn Exchange Regiment*, pp. 323-325; Judson, p. 77; Miller, p. 19; Swinton, pp. 383, 384.

"Oscillation" marches: Judson, pp. 77, 78; Miller, p. 19.

The battle of Rappahannock Station: OR, XXIX, Part 1, 575, 576, 584-588, 591, 596, 599, 600; *Rebellion Record*, VIII, 161-164; *Corn Exchange Regiment*, pp. 336-339, 343; Whitman and True, pp. 136, 152-154; Stanley and Hall, p. 133; *Maine at Gettysburg*, pp. 419-421; Gerrish, *Army Life*, pp. 129, 130; 1863 MeAGR, p. 91.

Walter G. Morrill: 1862 MeAGR, App. D, p. 656; 1864-65 MeAGR, I, 1128, 1129; Will to Abbie Owen, Dec. 4, 1862, and Jan. 28, 1863; Regimental records, Ames to Governor Coburn, Mar. 10, 1863; *Medal of Honor*, p. 146; *Biographical Review*, XXIX, 583-585.

Joshua Chamberlain at Rappahannock Station, his hospitalization and transfer to Washington: 1864-65 MeAGR, I, 332, 333.

The Mine Run campaign: Swinton, pp. 390-398; Judson, p. 81; Parker, pp. 181, 182; Powell, p. 585; *Corn Exchange Regiment*, p. 371; Gerrish, *Army Life*, p. 133.

Camp at Rappahannock Station: Gerrish, *Army Life*, p. 136; Miller, p. 20; Will to Abbie Owen, Dec. 27, 1863.

Letter writing for furloughs: *Under the Maltese Cross*, pp. 221, 222.

Fat in the fire incident: Gerrish, *Army Life*, p. 143.

Exchange of compliments with Ames: Miller, p. 20; Ames to officers of the 20th Maine, Aug. 18, 1863; Gerrish, *Army Life*, p. 134.

Chapter 10. RIVER OF NO-RETURN

"HELL on the Rappahannock": Rauscher, p. 67.

Description of the Wilderness area: Melcher, p. 73; Schaff, pp. 57-62; Swinton, pp. 428, 429.

Grant and his ideas about strategy: Swinton, p. 440. There are characteristic pictures of the general in *Photographic History of the Civil War*, X, 30, 47.

Composition of the army and the 3rd Brigade: Swinton, p. 410; Powell, p. 594.

Corn Exchange Regiment: *Corn Exchange Regiment,* pp. 2-24; Carter in *Maine Bugle,* Jan. 1898.

Strength and condition of the 20th Maine: Regimental records, monthly returns for 1864; Melcher, p. 75; Livermore diary, entries of February, March and April, 1864.

Ellis Spear: Powell, p. 594; Eaton, *Annals of the Town of Warren,* p. 404.

Preparations for the spring campaign and attitude of the men: Will to Abbie Owen, April 12, 16 and 23, 1864.

March to the Rapidan: Gerrish, *Army Life,* pp. 156, 157; Judson, p. 93.

Grant's plan: Steele, I, 471.

Crossing of the Rapidan: Gerrish, *Army Life,* p. 157; Schaff, pp. 83-93.

Camping in the Wilderness, night of May 4-5: *Under the Maltese Cross,* pp. 236, 237; Gerrish and Hutchinson, *Blue and the Gray,* p. 582; *Corn Exchange Regiment,* p. 397.

Tactical situation, night of May 4-5: Swinton, pp. 417-419; OR, XXXVI, Part 2, 371; Powell, map opposite p. 631; *Corn Exchange Regiment,* pp. 396, 397.

The 1st Division and General Charles Griffin: Powell, pp. 19, 593, 594; *Corn Exchange Regiment,* pp. 211, 319.

Discovery of Confederates on morning of May 5: Gerrish, *Army Life,* p. 158; Judson, p. 94; Powell, p. 606.

Series of messages: OR, XXXVI, Part 2, 403, 413, 415, 416.

20th Maine's preparations on the Orange Turnpike: Gerrish, *Army Life,* p. 159.

Attitude of men going into battle: Gerrish, *Army Life,* pp. 158, 159; Judson, p. 91.

Disposition of 3rd Brigade in advancing to the attack: Judson, p. 94; *Corn Exchange Regiment,* p. 401; Nash, p. 184; OR, XXXVI, Part 1, 580, 584, 587. The 1st Michigan did not participate in this attack, since it had been fighting out on the skirmish line with severe losses and was now relieved. And the 16th Michigan was off somewhere guarding a wagon train that day.

Musketry and shouting: *Corn Exchange Regiment,* p. 399; Judson, p. 94.

Charge across the open field: Melcher, p. 77; Schaff, p. 149; Powell, p. 594; Gerrish, *Army Life,* pp. 161, 162.

Bartlett "circus" anecdote: Gerrish and Hutchinson, *Blue and the Gray,* p. 405.

Advance beyond the field and dispositions to meet counterattack: Will to Abbie Owen, May 14, 1864; Judson, p. 94; *Under the Maltese Cross*, p. 248; Schaff, pp. 155, 165, 166; Gerrish, *Army Life*, pp. 162, 163; OR, XXXVI, Part 1, 573.

Holman Melcher's adventure with Company F: Melcher, pp. 78-84.

Experience of a wounded man: Gerrish, *Army Life*, pp. 166-169.

The night of May 5-6: *Corn Exchange Regiment*, p. 403.

Events of May 6: Powell, p. 616; *Corn Exchange Regiment*, p. 404; OR, XXXVI, Part 1, 573; Judson, pp. 94, 95.

Events of May 7: Schaff, p. 330; *Corn Exchange Regiment*, pp. 404-406; Judson, p. 95; *Under the Maltese Cross*, p. 251; Gerrish, *Army Life*, pp. 170, 171; Powell, p. 631.

Day-by-day losses of the 20th Maine in the Wilderness: 1864-65 MeAGR, I, 284.

Army losses: Fox, p. 546.

Chapter 11. ON THE GRINDING WHEEL

EVACUATION of the wounded: OR, XXXVI, Part 1, 217, 220, 221, 234; Gerrish, *Army Life*, pp. 81, 171. Livermore diary, entries of May 8-10, 1864.

Mrs. Sampson's report: 1864-65 MeAGR, I, 123, 128.

Movement of Herring's force from the Wilderness to Spotsylvania, and events of the daylight hours, May 8: *Corn Exchange Regiment*, p. 681; OR, XXXVI, Part 1, 226, 573; Steele, I, 489; Gerrish, *Army Life*, p. 175.

The fight on Laurel Hill: *Corn Exchange Regiment*, pp. 408-412; OR, XXXVI, Part 1, 574, Part 2, 543, 544; Gerrish, *Army Life*, pp. 176-178.

Entrenchments around Spotsylvania and effect on tactics: *Corn Exchange Regiment*, p. 418; Steele, I, 492, 493; OR, XXXVI, Part 1, 9; Gerrish, *Army Life*, p. 193.

The attack that didn't get started, on the evening of May 10: Judson, p. 98.

Events of May 11-13: Swinton, pp. 451-455; OR, XXXVI, Part 1, 574.

"Jug handle": *Corn Exchange Regiment*, p. 432.

Private Mero's poem: *Maine Bugle*, April issue, 1894, pp. 140-142.

Events of May 13-20 and description of the country: *Corn Ex-*

change Regiment, p. 426; 1864-65 MeAGR, I, 285; Swinton, pp. 19, 457.

Chamberlain's skirmish on May 22: *Joshua Lawrence Chamberlain, a Sketch*, pp. 15, 16; *Corn Exchange Regiment*, pp. 435-438; Judson, p. 99.

Flanking moves: crossing of the North Anna and the Pamunkey: Swinton, pp. 470-481; Miller, p. 23; Powell, p. 664; Gerrish, *Army Life*, pp. 192, 193; Nash, p. 199.

Exhaustion of the men: OR, XXXVI, Part 1, 246, 247.

Typical bivouac: Gerrish, *Army Life*, pp. 187-191.

Cold Harbor, Bethesda Church, the Chickahominy: Steele, I, 502, 503; 1864-65 MeAGR, I, 285.

The movement across the Chickahominy and James: Swinton, pp. 498, 499; Gerrish, *Army Life*, pp. 197, 198.

Depletion of the regiment: Regimental records, return for June, 1864; Powell, pp. 679-695; Joshua Chamberlain, *Passing of the Armies*, p. 3; Gerrish, *Army Life*, p. 187.

Chapter 12. WOODCHUCK WARFARE

APPROACH to Petersburg and attack of June 18: Miller, p. 24; *Under the Maltese Cross*, pp. 307, 308; Swinton, pp. 497-511; Powell, p. 699; Steele, I, 518, 519; OR, XL, Part 1, 464.

Chamberlain's attack and near-fatal wound: 1864-65 MeAGR, I, 333, 334; copy of Chamberlain's letter protesting the attack with a single brigade, in Chamberlain's Papers, Library of Congress, Manuscripts Division; OR, XL, Part 1, 455-457, Part 2, 216; *In Memoriam, Joshua Lawrence Chamberlain*, pp. 5, 6; Nash, p. 201; information provided by Alice Farrington; *Corn Exchange Regiment*, p. 479; *Medical and Surgical History of the War of the Rebellion*, II, Part 2, 363.

Sniping and death of Captain Keene: 1864-65 MeAGR, I, 407; Judson, p. 105; Nash, p. 202.

Entrenching operations: Steele, I, 519; *Corn Exchange Regiment*, p. 480; *Under the Maltese Cross*, p. 310.

Mortars, bombproof shelters and bombardment incidents: Billings, pp. 58-60; Nash, p. 202; Gerrish, *Army Life*, pp. 203-205; *Corn Exchange Regiment*, pp. 490, 491.

Living conditions in the trenches: *Corn Exchange Regiment*, pp. 482, 497.

Relations with enemy pickets and "criminal" shooting incident: Judson, p. 105; Sec. III, Para. 69, General Order No. 100, WDAGO, April 24, 1863; *Corn Exchange Regiment*, pp. 485-487.

The mine explosion: *Under the Maltese Cross*, pp. 311, 312; Lykes, pp. 16-22; Judson, 106; *Corn Exchange Regiment*, pp. 495-497; Gerrish, *Army Life*, pp. 207, 208; Powell, pp. 708, 709.

Withdrawal of 20th Maine from entrenchments: Powell, p. 710; Gerrish, *Army Life*, p. 211.

Tactical situation at Petersburg: Lykes, pp. 5, 6; Joshua Chamberlain, *Passing of the Armies*, p. 40.

The battle of the Weldon Railroad: Gerrish, *Army Life*, pp. 212-214; *Corn Exchange Regiment*, p. 498; Judson, pp. 106, 107; Miller, p. 25; OR, XLII, Part 1, 430-433.

The fighting on September 30, including the battle of Peebles' Farm: *Corn Exchange Regiment*, pp. 513-514, 518, 519; *Under the Maltese Cross*, p. 320; Judson, pp. 108, 109; Gerrish, *Army Life*, pp. 215-219; Will to Etta Owen, Oct. 14, 1864; Nash, pp. 209, 210; 1864-65 MeAGR, I, 285, 286, 469; Powell, p. 731.

The battle of Hatcher's Run in October: Swinton, pp. 541-547; Powell, p. 743; 1864-65 MeAGR, I, 286.

The presidential election: Gerrish, *Army Life*, pp. 209, 219, 220; Swinton, pp. 491, 492, 495; *Cyclopaedia of Political Science*, I, 783; McPherson, pp. 419-421; OR, XLII, Part 3, 533, 549, 570, 572, 577; Tilney, pp. 151, 152; Joshua Chamberlain, *Passing of the Armies*, p. 12.

The expedition down the Weldon Railroad, or "Applejack Raid": Gerrish, *Army Life*, pp. 220-222; Judson, p. 109; *Corn Exchange Regiment*, pp. 533, 534, 543; Tilney, pp. 162, 163; Parker, p. 241; 1864-65 MeAGR, I, 334; OR, XLII, Part 1, 459, 460.

Departure of Chamberlain: 1864-65 MeAGR, I, 334.

Chapter 13. THE WINDS OF MARCH

MOOD of the men at the end of 1864: Joshua Chamberlain, *Passing of the Armies*, pp. 18, 19.

Condition of the 20th Maine: Regimental records, monthly returns Sept.-Dec. 1864; Gerrish, *Army Life*, pp. 227, 228.

Attitude of recruits: Regimental records, Court Martial Order No. 1, Hq. 20th Me. Vols., March 11, 1865; Ezekiel to Augustus Benn,

Jan. 28, 1865, also information provided by Clara B. Holden and Algernon E. Holden.

Composition and character of 3rd Brigade: Powell, p. 764; Parker, p. 238.

Battle of Hatcher's Run: *Under the Maltese Cross*, pp. 332, 333, 336; Gerrish, *Army Life*, p. 223; Judson, p. 110; 1864-65 MeAGR, I, 370, 371; Powell, p. 764; Swinton, p. 549.

Weather and life in camp on Hatcher's Run: Gerrish, *Army Life*, p. 229; *Under the Maltese Cross*, p. 338; Tilney, pp. 189-191.

Private Edmund Morrison: Gerrish, *Army Life*, p. 230.

Location of the Confederate lines: Joshua Chamberlain, *Passing of the Armies*, p. 41; Swinton, pp. 582, 583.

Grant's plan: Swinton, pp. 578-581; OR, XLVI, Part 1, 50-52.

Description of Sheridan and Custer: Gerrish, *Army Life*, pp. 248, 249, 251, 348; Pray.

Story about George Washington's ghost at Gettysburg: *Bangor Daily News*, issue of July 1, 1913.

The fight on the Quaker Road, March 29: Parker, p. 245; Joshua Chamberlain, *Passing of the Armies*, pp. 40-59; Powell, pp. 776, 777.

Modification of Grant's plan for Sheridan and reactions of officers in Fifth Corps: Swinton, pp. 583, 584; OR, XLVI, Part 1, 53; Joshua Chamberlain, *Passing of the Armies*, pp. 61-63.

Experiences of 20th Maine, March 29 and 30: 1864-65 MeAGR, I, 286; Gerrish, *Army Life*, pp. 235, 236.

Fighting on March 31: Powell, pp. 780-784; Swinton, pp. 588-590; Gerrish, *Army Life*, pp. 237, 238; Joshua Chamberlain, *Passing of the Armies*, pp. 72-79; 1864-65 MeAGR, I, 335.

Sheridan's retreat and the conversation between Chamberlain and Warren about going to his aid: Joshua Chamberlain, *Passing of the Armies*, pp. 87-89.

Move of Bartlett's Brigade and its contact with the enemy: Powell, p. 786; Gerrish, *Army Life*; p. 239; *Corn Exchange Regiment*, pp. 572, 573.

Withdrawal of the Fifth Corps from the White Oak Road and its move to the support of Sheridan: Joshua Chamberlain, *Passing of the Armies*, pp. 89, 90, 98-105, 114, 118, 119; Powell, pp. 786-799; OR, XLVI, Part 1, 817-826, 1104, 1105.

The battle of Five Forks: Powell, pp. 799-809; Joshua Chamberlain, *Passing of the Armies*, pp. 120-131; Parker, p. 249; Lykes, p. 41; Gerrish, *Army Life*, pp. 241-245; *Corn Exchange Regiment*, p. 580; OR, XLVI, Part 1, 829-837, 849, 850, 860, 861, 865; *Medal of Honor*,

p. 190. Five Medal of Honor winners served in the 20th Maine: Adelbert Ames, Joshua L. Chamberlain, Walter G. Morrill, Albert E. Fernald, and Henry C. Merriam. However, Ames won his medal prior to joining the regiment, and Merriam after he left it.

Warren's dismissal: Powell, pp. 804-808; Joshua Chamberlain, *Passing of the Armies*, p. 142.

Burial of Morrison and Gilmore: Gerrish, *Army Life*, p. 246.

Chapter 14.   HUNGRY VICTORY

EVENTS of April 2: Joshua Chamberlain, *Passing of the Armies*, pp. 192, 193; Gerrish, *Army Life*, pp. 247, 248.

Lee's plan for continuing the war: Steele, I, 526.

March of the Fifth Corps on April 4, and the position at Jetersville: Joshua Chamberlain, *Passing of the Armies*, pp. 197-199; Swinton, pp. 609, 610.

Overshadowing of Meade and employment of the Army of the Potomac in the pursuit; Meade, II, 269, 271; Joshua Chamberlain, *Passing of the Armies*, pp. 201, 205; Powell map opposite p. 838.

Urgency of the march: Joshua Chamberlain, *Passing of the Armies*, pp. 212, 213, 219.

Condition of the Confederate army: Swinton, pp. 610-613.

March of April 6: Powell, p. 843.

Foraging: Gerrish, *Army Life*, p. 252.

March during daylight hours of April 8; Powell, p. 849; Joshua Chamberlain, *Passing of the Armies*, pp. 226-229.

March during the night of April 8-9 and arrival at Appomattox: Gerrish, *Army Life*, pp. 252-254; *Corn Exchange Regiment*, p. 587; *Maine at Gettysburg*, p. 283; Joshua Chamberlain, *Passing of the Armies*, pp. 230-233; Boykin, p. 55.

Positions of troops at Appomattox: Joshua Chamberlain, *Passing of the Armies*, pp. 233-235; OR, XLVI, Part 1, 1109; *Under the Maltese Cross*, p. 358; Cilley.

Description of cavalry moving across battlefield: *Maine at Gettysburg*, pp. 283-284.

Advance of the 20th Maine toward enemy lines, including the incident of the poultry chase: Gerrish, *Army Life*, pp. 255-258.

Battlefield and events including arrival of white flags as witnessed by Chamberlain: Joshua Chamberlain, *Passing of the Armies*, pp. 237-242.

Death of 155th Pennsylvania skirmisher: *Under the Maltese Cross*, p. 615.

Reaction of men in the 20th Maine to news of surrender: Dunn.

Truce period and arrival of Lee and Grant: Joshua Chamberlain, *Passing of the Armies*, pp. 243-247.

Descriptions of Confederate officers and men: Thomas to John Chamberlain, April 14, 1865; Gerrish, *Army Life*, pp. 261, 262; Dunn.

Mingling of men, sharing of rations: Gerrish, *Army Life*, pp. 259, 260; OR, XLVI, Part 1, 674.

Arrangements for surrender: OR, XLVI, Part 3, 666; Joshua Chamberlain, *Passing of the Armies*, pp. 248, 249.

Veteran regiments in 3rd Brigade: Powell, pp. 303, 304, 770, 771.

Agreement between Union and Confederate pickets: Dunn.

Scenes in Bangor and Brewer, Maine, as victory news arrived: Stanley and Hall, pp. 191-193, 199.

The surrender ceremony at Appomattox Court House April 12: Joshua Chamberlain, *Passing of the Armies*, pp. 257-270, *Third Brigade at Appomattox* (appended to Norton, *Army Letters*, pp. 352-355) and "The Surrender of General Lee" (see ¶ below); Boykin, p. 65; Parker, pp. 255, 256; *Under the Maltese Cross*, p. 367; Gerrish, *Army Life*, pp. 262, 263.

The exchange between Chamberlain and General Wise: This incident is related, without naming the Confederate general, in Chamberlain's *The Passing of the Armies*, pp. 266-269. In a lecture entitled "The Surrender of General Lee," a newspaper report of which is included in Chamberlain's Papers at the Library of Congress, Chamberlain gave another account of the conversation and identified the officer as General Henry A. Wise. Other references to General Wise at Appomattox: Meade, II, 270; and Gerrish, *Army Life*, pp. 263, 264.

Chapter 15.   THE LAST REVIEW

CHAMBERLAIN quotation: Joshua Chamberlain, *Passing of the Armies*, pp. 358, 359.

Conditions at Appomattox and the march to Farmville: Gerrish, *Army Life*, pp. 264-270; Powell, pp. 869, 870.

Reactions to news of Lincoln's assassination: Gerrish, *Army Life*, p. 271; Joshua Chamberlain, *Passing of the Armies*, pp. 277, 280-286.

The sutler: Billings, pp. 224-230; Act of Congress, March 19, 1862.

The fight at Sutherland Station: *Corn Exchange Regiment*, pp. 599-602; Gerrish, *Army Life*, pp. 273, 274.

Experiences with Negroes: Gerrish, *Army Life*, p. 275; Rauscher, p. 251.

The march through Petersburg and salute to General Warren; Joshua Chamberlain, *Passing of the Armies*, pp. 300-303; Gerrish, *Army Life*, p. 277. See Powell, pp. 811-828, for a detailed account of Warren's removal and the court of inquiry.

The march through Richmond: Gerrish, *Army Life*, p. 287; Joshua Chamberlain, *Passing of the Armies*, p. 306.

Incident of the bones: Powell, pp. 63-67; Joshua Chamberlain, *Passing of the Armies*, pp. 307-309.

Soldiers' visits to Stoneman's Switch and the Fredericksburg battlefield: *Corn Exchange Regiment*, p. 603; Gerrish, *Army Life*, pp. 83, 84.

Accidental death of Lieutenant Wood; Gerrish, *Army Life*, p. 289; Joshua Chamberlain, *Passing of the Armies*, pp. 313-314; Smith, p. 394.

The march on May 11 and arrival in Washington on May 12: Joshua Chamberlain, *Passing of the Armies*, pp. 312, 313; *Corn Exchange Regiment*, pp. 603, 604; Rauscher, p. 254; Gerrish, *Army Life*, pp. 289-294.

Preparations for the Grand Review: Joshua Chamberlain, *Passing of the Armies*, pp. 318, 330, 331.

Comparison of the Army of the Potomac and Sherman's army, and relations between the two: Joshua Chamberlain, *Passing of the Armies*, Introduction, 13, 319, 372, 373; Gerrish, *Army Life*, pp. 299, 300.

The Grand Review: Joshua Chamberlain, *Passing of the Armies*, pp. 328-331, 338-343; Meade, II, 281; Gerrish, *Army Life*, pp. 297, 298.

Chamberlain's record and his opinion on war: 1864-65 MeAGR, I, 502; Joshua Chamberlain, *Passing of the Armies*, pp. 385, 386; *In Memoriam, Joshua Lawrence Chamberlain; Medal of Honor*, pp. 138, 139.

List of engagements of the 20th Maine: Powell, pp. 876, 877.

The candlelight parade: Tilney, pp. 239-241; *Under the Maltese Cross*, pp. 382, 383; Livermore diary, entry of May 26, 1865.

Mustering out of the 20th Maine: 1864-65 MeAGR, I, 287; Gerrish, *Army Life*, p. 303.

INDEX

Falmouth (Va.), 75, 142
Farmville (Va.), 277
"Fat in fire" incident, 169
Fence burning, 91
Fernald, Lt. Albert E., 226, 256
Fever, 39, 206
Fife and drum corps, *see* Drum
    corps
Fifth Corps:
    at Antietam, 25, 26
    on "applejack raid," 232, 233
    at Appomattox, 264, 270
    badge, 71, 72
    at Bristoe Station, 159, 160
    in candlelight ceremony, 288
    in election of 1864, 230, 231
    at execution of deserters, 155-157
    in final pursuit of Lee, 259-261,
        263, 264
    at Five Forks, 251-253, 256
    at Fredericksburg, 46, 47, 50-52
    at Gettysburg, 97, 106, 108, 109,
        135
    at Grand Review, 285, 287
    at Gravelly Run, 247
    at Hatcher's Run (Feb.), 238
    Lincoln's inspection of, 72
    and McClellan, 42, 231
    at Manassas Gap, 149
    on march to Gettysburg, 84, 85,
        87-89, 94-96
    on march south from Gettysburg,
        146, 149
    in Mud March, 68-70
    at Petersburg, 209, 219, 221-224,
        230-232
    returning through Petersburg, 280
    on Quaker Road, 246
    at Rappahannock Station, 161,
        163, 166
    Regular troops in, 284
    at Shepherdstown Ford, 27
    soldierly bearing, 283, 284
    cuts Southside R.R., 258
    at Spotsylvania C.H., 197, 201,
        202
    supporting Sheridan, 241, 248-
        253, 259, 263, 264
    in Weldon R.R. battle, 221-224
    at White Oak Road, 247-250

    in Wilderness, 174, 178, 181, 182,
        193, 194
File closers, 34
Fire, in Wilderness forest, 187, 191,
    192, 197
1st Brigade, 1st Division, Fifth
    Corps, 65, 66, 202, 209-211,
    234, 240, 250, 253, 258, 272
First Corps, 95, 99
1st Division, Fifth Corps:
    in "applejack raid," 233, 234
    at Appomattox, 269, 272
    badge, 72
    in candlelight ceremony, 288
    at Chancellorsville, 77
    commanded by Chamberlain, 278
    destroying Weldon R.R., 232, 233
    in final pursuit of Lee, 263
    fist fight in, 69, 70
    at Five Forks, 252, 253
    at Gettysburg, 109
    in Grand Review, 285
    losses on "applejack raid," 234
    at Manassas Gap, 149
    at Mine Explosion, 217
    in mourning for Lincoln, 277, 278
    at Peebles' Farm, 227, 228
    preparing for Grand Review, 283
    on Quaker Road, 243
    reconnaissance to Richards Ford,
        65, 66
    at Spotsylvania C.H., 201
    in surrender ceremony, 272
    at Weldon R.R. battle, 222-224
    on White Oak Road, 247
    in Wilderness, 179, 182, 191, 192
    wounded from Wilderness, 195,
        196
    see also Griffin's Division
Fisher, Col. Joseph W., 129, 130,
    131
Fisher's Brigade, 129-131
Five Forks (Va.), 241, 246, 251,
    252, 253, 256, 258; battle of,
    251-257, 287
Flag, of 2nd Maine, 78; of 3rd Bri-
    gade, 1st Division, Fifth Corps,
    83, 109; of 20th Maine, 170
Flags at Appomattox, 265, 266

Made in United States
North Haven, CT
26 February 2022

16513236R00219